JEFF BALL'S 60-MINUTE VEGETABLE GARDEN

Photographs by Liz Ball

Illustrations by Frank Rohrbach

Collier Books   Macmillan Publishing Company   *New York*

Maxwell Macmillan Canada   *Toronto*

Maxwell Macmillan International   *New York*   *Oxford*   *Singapore*   *Sydney*

Collier Books   Maxwell Macmillan Canada, Inc.
Macmillan Publishing Company   1200 Eglinton Avenue East
866 Third Avenue   Suite 200
New York, NY 10022   Don Mills, Ontario M3C 3N1

Macmillan Publishing Company is part of the Maxwell Communication Group of Companies.

Library of Congress Cataloging-in-Publication Data
Ball, Jeff.
    [60-minute garden]
    Jeff Ball's 60-minute vegetable garden / photographs by Liz Ball ; illustrations by Frank Rohrbach—1st Collier Books ed.
        p.   cm.
    Originally published: Jeff Ball's 60-minute garden. Emmaus, Pa. : Rodale Press, 1985.
    Includes bibliographical references and index.
    ISBN 0-02-030376-9
    1. Vegetable gardening.   2. Organic gardening.   I. Title.
II. Title: Jeff Ball's sixty minute vegetable garden.   III. Title:
60-minute vegetable garden.
[SB324.3.B35   1992]   91-45972   CIP
635—dc20

First published by Rodale Press in 1985 as *Jeff Ball's 60-Minute Garden*

Macmillan books are available at special discounts for bulk purchases for sales promotions, premiums, fund-raising, or educational use. For details, contact:

Special Sales Director
Macmillan Publishing Company
866 Third Avenue
New York, NY 10022

First Collier Books Edition 1992

10 9 8 7 6 5 4 3 2 1

Printed in the United States of America

CONTENTS

ACKNOWLEDGMENTS

Developing something new, whether it be an idea or a device, cannot be done alone. Yes, the germ of the new idea begins in a single head, but it must get sustenance from others before it can be considered a final product. The 60-Minute Garden incorporates many new ideas and devices, and they all have been filtered through a network of family and friends who have tested these ideas for validity and substance.

My father, Ed Ball, has had the most influence in the development of the devices described in this book. He not only made major design contributions to the devices in the 60-Minute Garden, but he worked at my side, as we built and tested every device described in these pages. I am grateful for his enthusiastic support and willing labor. But I am especially thankful that he could share his wisdom from his 70 years as a craftsman and teach me some more of those craftsman's skills that can only come from experience.

As with my first book, my wife, Liz, has been my exuberant collaborator and tough but sensitive first draft editor. With much love and patience she has endured a year of sawdust throughout the house, chaotic household routines, and a husband often more preoccupied with some esoteric design problem like the roof of a compost bin than the fact that the car desperately needed a tune-up.

But most of all, I thank Liz for her photographs. With only a few exceptions, the photographs in this book have been taken by my wife, the professional photographer. Because of her diligence and attention to detail, these photographs make a major contribution to communicating the ideas and devices that make up the 60-Minute Garden. It was fun working as a team on this project with as loving and talented a person as Liz.

Special thanks go to Bob and Lissa Olson who not only gave me critical encouragement for my ideas, but eagerly adopted many of the 60-Minute Garden designs for use in their own garden. Their suggestions and recommendations for revisions have been invaluable.

INTRODUCTION

Vegetable gardening is second only to flower gardening as America's favorite pastime. At the same time there are many people who do not have a garden but who indicate a desire to have a garden. When surveys and polls are taken about the subject, many millions of Americans confess to not having a garden because they don't have enough time to take care of it. They understand the value and satisfaction to be found in gardening, but they believe that they are too busy with other responsibilities in their lives to add a vegetable patch to their schedule. Lack of time is one of the key reasons that the number of vegetable gardens in this country has dropped in the past few years.

Another phenomenon occurring in this country, especially in the suburbs and the cities, is that our living space is getting smaller. The average size of a new house is smaller than the average house built in the 1950s and 1960s. The size of the average lot for a new house is also smaller than it was just ten years ago. We have less space for that vegetable garden than our parents did.

There is another interesting trend developing while we have been worrying about having enough time to garden and while we have less space to garden. Americans are eating more fresh vegetables than they did ten years ago. The popularity of salad bars in restaurants, the expansion of the size of the fresh vegetable sections in most large supermarkets, and the year-round availability of our favorite vegetables have all contributed to this trend. We do like vegetables in this country. While it is difficult to get any kind of accurate measure, the best estimate of our vegetable consumption each year is between 300 and 400 pounds for each person. That figure includes canned and frozen vegetables. It also includes potatoes, which are not often grown in the backyard vegetable patch.

If we look at just fresh fruits and vegetables, Americans probably eat an average of about 200 pounds per capita. A couple with no children would then need about 400 pounds of fresh vegetables to satisfy their family's needs for the entire year. The 60-Minute Garden can produce over 400 pounds of food on only 200 square feet of space, while requiring only 60 minutes of work a week to maintain!

That's what this book is about. It is a new gardening system that addresses the needs of modern Americans, especially in the cities and the suburbs. It addresses their concerns about limited time and space and responds to their desire for fresh, healthful vegetables.

THE EVOLUTION OF THE 60-MINUTE GARDEN

Jeff Ball's 60-Minute Vegetable Garden contains a number of revolutionary ideas about how to raise vegetables in your backyard. In many cases, these ideas fly against the standard and accepted vegetable-gardening practices used in this country. Nevertheless, the 60-Minute Garden works very well. I know, because I use the system myself.

The concept of the 60-Minute Garden has evolved slowly in my mind over the past ten years. In that time I have been collecting new ideas and information about vegetable gardening. I've always been interested in how to make the vegetable garden more productive while at the same time taking up less of my time to manage it. Consequently, I have accumulated in my files a fair number of designs for devices that would seem to either increase productivity or save time or both. I've been gardening seriously now for over a decade and have learned a great deal about how vegetable gardens work.

About a year ago it seemed that it was time to put all of these ideas and designs into action and to build the ideal garden system.

My father, Ed Ball, is a retired engineer and is a master craftsman when it comes to building almost anything. Since he lives nearby, I enlisted his numerous talents and skills in the project. In the beginning, what I thought I was doing was simply building and testing 20 devices that I had either read about or designed myself. We started from scratch and tore up my entire garden and rebuilt it using boxed beds. Then we constructed tunnels for extending the growing season and trellises for vertical gardening. Several things happened as we proceeded to construct these various gardening devices.

The first thing I found was that few of the designs that I had read about could relate to each other. They stood by themselves, and when we attempted to coordinate them into a single garden system, they had design deficiencies. The trellis designs required completely different materials and separate supports from the cold frames. The shading devices had no compatability with the bird netting barrier devices. We would have wasted considerable time, energy, and materials if we had proceeded to build each device as it was originally conceived.

The second thing I learned was that I couldn't separate the design of a garden device from the actual garden management practices that would be used to grow plants. Plastic mulch is great, but how do you make it compatible with intensive succession-planting techniques that require setting new transplants in the bed through the plastic all throughout the season? A compost sifter is handy, but how does it relate to the design of the compost bin and how one generally uses compost in the garden throughout the year? I had to evaluate the designs of each of the proposed devices against the gardening principles that I use.

A third thing I discovered was that new research affected the designs in many ways. I had been collecting lots of information about experiments in vegetable gardening, and in many cases, this new information also affected some aspect of the design of many of these devices. Mulch became more important as a soil temperature control device than as the more traditional device for weed suppression and moisture control. The design of mulch had to change to accommodate this new development. There were many instances of the influence of new research on the design of many of the garden devices.

What evolved over the years of constructing the 20 gardening devices presented in this book was that there also developed some 10 new or revised garden management practices that were integrated with the designs of the 20 devices. In addition, the devices were revised so that they were much more interrelated and allowed for maximum interchangeability among the parts of the system. A brand new gardening system was developed. This new system, the 60-Minute Garden, has been built and tested. In the course of a year, we found a number of design refinements that needed to be made as we gained practical experience with this new gardening system. So the system has stood the test of practical experience.

ORGANIC GARDENING

I am an organic gardener. I have not made that choice for philosophical reasons, although I do have a philosophy that is concerned with the relationship of man to nature. I am not an organic gardener because I am worried about additives and chemicals in my diet, although I am concerned about such things. I am an organic gardener because it makes good business sense. I am an organic gardener because the technique allows me to get excellent production from my garden with a decrease in my costs and my time requirements every year. For me, organic gardening is an investment in my future in terms of real dollars and cents.

I don't want to dwell on this issue. Other authors have been far more eloquent on the subject. At the same time, while the 60-Minute Garden will work just fine using traditional chemical fertilizing and pest control techniques, it will work much better using organic gardening techniques. I feel it's important to explain why at the outset.

I am fully aware that plants will grow well whether they get their nitrogen, phosphorus, and potassium (NPK) naturally from the breakdown of organic materials in the soil or from the introduction of water-soluble chemical fertilizers. If that were the only consideration, then I would have no argument. There happen to be a number of additional considerations that have convinced me that the organic gardening method is the only way to go.

The first fact that I found significant was that most commercial chemical fertilizers kill a large portion of the microbiotic life in the top 6 inches of soil. They drive out the earthworms and most of the other creatures in the soil that normally live there. The soil becomes just a medium for holding up the plants, and the plants become totally dependent on man's continued application of fertilizer to keep them healthy.

I want the microbiotic life to remain in my soil. I know that in 200 square feet of healthy organically treated soil, the earthworms will produce over 150 pounds of manure every year all by themselves! I appreciate their saving me the trouble. I know that the microbiotic life in the top 6 inches of soil includes predators and parasites that help control the larvae of overwintering pest insects. If they are not there, I have more pest insects to cope with, which take up my valuable time. Finally, I don't want to spend the time having to provide all the nutrients my plants need throughout the seasons, year in and year out. I want to be able to encourage the soil to grow in fertility each year so I can spend less time each year, rather than more time, keeping my plants supplied with nutrients. I feed my soil and then let my soil feed my plants. It takes less time and in the long run it is cheaper.

The primary source of food for my garden is compost. My compost is free. Chemical fertilizers are not free, and their cost will rise significantly in the next decade. The time it takes me to make my compost and apply it once a year is about the same as the time it takes to go and buy the fertilizer and spread it appropriately throughout the growing season. However, the active organic soil enriched by the compost, with its millions of micro pals, helps me control my insects. It's reducing my plant's vulnerability to drought and disease. And in the 60-Minute Garden, the soil doesn't even have to be dug anymore. I save some time with no digging, with fewer problems from insect pests, less need to water so often, and less concern about dealing with diseases. I get as good or even better productivity in my crops; I save valuable time; and in the long run (over five years) I save money. That is a good business deal, and that is why I am an organic gardener.

HOW TO USE THIS BOOK

The 60-Minute Garden is built literally from the ground up and is composed of eight broad components, which are specifically listed in chapter 1. Throughout this book I thoroughly discuss how these components can be integrated into your own 60-Minute Garden. Also, at the ends of chapters 2 through 8, there are explicit construction directions for building the 20 devices found in the 60-Minute Garden. In some cases you will just follow the directions as given while in others you may have to modify the designs for your particular situation. In either case, the devices, with the exception of the compost bin, the raised bed for special gardeners, and the garden sink can be built by anyone who can read and follow directions and who can use a hammer and saw. The compost bin, raised bed for special gardeners, and the garden sink require just a bit more building experience—but even they are not out of the reach of backyard gardeners ready to tackle something new.

The cultural practices and the garden devices found in the 60-Minute Garden accomplish two objectives simultaneously. They save time in the day-to-day caring of a backyard vegetable garden, and they increase the productivity of the small vegetable patch. An additional accomplishment is that the 60-Minute Garden makes gardening an enjoyable experience—free from frustrations and drudgery. I hope you enjoy building your 60-Minute Garden as much as my father and I have enjoyed developing it. It has been an exciting time for us.

CHAPTER 1
THE 60-MINUTE GARDEN:
AN OVERVIEW

The 60-Minute Garden is an amalgam of ideas from the ancient Chinese and Greeks as well as from the most recent research in the finest agricultural laboratories in this country. The system is an integration of 8 improved gardening techniques with 20 garden devices that have been designed and built for this particular system. The 60-Minute Garden is a permanent installation in your backyard and will reward you with bountiful harvests, while requiring only 60 minutes of work each week to maintain. The raised beds, tunnels, trellises, and other various devices are all designed to last for decades, and the small amount of money that you spend to build them will be amply paid back in terms of fresh vegetables that you can easily grow throughout *five* growing

seasons: early spring, spring, summer, fall, and early winter. The 60-Minute Garden is attractive as well as productive. Flowers, birdbaths, and even colorful flags make this vegetable growing system a beautiful addition to your backyard. So if you are ready to move into the future using the very latest technology in producing vegetables in your backyard, read on.

While this system will work just as well in a 1,000-square-foot garden as it does in 200 square feet, I use a 200-square-foot model garden throughout this book to describe the various components of the system. All of the data, where possible, has been translated to apply to a 200-square-foot space. If your garden is 600 square feet, then you multiply the data in this book by three, and you have a 180-minute garden system. The 200-square-foot garden using the 60-Minute system is considered ideal for a couple with no children or for a single-parent family.

The 60-Minute Garden has three primary goals—to save time, to increase productivity in a small space, and to reduce frustration with gardening problems.

SAVE TIME

Many people garden for the pleasure and the relaxation it gives them, and consequently they are not terribly concerned about how much time the garden takes each week. For others of us, time is always in short supply. We have jobs, families to care for and enjoy, and a desire for some fun and recreation once in a while. Whether or not we even have a garden may come down to the question of the availability of our time.

The most common practices in vegetable gardening waste time rather than save time. The 60-Minute Garden reduces the time needed to establish a vegetable garden in the spring and manage it throughout the growing season.

The 60-Minute Garden is based on a system of boxed raised beds that have been double dug and amended with organic materials such as compost. Once these permanent beds are established, they are not dug again. So while your neighbor is out there every spring digging the garden for the umpteenth time, you are not bothered with that time-consuming and generally unpleasant task.

There are no weeds in the 60-Minute Garden. It uses a system of mulching throughout the entire year that virtually eliminates any weeds in the vegetable garden. That is a significant time saver in any garden. Watering and feeding the 60-Minute Garden are easy tasks that take very little time each week because of the drip irrigation system, which is attached to a me-

chanical timing device that allows you to turn on your watering system and forget about it. It turns itself off. The 60-Minute Garden is designed to require very little additional fertilizing after setting up the beds each spring. Again, more time is saved. The beds in the system have permanent foundations installed that are the base for many of the timesaving devices such as season-extending tunnels and trellises. In 15 minutes you can set up 100 square feet of tunnels covered with polyethylene film, giving you an extensive growing area for early crops in the spring and late crops in the fall. It only takes another 15 minutes to remove those tunnels and install trellises along the edge of every bed in your 200-square-foot garden.

The system, therefore, eliminates or greatly reduces the need to dig the garden, eliminates weeding, makes watering a task done in minutes, and reduces feeding requirements; and the devices are designed to be installed and dismantled with maximum concern for keeping time requirements down. In short, the 60-Minute Garden, in a 200-square-foot area, will take the average gardener about 60 minutes of work each week, while producing the optimum level of from 300 to 400 pounds of food. That is a time-efficient system.

INCREASE PRODUCTIVITY

Productivity of a vegetable garden is difficult to quantify in an accurate fashion. Most of us do not weigh everything we harvest, nor do we keep track of the dollar value of our produce compared to local vegetable prices in our supermarket. We think in terms of what is "enough." Do we need to plant a few more tomato plants next year because this year we didn't have quite enough? Next year we plant fewer peppers since this year we had enough to feed an army. Most vegetable gardeners are looking for just enough

Photo 1–1: The 60-Minute Garden uses permanent boxed raised beds that are double-dug and enriched with compost. A system of mulching eliminates weeds, and a drip irrigation system makes watering and feeding the garden an easy task. The 60-Minute Garden is very productive, although it requires little work to maintain once it is established.

of each of their favorite foods and maybe a little extra for the neighbors. Productivity is a pretty subjective concept in most gardeners' minds.

Nevertheless, most of us have a sense of the value of our efforts even if we can't quote precise dollars and cents in total production for a season. Most gardeners who use the system described in this book will produce more food than they are now getting in the same space with traditional methods, and they won't have to work as hard. For those gardeners who are curious about how much we are really producing, let's talk about some statistics.

The average vegetable garden in this country is about 600 square feet or 20 by 30 feet. The latest studies estimate that the value of produce from that average American garden is $360 to $480 or about $0.60 to $0.80 a square foot, using 1984 food prices. This comes from about 1 to 1½ pounds of food produced in each square foot of garden. The most important fact to note is that this "average American garden" is still laid out in rows, doesn't use mulch, uses very little vertical space except for tomatoes, and produces primarily during a growing season that begins with the last frost and ends with the first frost. Unfortunately these are all

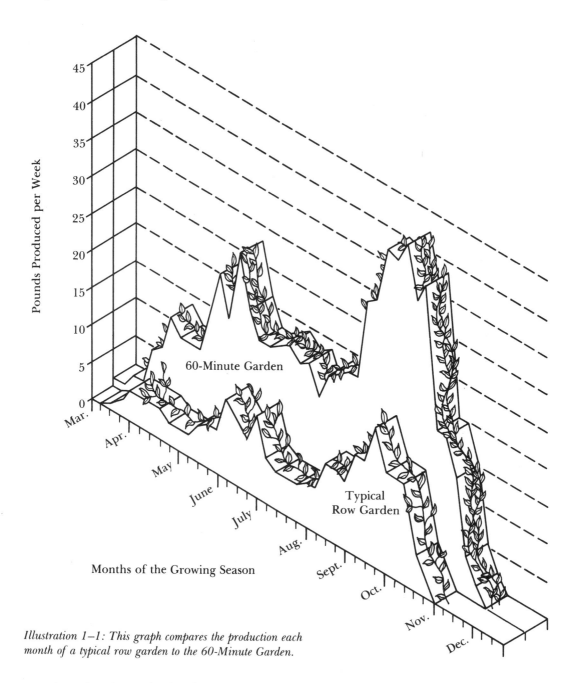

Illustration 1–1: This graph compares the production each month of a typical row garden to the 60-Minute Garden.

practices that keep the level of food production down, as I demonstrate in this book.

If the 60-Minute Garden were incorporated into that average American garden, the productivity of that garden would increase three to five times with no increase in the size of the garden! More dramatically, a master gardener, using this system, could

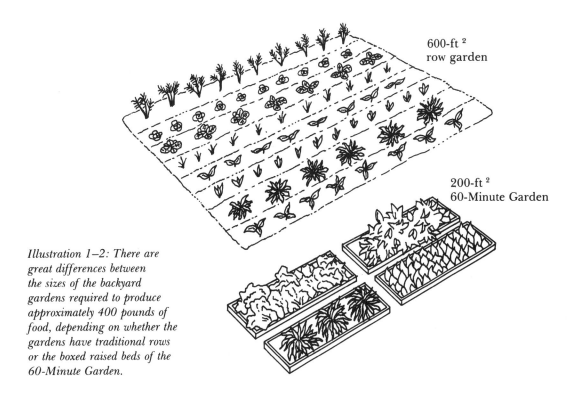

600-ft² row garden

200-ft² 60-Minute Garden

Illustration 1–2: There are great differences between the sizes of the backyard gardens required to produce approximately 400 pounds of food, depending on whether the gardens have traditional rows or the boxed raised beds of the 60-Minute Garden.

produce at least the same amount of food in only a 200-square-foot garden as is now produced in the average 600-square-foot garden in this country!

If the average 600-square-foot garden made use of the 60-Minute Garden, it would produce over $1,000 worth of vegetables instead of $360 to $480. This adds up to about 3½ to 4 pounds of food, worth about $2 a square foot!

How does the 60-Minute Garden achieve such an increase in productivity? The boxed raised beds provide more growing area for plants than does a garden of the same size using rows. The tunnel system extends the growing system one to two months on both sides of the growing season, increasing the total production of the garden just because it is producing food for two to four

more months a year. The trellis system effectively doubles the growing area of the garden by having vertical crops in every bed in the garden. The advanced growing practices such as succession planting, interplanting, drip irrigation, foliar feeding, and mulching all contribute to an increase in vegetable production over traditional gardening practices.

Another way to take advantage of the benefits of this gardening system is to view it as a means to reducing the size of your backyard garden. If your current garden is providing enough produce for you and your family already, then this system will allow you to reduce the size of the garden by at least half. This frees up valuable space for other uses such as flower gardens, fruit trees, sandboxes, and storage sheds.

REDUCE FRUSTRATION

A vegetable garden can be a discouraging experience, especially for beginners. There are so many variables to keep track of, it is easy to lose control to the weeds, the bugs, and the wilt. The 60-Minute Garden doesn't eliminate garden problems, but it helps to ease them. There are a number of techniques and procedures for easily keeping track of what needs to be done in the garden each week. You don't need a home computer for this, but if you have one there is a whole chapter about how to use that computer to help you manage your garden.

There is the backyard Integrated Pest Management system that gives lots of ideas about keeping pests out of the garden, both

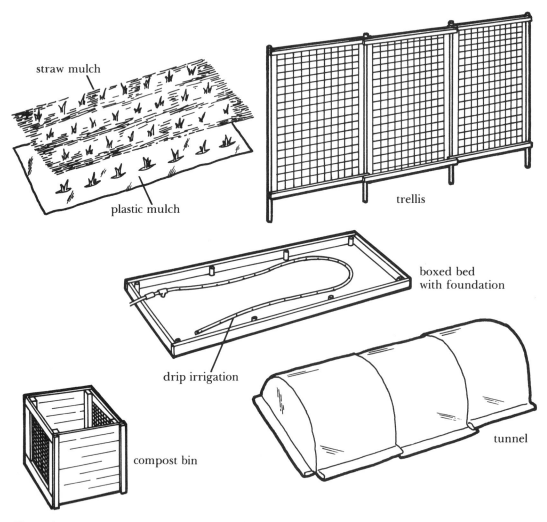

Illustration 1–3: The basic components of the 60-Minute Garden include boxed raised beds with foundations, a drip irrigation system, a mulching system, tunnels, trellises, and a compost bin.

insects and four-legged critters. There is nothing more frustrating than to come out to pick that fresh corn and find that the raccoon beat you to it by one night.

Disease is something that can be prevented by good gardening practices. The 60-Minute Garden is designed to help reduce the problems of disease in a vegetable garden. All of these things provide the gardener with ways to avoid frustration.

SO WHAT IS THE CATCH?

There has got to be a catch to all these wonderful ideas to increase the production of the vegetable garden while taking less time to manage it, and there is. The 60-Minute Garden requires some initial capital investment, both in money and in time. It's the old story—you have to spend some money and time to save some money and time. The beauty of this system, however, is that you can build it in pieces. The cost of each device described in this book is presented in terms of money and time. You can incorporate almost any component of this system into your existing garden and gain the benefits without having to include all the other devices and ideas. You can move toward the complete system at your own pace, over a period of years.

If you decide to develop the entire system at once, you will be spending approximately $3 a square foot in that first year of construction. Therefore, if you have a 200-square-foot garden, it will cost about $600 to install this comprehensive gardening system. At the same time, you will produce over $400 worth of food in that 200-square-foot garden, returning a good portion of your investment in the first year. If we look at a five-year investment plan, you would spend $600 to install this system and about $75 a year to maintain it. In return you would grow $2,000 worth of fresh food, about a 200 per-

Photo 1–2: One very important element of the 60-Minute Garden is the PVC pipe foundation, which supports season-extending tunnels and trellises.

cent return. You can't find a bank to give you that kind of payback.

Building this gardening system takes no special technical skills. My father and I have designed everything so that you can do the job with hand tools. A few power tools such as a power drill and a power saw are very helpful but are not essential. An individual can do everything required to build this system, but like everything else, it is easier and more fun when two are doing the job.

The best time to build your 60-Minute Garden is in the fall and winter when the garden is not in full swing. I built my own system throughout the main part of the growing season, and while I had the best year of my career in productivity, my gardening life was a bit more complicated than it would have been if I had taken on the job in the fall.

COMPONENTS OF THE SYSTEM

The 60-Minute Garden is divided up into eight broad components. Each component includes several devices that contribute to improved productivity and/or time saving. A separate chapter describes how to ap-

ply these components to the 60-Minute Garden, and at the ends of chapters 2 through 8 there are construction details for the various devices. The eight components of this garden system include the following items:

Permanent raised beds
Season extenders using tunnels
Vertical growing system
Advanced soil management techniques
Advanced growing techniques
Watering and feeding devices
Environmental management devices
Garden management techniques

Photo 1–3: One of the joys of the 60-Minute Garden is that it has five seasons: early spring, spring, summer, fall, and early winter. Season-extending tunnels allow you to grow peas in early spring and cold-hardy vegetables into the winter.

TABLE 1–1

OPTIMUM VERSUS MAXIMUM PRODUCTION
IN THE 60-MINUTE GARDEN

CROP	OPTIMUM PRODUCTION (LB)	MAXIMUM PRODUCTION (LB)
Beans, pole	33	50
Beets	17	25
Broccoli	19	29
Brussels sprouts	13	20
Cabbage	21	32
Carrots	27	40
Cauliflower	7	10
Celery	20	30
Chinese cabbage	11	17
Collards	14	21
Cucumbers	20	30
Eggplant	17	25
Kale	10	15
Kohlrabi	9	13
Leeks	13	20
Lettuce, leaf	19	28
Muskmelons	20	30
Onions	23	35
Parsnips	7	10
Peas, snap	10	15
Peppers	10	15
Spinach	23	35
Squash, acorn	13	20
Squash, butternut	13	20
Squash, yellow	10	15
Swiss chard	13	20
Tomatoes	33	50
Zucchini	20	30
Total garden production. for 5 growing seasons	465	700

Note: The figures in this table are for a 200-square-foot garden. Optimum production requires 1 hour of work a week in the garden, whereas maximum production requires 4 hours of work.

Redesigning your garden with permanent raised beds can almost double the growing area available for producing food. If you do nothing else, this change will make a major contribution to giving you more return for your energy in the backyard vegetable patch. Extending your growing season with the tunnels described in chapter 3 gives you some increase in quantity of your produce, but it also gives you fresh vegetables when the prices are generally higher in the grocery stores. Trellises often allow you to grow vegetables, such as winter squash and cantaloupes, which you normally can't grow because of space limitations. Using as much vertical space as possible adds almost 30 percent to your productivity in the garden.

The advanced techniques and devices discussed in the later chapters will add as much as 30 percent more to your productivity as you gain the skills necessary to implement these techniques. I want to emphasize that the data and the estimates of production used in this book are conservative figures. I estimate that you can produce over 400 pounds of food in a 200-square-foot garden using this system; however, I am confident that someone who is willing to put in a bit more time and take the trouble to develop all of these techniques to their fullest potential will be able to produce over 700 pounds from 200 square feet with just a few years of experience. That is close to a year's supply of fresh vegetables for a family of four. Not bad for a small piece of the average backyard in this country.

OPTIMUM VERSUS MAXIMUM PRODUCTION

One of the strengths of the 60-Minute Garden is its versatility. It is very simple in its concept and its design so any beginning gardener can use the entire system with ease and confidence. At the same time, the system incorporates advanced techniques available for vegetable gardening, giving the master gardeners a new tool for producing their county fair champions.

There is a distinction made throughout this book between optimum production and maximum production. I believe that there is considerable confusion created by many of us garden writers as we attempt to educate our readers about vegetable gardening. In our dedication to giving our readers the very best information, we often tend to write about those techniques designed to yield maximum production possible—the biggest tomato and the highest yield of green beans. We seldom write about those techniques that just give us the average production. Many of us don't need the biggest tomato. We just want nice tomatoes and enough green beans. Most of us are not interested in spending the extra time and trouble to get the absolute maximum out of our vegetable garden. For us, "optimum" is fine.

The 60-Minute Garden is designed for both groups of gardeners, the majority of gardeners who want an optimum production for the minimum time invested and the master gardeners who are willing to spend the extra time to get the very best productivity for their effort. The 60-Minute Garden, applied to a 200-square-foot area can give you an optimum production of between 300 and 400 pounds of food while taking only 60 minutes a week to manage. If you want to use some of the more advanced and time-consuming gardening techniques, you can produce over 700 pounds of food in that same 200 square feet! It will take a few years to gain the necessary knowledge and skills, and you will spend 3 or 4 hours a week to do it. However, for that kind of productivity, 3 or 4 hours a week is still not a bad investment for a lot of folks.

Now, let's get started on the basic layout of the 60-Minute Garden and talk about building some raised beds.

CHAPTER 2

RAISED BEDS: THE FOUNDATION OF THE SYSTEM

Raised growing beds are unquestionably the best design for a backyard vegetable garden. Simply by shifting the design of a vegetable garden from traditional rows to raised beds, productivity is increased from 60 to 80 percent. So why are the majority of America's backyard gardens still laid out in rows? Probably because that is the way our parents did it, or because many gardening books, gardening magazines, and garden writers still recommend that approach. Whatever the reason, using rows for laying out a vegetable garden is the worst waste of space possible!

What is a raised growing bed anyway? Most simply, it is a wide row of soil that is anywhere from 2 to 5 feet wide. It is dedicated exclusively to growing plants and therefore is never, *never,* walked on. The soil is loosened by digging or rotary tilling, which causes the bed to rise anywhere from 2 to 4 inches above the level of the surrounding soil that becomes the permanent path.

There are many reasons for establishing raised beds in the vegetable garden. The most important is that they significantly increase the productivity of the garden, simply because they provide more area for growing vegetables than the same size row garden does. Simply by laying out a row garden into beds, you have almost a doubling of the amount of area for growing plants. The additional space comes from area that previously was used for paths in the row garden.

Conversely, raised beds will allow for decreasing the space needed for your gar-

Photo 2–1: The surface of these raised beds is about 3 to 4 inches above the level of the paths. These beds are about 4 feet wide.

den, if you are satisfied with your garden's current level of productivity. If you have 400 square feet in rows and you are getting the amount of vegetables your family desires, then you can shift to a raised-bed system and grow the same amount in less than 200 square feet, freeing the remaining 200 square feet for other uses.

Each part of the 60-Minute Garden, whether it is the growing tunnel, the trellis system, or the mulching system, is dependent upon having a raised bed with some kind of foundation device to support all the other parts. A critical issue in building this system is to establish some degree of uniformity in laying out the beds. It really doesn't matter how wide you make them, as long as you can comfortably reach into the center of the bed. What does matter is that all the beds are the same width throughout the garden, allowing for the important interchangeability of all the devices that are part of the 60-Minute Garden design.

OLD TECHNOLOGY FOR MODERN GARDENS

For many of us, using raised beds seems like a modern innovation—a new way of growing vegetables. In fact, beds were used in China thousands of years ago, and in that country they are still the basic form for growing vegetables in a small space. The Greeks developed raised beds 2,000 years ago after observing that plants thrived in areas struck by landslides. The loosened soil left by the landslide offered a better environment for healthy roots to grow. In the late nineteenth century, the French market gardeners outside of Paris refined the use of raised beds to an art. Using the permanent raised bed, they developed what is called the *French intensive growing system*, which encourages crowding plants much more closely than is commonly done in this country. Some of the permanent raised beds outside of Paris have been extremely productive for over 125 years! Something must be working.

The use of raised beds didn't begin to become popular in the United States until the 1960s. On the West Coast, Alan Chadwick, a brilliant British horticulturist, led a number of research projects demonstrating the spectacular benefits of what he called the *biodynamic/French intensive method,* which made use of beds. This work was popularized by one of Chadwick's followers, John Jeavons. For over 12 years, Jeavons has directed the work of the Common Ground Garden of Ecology Action of the Mid-Peninsula in California. Their research has clearly demonstrated that raised beds, which allow for intensive planting, will produce over four times the vegetables per acre that can be produced by farmers using modern agricultural techniques, chemical fertilizers, and modern machines. Their approach uses less fertilizer, less water, and much less energy.

In the past decade, other groups around the country have developed important demonstrations using raised-bed gardening. The New Alchemy Institute on Cape Cod in Massachusetts has a major demonstration that also includes solar greenhouses, windmills, and aquaculture. The Research Center of Rodale Press in southeastern Pennsylvania has extensive raised-bed gardens to test various designs and approaches that improve production levels.

HOW DO RAISED BEDS WORK?

Before we get into how to build raised beds, it's important to understand a little more about just how they work so that you can decide which particular design is suitable for your garden.

Raised beds work because the vegetables have an ideal growing medium: loose and fertile soil. While beds can be flat, I believe that the advantages of the raised beds outweigh the extra effort it takes to construct

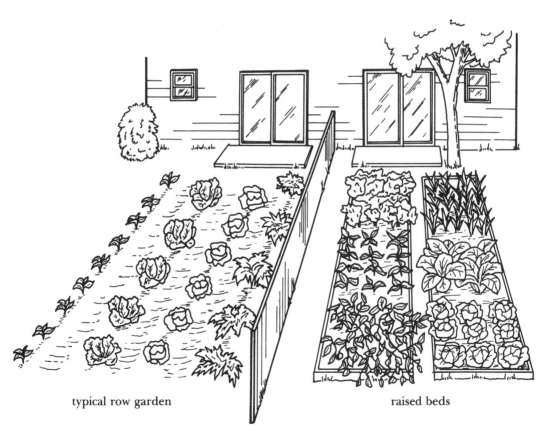

typical row garden   raised beds

Illustration 2–1: Both of these gardens require 200 square feet. The garden on the left uses the traditional row method, while the garden on the right, using intensive planting techniques in boxed raised beds, has significantly more vegetable plants in it.

them. Raised beds have at least five distinct advantages over level row gardens:

Concentrate water and nutrients

Drain faster

Heat up earlier in the season

Avoid the problem of compaction

Reduce or even eliminate the need to dig the garden

CONCENTRATION OF FERTILIZER AND WATER

Raised beds conserve fertilizer and water, and they are permanent, just as the paths between them are permanent. Water, fertilizer, and compost go only on the beds and not the paths. The beds not only get maximum benefit from the fertilizer and water that you use, but there is an important benefit accruing over the years. As a raised bed is enriched with compost, mulch, and other nutrients, the microbiotic life within that bed grows more active each year. In effect the bed becomes more fertile and more productive every year, until it reaches a high level of productivity that will never deteriorate with proper care. Remember the French beds that have been going for over 125 years.

IMPROVED DRAINAGE

The raised bed serves in a modest but measurable way to raise what is called the "head" of the water in the raised bed compared to the "head" of the water in the garden paths. This allows gravity to exert slightly more pressure on the water in the raised beds, pulling it down into the soil a bit faster than water is pulled by gravity in the ground surrounding the raised beds.

The ability of a soil to drain properly is also dependent upon the percentage of humus it contains. In sandy soil humus helps to retain moisture. In clay soil it also sepa-

rates the clods, helping that kind of soil to drain better. No matter what kind of soil you have, it doesn't have to take very many years to get the humus content of it up to the proper level. Soil with a humus percentage of 10 percent is considered good for gardening. The secret is to simply keep adding as much compost and mulch each year as possible. It is really impossible to have too much organic material in a vegetable garden soil. In chapter 5 I recommend that you put 1 inch of compost over your entire 200-square-foot garden every year. This amounts to about 17 cubic feet of compost, which represents about 8 percent of the first 12 inches of your garden's soil. If you add 8 to 10 percent humus or compost to your garden every year, you will have no drainage problems.

EARLIER HEATING

Raised beds will heat up faster in the spring than the surrounding soil. This phenomenon occurs for two reasons. The raised beds stick up from the surrounding surface of the ground, giving them more access to the rays of the sun in the late winter and early spring. In addition, raised beds very often have been amended with compost, manure, and other organic materials over the years, making the color of the soil in the beds much darker than the surrounding soil. This causes more heat to be retained by the darker soil of the raised beds than by the soil surrounding the beds. Of course, in the 60-Minute Garden, the raised beds will warm up even faster because of the tunnels and plastic mulch treatment described in the next chapter.

NO COMPACTION

Compacted soil is no friend of the vegetable gardener. Compaction is caused by pressure from equipment or even from

Photo 2–2: A garden layout featuring permanent raised beds—here they are boxed— with paths between them produces more and healthier plants.

the weight of a footstep. It has the effect of strangling the roots of vegetables. In compacted soil, roots can't get enough water or oxygen to grow properly. Folks who use rows compact the soil in the paths one year while the next year that same area is used to grow vegetables. These gardeners risk stunted plants as roots struggle to penetrate the soil. Rotary tilling does not get down to the levels where compaction does its damage. Organic matter cannot decompose properly in compacted soil because water and oxygen are needed for the decomposition process. So you can add all the organic material you want on top, but down a foot or so, a compacted soil can get little benefit from the organic material.

When I say, never walk on your beds— ever—I mean it! Research completed by Al Trouse of the United States Department of Agriculture's National Tillage Machinery

Laboratory has demonstrated that just normal everyday compacting can slow growth of the plants to at least one-tenth of what it should be. This kind of compacting can occur just from walking on the beds. So the best cure for compaction is to eliminate walking on the beds at all. If, over the years, you add lots of organic material and if you avoid pulling the roots of plants such as broccoli and tomatoes by cutting the stems just below the soil surface, you can begin to solve any compacting problem you already have. What you are striving to achieve is a soil that is loose and porous. Walking on it destroys those conditions. One excellent way to avoid walking on a raised boxed bed is to use a standing board, which is specifically designed to help you avoid compacting the soil by allowing you to stand over the bed to work (directions for making a standing board are found at the end of this chapter).

Photo 2—3: Because the soil is never walked on, it can support plants that are much closer together—intensive planting.

NO DIGGING

Here we get into what might be a controversial subject among some vegetable gardeners. I believe that after a raised bed has been properly built and has had sufficient time to get enriched it does not have to ever be dug up again. However, there are a couple of important exceptions to my position. If you are starting out with very heavy clayey soil that has never been used for gardening, you will have to spend one or two years adding considerable amounts of organic matter to make that soil loose and friable, and it will take several repeated diggings to mix that organic matter with the clay. The same applies to gardens in very sandy soil that won't hold moisture.

In these situations, where the soil is in poor condition in the beginning, you will need to apply at least 2 inches of compost, manure, peat moss, and/or any other organic material that will provide the necessary humus to improve your soil for gardening. This is discussed more thoroughly in chapter 5. Double-digging helps to mix the organic material faster. In both these cases, soil conditions will be improved enough in two years to reach a point where digging the garden becomes a task only for your next door neighbor who still uses rows.

Let me describe double-digging, since it is the best technique for quickly getting a raised bed in shape. There are many advocates for double-digging a garden every single year or even every time a new crop goes in. I believe this is unnecessary. Double-digging is important in establishing a bed for the first time, and it is especially important if you have hardpan to break up below the topsoil in your garden. However, if hardpan is not a problem, I have no trouble with recommending beginning a garden with a rotary cultivator to build your raised beds. Double-digging is still the most thorough method for the beginning garden, but rototilling will suffice.

There is no getting around the fact that double-digging is hard work. But if you are willing to spend 2 to 4 hours double-digging your 200-square-foot garden for a year or possibly two, your garden's productivity will reflect the value of the effort. Double-digging simply means lifting a shovelful of topsoil out of the garden so that you can take a spading fork and loosen, without removing, the second layer of soil below the topsoil. This technique, shown in illustration 2—2, allows you to move down the bed making consecutive trenches, loosening the subsoil, and then refilling the trenches. Double-digging your beds will raise them about 3 to 4 inches because this technique thoroughly loosens and aerates the soil.

I have concluded that digging is not essential, after learning about some recent research on the subject. There are two issues at stake here—the microbiotic life of the soil and the structure of the soil. Extensive and repeated digging or tilling disrupts both.

Again, Al Trouse of the USDA National Tillage Machinery Laboratory has learned that turning the soil dismantles the soil's structure—crumbs that were stuck together come apart. Many of the crumbs are shattered into smaller pieces, making a very

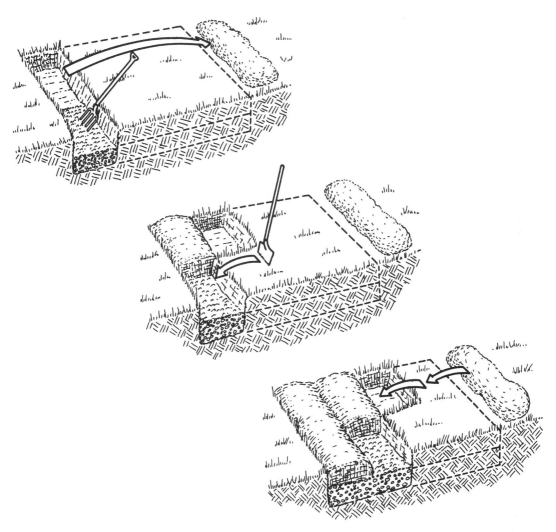

Illustration 2–2: Although double-digging means a lot of hard work, it is the best way to prepare a bed for the first time. The first step is to dig a trench at one end of the bed and move that soil to the other end as in the top illustration. Use a spading fork to loosen the subsoil after removing the topsoil. Next, dig a second trench beside the first one, and place the soil from the second trench into the first trench as in the middle illustration. Continue digging trenches and moving the soil into the previous trench as in the bottom illustration. The final step is to use the soil from the first trench to fill in the final trench that you dig.

Photo 2–4: If it is at all possible, lay out your raised beds with a north/south orientation. This way, as the sun moves daily east to west, it falls on the entire length of each bed. Here the crops on the trellises will not shade the lower growing flowers and herbs in the front of each bed.

fine and fluffy soil, which actually is also a very weak soil. It compacts more quickly, and water and oxygen have more trouble reaching the lower depths of root growth.

Most people don't appreciate the fact that about 75 percent of the beneficial microbiotic life in a soil inhabits the upper 6 inches—the very level we like to rotary cultivate. The worm's life cycle is disrupted by digging. Colonies of beneficial bacteria are slowed in their reproduction by digging, reducing their positive impact. In short, tilling or digging messes up the environment of the very creatures we want to encourage in our soil to keep it healthy and productive.

So what do I do instead of digging? I add organic material, I rotate crops, I leave roots in the ground, and I let the worms do their thing. I add enormous amounts of compost to my garden every year. Usually, I use it for mulch early in the season just before I lay down my black plastic mulch in the spring or the straw or hay mulch in the summer. Rotating the crops not only helps minimize disease problems, it also causes differing root systems to grow throughout the garden over the years. Tomato roots go down 6 feet, and many other plants have root systems going down 3 to 5 feet deep. By rotating those deep-rooted crops with the shallow-rooted crops, the whole garden is effectively being tilled by the very vegetables you are growing. I cut off plants where I can to leave the roots in the ground to decompose and produce channels or tunnels for water and oxygen next year.

An abundant earthworm crop is a marvelous tilling machine. Earthworms are constantly building tunnels in the soil, allowing oxygen, water, and other nutrients to go deep into the area where roots need sustenance. This tunneling includes passing the soil through their digestive system, liberating plant nutrients, and moderating soil acidity. Over time the earthworm population will deepen the topsoil layer by breaking up subsoil and hardpan. Finally, if that were not enough, by their tunneling, earthworms create access to deeper soil levels for countless smaller creatures, such as predatory mites, springtails, and flatworms, which are less able to move the earth but which are very beneficial to the health and vigor of the soil.

Other gardeners have developed additional methods for replacing tilling and digging. Letting your chickens, if you have any, into a portion of your garden effectively tills the top 1 to 2 inches of your soil while getting rid of weed seeds and lots of insects and grubs.

In the end, I am convinced that my garden does not have to ever be dug again. In the spring, I simply rake the top inch or so to prepare a seed bed, add ½ to 1 inch of compost, and away I go! No more backaches and blistered hands or rental costs for the rotary cultivator. Although I dug my garden a few times as I was building up my beds, I am now enjoying the fruits of that labor with some time to do other things.

GARDEN LAYOUT

Whether your garden is established or you are just starting out, it might be helpful to think through the overall layout of your new 60-Minute Garden with raised beds. Many gardeners have absolutely no choice about how their garden is laid out. Trees, small yards, location of the house on the property, and the position of the neighbor's garage all can define exactly the space you have available for a garden; however, if you do have some leeway, there are a couple of issues you might want to review before you start building your raised beds.

NORTH/SOUTH BEDS

Most gardening experts routinely recommend that a garden, whether it has rows or beds, be laid out on a north/south orientation. This allows the sun to come across the garden each day from east to west, causing minimum shading problems between the tall and short plants. This north/south configuration is even more critical in the 60-Minute Garden. Vertical gardening is a major component of the system. Having any orientation other than north/south greatly limits the value of the vertical growing capacity of a garden. Chapter 4 gives several hints to overcome the problem of having a trellis in an east/west layout if that is your only choice.

PATHS

While the beds are the main subject of this chapter, the paths are not an inconsequential consideration in designing your garden system. Both the width of the permanent paths and the material used in the paths are worth thinking about before moving ahead with bed construction.

The paths in my garden are 16 inches wide except for two main paths in the middle of the garden that are 38 inches, allowing me to take my garden cart into the middle of my plot. The widths of the paths are a function of how much space you want to take from growing plants to be used for com-

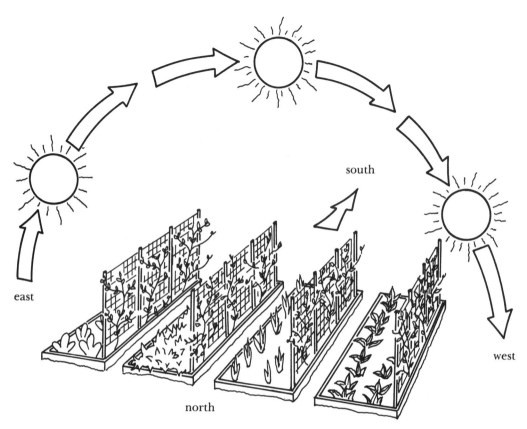

south

east

west

north

Illustration 2–3: For trellises to create the least amount of shade in the garden, orient them in a north/south direction. Consequently, this minimizes the amount of shade in any part of the garden during the day.

fortable access to the beds. I think a 12-inch path is a bit tight when you kneel down to work on a bed, but paths can be from 12 to 18 inches wide and still not take up more than 20 percent of your total garden area (compared to 40 to 50 percent in row gardens). Having wider paths for access by a wheelbarrow or garden cart is a very important consideration. The beds in the 60-Minute Garden are supposed to be permanent. Therefore, what you do now will take considerable trouble to change later. Being able to get a cart full of manure or compost or straw as near your bed as possible is an important convenience, since the goal is to build a garden that is easy to maintain.

Lots of folks have permanent paths of bare soil. It compacts down so much over the years that weeds will grow only with difficulty. Since these are permanent paths, I like having some kind of soft material in the paths to make walking more comfortable, to improve the garden's appearance, and to eliminate mud on my shoes during the wet spells. Some people use gravel, bricks, old carpeting, or boards to cover their paths. I like wood chips that come from the big shredders used by tree-trimming crews. I can often get a truckload for free, or at the most I would pay only $5 or $6 for a year's supply of wood chips.

These wood chips slowly decompose.

They drain very well, and their appearance is pleasing whether they are dry or wet. In addition, after five or six years of adding a fresh layer of wood chips to my paths, I will have a nice layer of beautiful black humus built up, which I can remove and use in my composting system. This is a form of what is called *sheet composting*. Organic materials are put in the paths with the intention that these materials, when later decomposed, will be used as compost.

In some areas of the country, gardeners may choose path material with the consideration of whether it harbors slugs or other harmful insects that may be particularly troublesome to them (see chapter 8 for more on controlling slugs). In that case, boards may be more attractive as path material because they can be picked up each morning so the slugs can be killed. Probably the biggest consideration in selecting a material for your garden paths is availability and cost. Whatever is available, especially if it is free, will probably be what you use for your paths.

Photo 2–5: Whether mounting the PVC foundations on the inside or outside of the boxed bed, fasten them with electrician's pipe brackets and screws.

BED DESIGN AND CONSTRUCTION

There are a variety of methods for building raised beds. Building raised beds does not have to be accomplished in a few backbreaking days. The beds can be introduced into your own backyard over a number of months or even years, spreading out the workload.

A bed can be any length and any width, though there are some limiting factors. A bed should be no wider than twice the distance you can comfortably reach. I emphasize the word *comfortably* because it is one thing to be able to reach 3 feet to pull a weed. It is quite another thing to spend 15 minutes reaching out 3 feet as you transplant seedlings or pick beans. Your arms can get very tired.

I recommend that a vegetable bed be either 3 feet or 4 feet wide—3 feet if there are any young people helping with the garden or grownups of diminutive stature. My beds are 4 feet wide. At the end of this chapter, there are design and construction details for a comfortable sitting board that you can use to make working on the beds easier. I have three of these boards lying around in different parts of the garden so there is always one close by when I need it. They are very easy to make.

The length of beds can vary, as can the width. The primary issue in determining the maximum length of a bed is how far you want to walk to get to the other side of the bed. A 25-foot bed is nice, but you have to walk a bit to get to the other side, and when it is filled with plants, you can't easily step over it. While it is not critical for the 60-Minute Garden, it is helpful to have the length of the beds be evenly divisible by the width of the bed. If you have 4-foot-wide beds, then 8, 12, 16, 20, and 24 feet are good lengths. If you have 3-foot-wide beds, then 6-, 9-, 12-, and 15-foot-beds will work nicely. This allows for easier applications of the tunnel system and the trellis system as you will see in later chapters.

There is no single best design for a growing bed, although there are three designs (flat beds, raised beds, and boxed raised beds) that are the most common and easiest to build. Nevertheless, most of my discussion will dwell on the boxed raised bed, since that is the design I prefer.

FLAT BEDS

Whether for aesthetic reasons or because of time pressures, a perfectly flat permanent bed can be used in this growing system. The flat bed is a bit less obtrusive in a backyard layout.

The borders of a flat bed can be beams much like railroad ties (never use new ties that have been treated with creosote; old ties treated with creosote should not be toxic) or bricks sunk into the soil flush with your yard surface. The paths can be made as wide as your lawn mower and left to grass. The trellis and tunnel foundations I describe in chapter 3 can be used in this form of bed construction just as well as with the other designs. My resistance to flat beds is simply that those beds don't remain flat. They tend to rise a little bit each year because I add so much organic material to my garden. This produces the more common raised bed, which is fine except I prefer to have boxes on my raised beds so I don't have to keep dressing up the sides as they slowly erode from the weather. This is just another task for which I don't have time.

RAISED BEDS

The raised bed without any box or sides (see photo 2–1) is the design that was used by the ancient Chinese. It is sometimes called the *Chinese mound system*. There is an excellent description of this form of bed in Peter Chan's delightful book *Better Vegetable Gardens the Chinese Way* (Graphic Arts Center Publishing Co., 1977). I have used this form of bed for seven years. It works very well except, as I said before, the sides tend to erode down each winter, and dressing up the sides of all the beds in a large garden is almost like work. That is one reason for my moving to boxed beds.

For those of you just beginning your vegetable garden, there is an easy method for building raised beds if you wish to avoid, or at least delay, the task of double-digging your garden. You simply till your entire garden plot with a rotary cultivator. Then, with string and stakes, lay out your permanent beds using whatever length and width you desire. Next, take a shovel and dig the top soil that is in the paths up onto the adjacent bed—giving you instant raised beds. This may not be the best way to get a good raised bed, but it will serve for folks short on time.

BOXED RAISED BEDS

Boxed raised beds have a number of advantages that distinguish them from raised and flat beds. Once the soil is in good shape, you don't have to dig the beds each year (see chapter 5 for soil management tips). The box prevents the sides from eroding, eliminating the need to dress them up each spring. The polyvinyl chloride (PVC) pipe foundations described shortly are easy to install. You get a nice separation between the bed and the path so that the material in the path, such as wood chips, does not get into the bed and vice versa.

There are a number of materials that can be used to box in the bed. The best material of course is free material, but many of us don't have access to old barn boards or free railroad ties, so I will describe the use of planks. The primary issue is cost, but aesthetics and ease of construction are also important considerations in your choice of design.

BEDS MADE
WITH PLANKS

Boards or planks make a nice box and are relatively easy to work with. I've used 1 × 10 cypress boards, and I've used pressure-treated 2 × 8 pine or fir planks (a board becomes a plank when its thickness exceeds 1 inch). Whatever you use, it should

Photo 2–6: This raised bed is boxed with cypress boards that have PVC pipe foundations attached on the inside of the boards. The three white PVC poles will support the trellis netting described in chapter 4. The path between the beds is about 18 inches wide.

be able to withstand prolonged contact with the soil. All boards are going to need replacing sometime in the future but the farther in the future the better. The cypress should be good for 10 years at least. The pressure-treated lumber is more expensive but should be good for 25 years. Redwood is even more expensive, but it lasts 10 to 15 years and is very attractive. Thin boards tend to curl over and warp with time. A thickness of 1½ inches or more is the best choice.

The best time to build a boxed raised bed is in the fall so that your beds will be ready to go very early in the season next year. If you wait until spring, you must wait until the ground is no longer frozen, and you will have missed the head start that the 60-Minute Garden gives you. No matter when you build them, boxed raised beds are not very difficult to construct. Detailed construction information is found at the end of this chapter.

PVC FOUNDATIONS

The PVC pipe foundations give the raised bed its final component and provide the structural base for many of the system's key devices described in the following chapters. For example, the foundations support the tunnel system and the trellis system. All the parts are interchangeable. PVC pipe was chosen for this function because it is durable, strong, easy to work with, safe, and comes in a number of sizes. I prefer the 1½-inch diameter PVC, though 2-inch pipe would also work. Anything smaller would be difficult to work with. The key to the whole design is that the distance between the foundations be uniform, making all the tunnels and all the trellises interchangeable. The importance of this feature will be clearer after reading the chapter on the tunnel system and the chapter on the vertical trellis system.

There are several design options for these foundation devices. The basic issue is

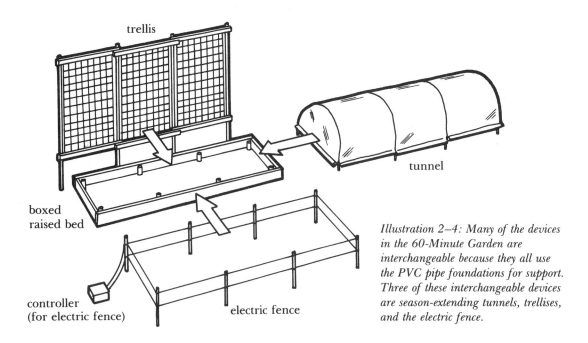

trellis

tunnel

boxed
raised bed

controller
(for electric fence)

electric fence

*Illustration 2–4: Many of the devices
in the 60-Minute Garden are
interchangeable because they all use
the PVC pipe foundations for support.
Three of these interchangeable devices
are season-extending tunnels, trellises,
and the electric fence.*

how to mount the PVC pipe so that it will hold an 8-foot trellis loaded with big fat tomatoes or even winter squash. I have done considerable experimenting with this design, which I hope will help you avoid some of my mistakes. There are two methods for establishing foundations for your 60-Minute Garden. You can strap the PVC pipe to the planks or beams of your raised bed, or you can sink them in the soil, embedded in concrete, to use if you have flat beds.

STRAP PVC
AGAINST THE BOARDS

As you can see in photos 2–7 and 2–8, the PVC pipe can be mounted either on the inside or the outside of the boxed bed. I used PVC pipe that had been cut to 12 inches, which when mounted, is long enough to support the 8-foot poles I use in the trellis system. I prefer mounting the PVC pipe on the inside of the bed, since it has more stability

when used to support the trellises; however, if you have existing beds, you might find that installing the PVC pipe on the outside is considerably easier and less time-consuming. Details for mounting the foundations can be found at the end of this chapter.

IMBED PVC IN CONCRETE

If you don't use a boxed raised-bed design, you can still use the PVC foundations, although they are a bit more time-consuming to install. If you are using the Chinese mound design and have no boards around your beds or if you have flat beds, then the PVC pipe can be embedded in concrete and sunk into the ground. I've tried several methods for setting the PVC pipe in cement. You can probably come up with some of your own as well.

The best design uses PVC pipe embedded in a standard concrete construction block. Set the pipe in one of the existing holes in the concrete block, and pour concrete to fill the hole. To install this foundation you simply bury the block so that the PVC pipe sticks above the ground an inch or so. If you don't want to construct the concrete foundations, you can use the soda bottle version. You use a 2-liter plastic soda bottle as a mold for the concrete and the PVC pipe. You need to have at least 18 to 24 inches of pipe for this design so the foundation can be buried deeply enough to give good lateral support to the trellis system. This unit is simple to install using a

Photo 2–8: These PVC foundations are on the outside of the boxed raised bed. They work satisfactorily, but the foundations will be stronger if mounted on the inside.

Photo 2–7: In the 60-Minute Garden the PVC pipe foundation is either on the inside or the outside of the planks boxing a raised bed. Here the foundation is on the inside, attached with pipe brackets available in most hardware stores. The top of the foundation is even with the top of the plank. A wooden trellis pole sits in this foundation.

posthole digger. I use this method for setting foundations in my permanent strawberry bed, which does not need to support poles but simply needs to support a tunnel system for the netting to keep out the birds.

Making the soda bottle foundations is simple. Mix some concrete to a fairly loose consistency. Cut off the top of the bottle and fill it about two-thirds full with concrete. Then, press the PVC pipe down into the bottom of the bottle, using a piece of paper on the bottom of the pipe to keep the concrete from oozing up into the pipe. This forces the concrete up to the very edge of the bot-

Photo 2–9: You can see the tips of the PVC foundations sticking up above the level of the soil in this newly constructed boxed raised bed. The foundations need to stick up an inch or two to prevent soil from falling down into them as you prepare and work your garden during the year.

tle. When the concrete dries, take a masonry drill and drill a hole in the bottom so water can drain from the pipe when it rains.

TIME AND COST CONSIDERATIONS

The beds and the foundations described in this chapter serve as the base for many of the devices described throughout the remainder of this book. They have been tested, and they work.

It is very difficult to estimate how much time this phase of construction will take for an individual gardener. Digging 200 square feet of new beds can take an hour with a rotary cultivator or can take 8 hours double-digging by hand if the soil is difficult. Constructing the boxes for the beds and mounting the foundations can take a day or even two, depending on the design and on how much help you have.

The best time to do this work is in the fall. Wintering over gives the beds a chance to settle, and you don't feel so rushed as you might if you were building them in the spring. The beauty of this system is that you don't have to do your entire garden all at once. You can transform an existing garden one bed at a time over a period of a few years. When you build a permanent growing system such as this, taking a few years for construction is insignificant compared to anticipating decades of high-level production.

Using the model 200-square-foot garden, building these beds and foundations will cost you about $150 or $0.75 per square foot.

Speaking of production, what kind of harvest can you expect after this phase of bed building? Estimating how much food you will produce in a given space is a little bit like trying to predict the weather. We can make an intelligent guess, but the reality can be considerably different from the prediction. Throughout this book, I estimate production levels in terms of value per square foot of garden and weight of food per square foot of garden. Both of these are clearly just estimates, but they should give you some indicators for comparison.

A 200-square-foot garden, using beds, can produce about 400 pounds of food, worth approximately $200. This assumes average soil, average gardening skills, normal weather, and some good guessing. This means that your initial investment in constructing the beds and foundations is covered in the first year of production.

If you just stopped here in developing your gardening system, you would be considerably ahead of the game in improving your vegetable garden's performance. But why settle for only half the benefits? The next step is to develop the capacity to extend the growing season so that you can take greater advantage of this increased growing area you have gained by building raised beds. That is what chapter 3 is all about.

FOUR BOXED BEDS (USING PLANKS) WITH PVC FOUNDATIONS

For a 200-square-foot garden, you could easily build four boxed beds, each 12 feet by 4 feet (both outside dimensions). The construction details that follow describe the materials, tools, and procedures necessary to build four beds.

The general procedure when constructing boxed beds with PVC foundations is to dig the bed first, piling the dirt up away from the edges. This leaves a relatively flat surface upon which to lay the box. Then build the box and install it in place around the bed. Use a level to make sure that the box is level, making adjustments as needed. When everything looks square and level, pack dirt along the outside of the boards, and rake the soil inside the bed up to the edge, giving the boards support on both sides. A few rains complete the settling of the whole rig.

The box for raised beds is easy to construct. Use 16-penny galvanized nails to join the corners. Constructing a bed up to 12 feet long is easy. If you decide to make beds longer than 12 feet, construction includes a few more steps. At 16 feet and 24 feet, you get into the problem of having

to connect two or three planks together because it is difficult to buy single pieces of lumber long enough. Simply line up the two pieces, and nail a small piece of board to each side, using 8-penny nails. It is not difficult, but it is somewhat awkward and definitely needs two people for the job.

If you choose to use boards instead of planks, you will want to mount a triangular gusset on each corner to avoid having the boards curl over after a few years. This gusset can be a triangle with sides of about 5 inches, and it is attached with nails.

PVC foundations are stronger and they look neater when they are installed on the inside of the box. The easiest way to install them on the inside is to mount the foundations when you are building the box. That way you can do the drilling and mounting all at once up on sawhorses, which is much more comfortable.

Mount the PVC foundations so that the top of the open pipe is flush with the top of the boards surrounding the bed. This minimizes the amount of soil that will inadvertently fall down into the pipe.

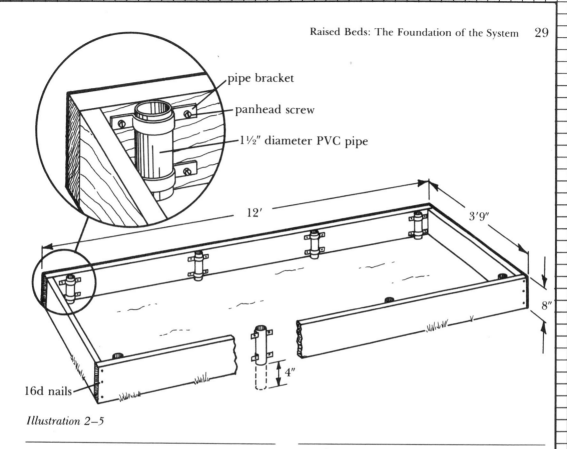

pipe bracket

panhead screw

1½″ diameter PVC pipe

12′

3′9″

8″

4″

16d nails

Illustration 2–5

SHOPPING LIST

Lumber
128 feet 2 × 8 × 12′ pressure-treated
   pine planks
Hardware
32 feet rigid PVC pipe 1½″
64 electrician's pipe brackets 1½″
128 panhead zinc-plated screws #10 × 1″
4 dozen galvanized nails 16d
     Total cost: $150
     Cost per square foot: $0.75

TOOLS

Drill
Hammer
Level
Saw
Screwdriver
Shovel
Spading fork
Square
12′ measuring tape

CUTTING LIST

Size	Piece	Quantity
12'	Side pieces	8
3'9"	End pieces	8
12" × 1½"	PVC foundations	32

CONSTRUCTION STEPS

1. Cut the planks: 8 side pieces that are 12 feet long and 8 end pieces that are 3 feet 9 inches. To prevent splitting the planks, drill three starting holes to receive the nails at the ends of the side pieces.

2. Attach the PVC pipe foundations on the inside of the side planks with pipe brackets. To ensure even distances between the PVC foundations, put the first one 4½ inches from each end of the planks, with 3 feet 9 inches between them. Locate and drill for the brackets so that the top of the pipe is flush with the top of the plank and the bottom clip is down about 6 inches.

3. Prepare the beds by digging holes where the PVC foundations will extend— about 4 inches below the bottom of the plank. You want the surface of the soil on which the planks will sit to be as level as you can make it, although you can adjust it easily later.

4. To build one bed, set one long plank in place, and level it by digging here and there or shimming with little stones. Then nail both end pieces to it with 16-penny galvanized nails, three to each joint. Make sure that the corners are square, and then make sure that they are level.

5. Attach the other 12-foot plank, checking level and squareness.

6. Back fill as necessary outside the planks to whatever level you wish to have your paths. I used wood chips to fill in the paths. Tamp the soil under the planks in those places that had been shimmed for leveling. Construct the other three beds in the same manner that you constructed this bed.

STANDING BOARD FOR WORKING WITH BOXED BEDS

This device allows you to work over your boxed raised beds without standing directly on the soil and compacting it.

SHOPPING LIST

Lumber
1 pc. 1½″ × 12″ × 5′ pressure-treated plank
2 pcs. 1 × 2 × 12″ scrap lumber
Hardware
6 flathead wood screws #10 × 1½″
    Total cost: $4

TOOLS

Drill, bits, and countersink
Saw
Screwdriver

CUTTING LIST

Size	Piece	Quantity
1½″ × 12″ × 4′2″	Standing board	1
1 × 2 × 12″	Blocks	2

CONSTRUCTION STEPS

1. Cut the plank to size.
2. Locate the two blocks so they are lined up on the underside of the standing board just inside the edges of your boxed raised bed. For a 4-foot-wide boxed bed, the blocks should be approximately 3 feet 8 inches apart. These prevent the standing board from sliding to one side or another when you are up on it. Screw the blocks to the standing board.

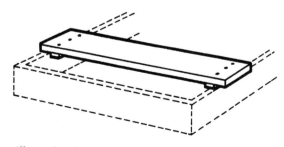

Illustration 2–6

SITTING BOARD FOR WORKING WITH BOXED BEDS

A comfortable sitting board makes working in the 60-Minute Garden an easy task. A bed that is about 4 feet wide allows a gardener to easily reach into it while sitting on the board. The paths between my beds are less than 2 feet wide, so my sitting board is 2 feet long. When you make your sitting board, be sure to make it long enough to accommodate the width of the paths between your beds.

SHOPPING LIST

Lumber
1 pc. 1 × 12 × 2′
Hardware
1 pc. cloth-backed plastic upholstery material 18″ × 30″
several upholstery tacks
1 pad of scrap cloth, old rug, or some similar cloth material that is about 1″ thick and the size of the sitting board
Total cost: $4

TOOLS

Hammer
Sharp knife

CUTTING LIST

Size	Piece	Quantity
1 × 12 × 2′	Sitting board	1

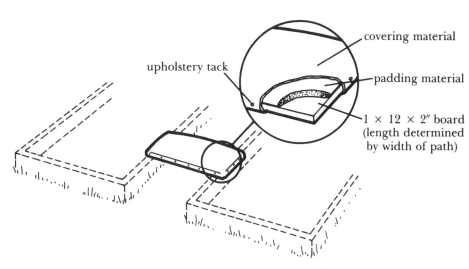

upholstery tack

covering material

padding material

1 × 12 × 2″ board
(length determined
by width of path)

Illustration 2–7

CONSTRUCTION STEPS

1. Fasten the plastic covering material along one long edge of the sitting board with upholstery tacks, spaced no more than 2 inches apart. The material should overhang each end of the board equally.

2. Form the packing material into a pad about 1 inch thick and evenly distributed over the full area of the sitting board.

3. Pull the plastic covering material tightly over the pad, maintaining the even distribution of the material on the board.

4. While keeping tension on the plastic covering material, tack along the other long edge of the sitting board, as in step one.

5. Pull one end of the covering material into position and tack it with several tacks in the middle section of the end piece. Then cut and fold the corners and finish tacking the first end.

6. Pull the covering material tightly over the other end and repeat step five.

7. Cut excess material flush with the bottom side of the board.

BOXED BEDS FOR GARDENERS WITH SPECIAL NEEDS

Gardening can be a pleasure for all people, old and young, active and infirm, but some folks have difficulty working in a garden that is down at ground level. This bed, for people who need to be able to work at waist level, is designed to make reaching the vegetable plants much easier. Construction of this raised bed, however, takes a strong back and some knowledge of masonry techniques. To form the ribs to support bird netting or polyethylene, push 1-inch PVC firmly into the soil as shown in illustration 2–8.

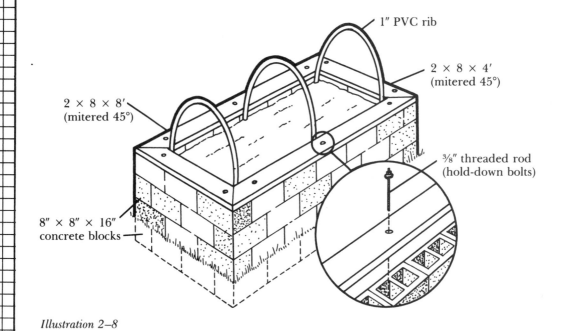

1″ PVC rib

2 × 8 × 4′
(mitered 45°)

2 × 8 × 8′
(mitered 45°)

⅜″ threaded rod
(hold-down bolts)

8″ × 8″ × 16″
concrete blocks

Illustration 2–8

_____ SHOPPING LIST _____

Lumber
3 pcs. 2 × 8 × 8' pressure-treated pine
    planks
Hardware
64 hollow concrete blocks 8″ × 8″ × 16″
    (24 of those 64 should be corner or end
    blocks)
200 pounds of mortar mix
10 washers ⅜″
2 36″ lengths of ⅜″ threaded rod
10 nuts ⅜″
        Total cost: $75

_____ CUTTING LIST _____

Size	Piece	Quantity
8'	Side pieces of top shelf, mitered 45°	2
4'	End pieces of top shelf, mitered 45°	2
6″	Threaded rod, chamfered (beveled) on one end	10

_____ TOOLS _____

Hoe
Level
Measuring tape
Mixing tub for mortar
1″ counter-boring bit
Saw
Shovel
Small 6″ mason's trowel
Square
⅜″ drill

CONSTRUCTION STEPS

1. Using a shovel, dig a level trench to a point 8 inches below the surface of the ground to accept 8-inch concrete blocks. The trench will be a rectangle with outside dimensions of 8 feet by 4 feet. While not essential, a layer of sand or fine gravel on the bottom of the trench is desirable. Use a hoe to level the bottom of the trench.

2. Using no mortar lay six blocks on each side with two blocks at each end enclosed by the side blocks, leaving about ½-inch space between adjacent blocks. The top surface must be level and even for all blocks.

3. Lay the first course of mortared blocks with the end joints broken so that there are five blocks on each side and three across each end. Check frequently to ensure the straightness of the line of blocks, squareness of the structure, and levelness of the structure. *Breaking the joints* means each joint between blocks is over the middle of the block in the course below.

4. Lay the other two courses of mortared blocks, breaking the joints as described above.

5. Let the structure stand at least one day before attaching the plank shelf on the top or filling with soil.

6. Backfill the outside of the trench up to ground level.

7. Planks are cut to fit the top of the structure with the corners mitered at 45 degrees—the two side pieces are 8 feet long

and the two end pieces are 4 feet long.

8. Mark the locations for hold-down bolts in the planks to correspond with block openings near the ends of the planks and in the center of the two long planks. Using the 1-inch-hole bit, counterbore about ½ inch in each location. Then drill through with a ⅜-inch hole for the bolts.

9. Set a washer in each counterbore; assemble a nut on one end of each bolt, leaving a few nut threads outside for later tightening, and pass the bolt through the washer and the hole in the plank.

10. After the structure has stood for at least one day, push tightly crumpled newspaper down far enough into each of the block openings selected for hold-down bolts to be below the end of the bolt, or about 5 inches.

11. Mix some mortar, and fill each of the holes with mortar up to ¼ inch from the top of the block. Place the planks with assembled bolts in position, making sure that the bolts are pushed down so that the nuts are in contact with the washers. Shim corners if necessary to make the boards all level and smooth at the joints. Let it sit for two days and moderately tighten the bolts. Fill the bed with soil, aged horse manure, and compost.

CHAPTER 3

GARDENING WITH TUNNELS

American vegetable gardeners have been extending their growing seasons in various ways and with various levels of success since the days of the colonists. Cold frames and cloches have been the most common devices used to add a few weeks to the growing season, especially in the North. A form of cloche that has been generally overlooked in the backyard garden until recently is the plastic tunnel. A tunnel is made by stretching polyethylene film over a series of ribs or supports that have been fastened into the ground in some way. Unlike a greenhouse these tunnels do their job without having to be completely airtight.

These tunnels have been used in Europe, especially by market gardeners, for many decades. While they are being ac-

cepted more and more in this country by commercial growers, these devices have had little impact on the backyard gardens of America. Yet they offer substantial benefits in extending the growing season and in protecting plants from flying pests. They cost very little to construct.

The tunnel not only helps us to extend our growing season, it allows us to take better advantage of the money-saving value of our gardens. If a person has a vegetable garden, at least partly to save some money, then growing vegetables during the summer months doesn't accomplish that objective very well. With the increase in the availability of farmers' markets and fresh vegetable stands around the country, we don't save a great deal of money from growing our own tomatoes, peppers, and zucchini in August. Where we begin to save money is in the winter and early spring when vegetable prices are at their highest. For example, our snap beans are worth about $0.40 a pound in the summer when we pick them but cost $1.00 a pound in December whether we buy them fresh or frozen. Therefore, to get the most from the money-saving value of our garden, we must either store much of our garden produce, extend our growing season, or do both.

The polyethylene tunnel can extend the productive growing season of most areas in the United States from one to two months beyond the frost dates on both ends of the season, or a total of two to four months each year! It almost doubles the growing season. That kind of extension means significant savings from the backyard vegetable production effort.

Tunnels perform a substantially different function from the traditional cold frame. The cold frame has been used to start or "harden off" early season seedlings. Most backyard cold frames have a growing area of less than 30 square feet. While tunnels can be used for these purposes as well, their primary function is to allow food production to begin directly in the garden one to two months before normal planting time. More importantly, the tunnel allows you to use your entire garden in your extended growing season, not just 30 square feet found in the typical cold frame.

The plastic tunnel has three functions in the vegetable garden. First, it allows you to begin your spring planting at least a month earlier than normal and allows you to keep producing food at least a month longer in the fall than normal. Secondly, by using a material other than clear plastic as a cover, the tunnel can also become a shading device for growing lettuce and other heat-sensitive crops during the heat of summer. Cheesecloth or mosquito netting works well for this purpose. Finally, the tunnel can be used to protect your plants from insects and birds.

Using netting instead of clear plastic protects strawberries from marauding birds just waiting to decimate your patch of juicy red berries. Mosquito netting over the zucchini patch, at the proper time, can repel the fly that lays the eggs that produce the destructive squash borer.

HOW DO TUNNELS WORK?

Essentially, plastic tunnels serve to soften the effects of the environment on plants. The tunnel increases soil and air temperature, protects plants from wind and frost, and reduces moisture loss. It effectively softens the impact of cold weather on plant growth.

Cold acclimation of vegetable plants takes place in two stages. Colder temperatures first tend to slow and then stop plant growth. At that point, the plant produces natural sugars within the leaf structure to help depress the freezing point of the water within the leaf. This tends to protect the leaf from the damage caused by freezing, which bursts the plant's cells. Those vegetables we call *frost hardy* or *cold hardy* have this sugar-producing capacity to protect themselves from some frost exposure and can survive colder temperatures.

The damage to many vegetables is directly related to how long a freezing temperature exists around the plant. A short period of freezing temperatures can be endured by many vegetable plants. The tunnel, therefore, helps these vegetables endure freezing periods by slowing down the impact of cold outside temperatures and thereby extending the period of growth.

However, for many vegetable plants, direct contact with frost causes serious, if not terminal, damage. The tunnel protects your garden from all frost damage, since any cover will prevent frost from forming on the plant. The ability to protect plants from frost, es-

Photo 3–1: Flexible PVC pipe ribs (that are mounted in the PVC pipe foundations attached to boxed raised beds) support these two tunnels. The panels of polyethylene film laid over the ribs overlap each rib about 6 to 10 inches. A piece of clear Plexiglas closes off the end of the tunnel on the right, while polyethylene film folded over like a gift package closes off the end of the tunnel on the left. Notice the slits cut into the plastic for ventilation.

pecially in the fall, has significant impact on the length of the growing season. Tomato plants, for example, will continue to ripen fruit for weeks under a tunnel after the first light frost of the fall, which normally completely knocks them out.

Another major benefit of the tunnel is as a wind protector. Most folks don't appreciate the potential harm to plants of a chilling wind. In the first place, wind causes the moisture in the soil to evaporate faster. More importantly, a windchill effect can have serious consequences for plant growth. According to some recent research, if protected

from the wind, a tomato in a tunnel at 68°F will grow better than a similar plant will grow at 77°F in the open.

Perhaps the greatest value of the tunnel is its capacity for warming the soil, especially when used in conjunction with black or clear plastic mulch. Experiments at the Rodale Research Center have shown that temperatures at the plant's root zone are more important to growth than air temperatures surrounding the leaves. Therefore, if we can get the temperature of our garden soil up to the level needed for growing plants earlier in the spring, we can begin planting and producing earlier. Likewise, in the fall, the longer we can keep soil temperatures at the proper level, the longer we can have growth and production of food.

The tunnel operates just like a greenhouse. It allows the sun's rays to pass through the plastic film and to heat up the soil and the air in the tunnel. When black or clear plastic is laid on the soil in a tunnel, that soil tends to absorb more heat than would be absorbed without the plastic being there. In addition, the plastic mulch helps the soil retain heat longer than if it were not there. So

while the temperature of the air in March can go below freezing at night, the soil under the black or clear plastic will not freeze in just one night.

A properly vented clear plastic tunnel with black or clear plastic mulch will protect plants when the outside air is down to 28°F. The air temperature during the day in a properly ventilated tunnel will be from 6° to 29°F warmer at midday than that outside the tunnel. The soil temperature will be from 6° to 8°F warmer because of the black or clear plastic. The combination of the tunnel and

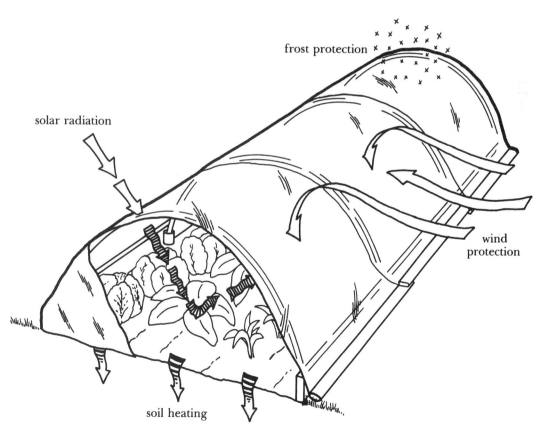

Illustration 3–1: A tunnel made of polyethylene film supported by PVC ribs protects the vegetables in the bed from the harsh environmental conditions found in late winter and in late fall. It protects the plants from the wind, from frost, and from evaporation of water in the soil. It also collects solar heat, which is then radiated into the soil to protect the plants from the overnight cold.

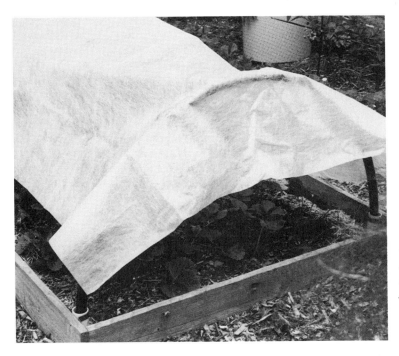

Photo 3–2: Tunnels made of polyspun row cover fabric protect cool-weather crops from hot summer sun. While it shades the bed, it allows air, light, and water through to the plants.

the plastic mulch can keep the ground from freezing two months on either side of the first and last frost.

BUILDING A PLASTIC TUNNEL

There are a number of designs for building plastic tunnels. Also, there are variations on the kinds of material used for the ribs of the tunnel and variations for how the clear plastic film is attached to the tunnel. All of these designs will work, but I am convinced that the design presented here is the best for a backyard application. My design uses the polyvinyl chloride (PVC) pipe foundations described in the previous chapter. The tunnel is constructed by simply placing the tunnel's ribs into the foundations and covering those ribs with some material. Once the materials are gathered and the pieces are

assembled, setting up the tunnel can be done in minutes.

RIBS OF THE TUNNEL

While some designs suggest using various kinds of wire or bent concrete rods, the best material for the ribs of a tunnel in a backyard vegetable garden is flexible PVC pipe. It is easy to use and will last forever. Unlike the stiff PVC pipe that was used for the foundations, flexible PVC can be easily bent into a semicircle to form the ribs. I have two sizes of ribs. For the plastic tunnel that is used like a greenhouse, I use 1-inch flexible PVC pipe (it usually is black). For tunnels to screen out insects or protect against birds, I use ½-inch flexible PVC pipe. I prefer the heavier ribs for the growing tunnel since it can support the wet snow that often graces my area in March. The lighter ribs could probably hold the weight, but they aren't quite solid enough for my conservative Yankee upbringing. On the other hand, the ½-inch pipe is cheaper.

GLAZING

The glazing material for a tunnel is some kind of clear polyethylene film. Any of these films will work, so the issue for me is how long it will last. Most plastic film will break down from ultraviolet radiation. Most clear plastic will last only about two seasons. However, there is on the market a clear polyethylene film that has an ultraviolet inhibitor that stabilizes the material. While estimates vary, depending on who you talk to, this plastic should last from five to ten years. It comes in 6-mil thickness, so it is pretty durable.

Most polyethylene films come in varying lengths but are usually 10 or 20 feet wide. You can find clear plastic in most garden centers, but the ultraviolet stabilized stuff is usually only found from mail-order houses. There is a list of sources in the appendix.

There are at least two ways to mount the clear plastic on the ribs of the tunnel—the method developed by commercial growers and my way. The commercial method, developed by market gardeners, is to lay the plastic film lengthwise over the ribs, securing the ends in a bunch and holding down the sides in some fashion.

This method works fine for large applications, but I believe it is not as flexible as it might be in a backyard application. My father and I have come up with a different approach that works very well and gives us much more flexibility in using tunnels throughout the garden area. Our method uses individual panels of clear plastic mounted on strips of wood at each end. One panel lies over each set of ribs, overlapping the adjacent panel. See illustration 3–3 near the end of the chapter, which is a detailed drawing of this design.

With these panels of plastic glazing, I can construct a tunnel of any length. I can take down part of a tunnel in the late spring, leaving a smaller section to be used a bit longer. I can build several smaller tunnel devices rather than having one long one. In other words, I have much more flexibility with this design than I had with the single long-sheet method.

The key to this scheme is making sure you take the correct measurements for cutting your panels of clear plastic. These panels will last from five to ten years, so you don't want to have them be less than perfect. There are two issues to keep in mind—have sufficient overlap between panels and make special panels for the end ribs of the tunnel.

I want to mention one alternative design that I find attractive, but because of the cost, it may not be so attractive to others. I use Plexiglas (one of several kinds of rigid acrylic sheets) to make the end pieces for my tunnels. I think they look a little neater, and I can see into my bed more clearly than with the semiopaque polyethylene. I simply make a semicircle of Plexiglas and mount it to one of my PVC ribs with sheet-metal screws. This becomes a permanent end to my tunnel. I use the Plexiglas device on the south end of my tunnel and a piece of Masonite or other solid material for the end piece that sits on the north end of the tunnel. These Plexiglas ends can cost from $16 to $22 and are a bit difficult to work with; however, I think they make the tunnel more attractive, and I was willing to spend the money for four Plexiglas end pieces.

VENTILATION

The tunnel needs to be ventilated because the air in the tunnel on a clear sunny day can become much too warm for effective growth of the plants. In addition, a tunnel can become a breeding ground for mildew and mold, if ventilation is not available. The humidity and the temperature buildup combine to create a perfect environment for these problems.

There are at least two methods for ventilating a tunnel. You can raise the sides of the plastic covering during the day when it is sunny, or you can cut permanent slits in the plastic cover. I prefer the latter method because I am not always at home and do not want to have to worry about venting my tunnels every time it is sunny. The slits are placed at about 5-inch intervals halfway down each side of the tunnel. The slits can be from 3 to 6 inches apart. The warmer your weather, the more slits you will need.

There is commercial polyethylene film available with the slits already cut. I prefer to make my own slits because I don't need as many cuts as there are in the commercial materials. I use a razor-sharp knife to make my ventilation slits. During cloudy days, the slits are not open very much, and the air inside the tunnel is almost always a bit warmer than the outside air, even with all those slits in the plastic cover. Remember, it is the soil temperature that is more important to plants in the tunnel than the air temperature. Air that is too warm and air that is too humid can be just as harmful to vegetables as a heavy frost or overnight freezing temperatures. Now let's talk about how to have better control of that soil temperature.

PLASTIC MULCH IN TUNNELS

I will talk more about mulches in chapter 5 when I get into advanced planting techniques; however, we need to talk about how to cut black or clear plastic mulch now because you will normally lay the plastic over the bed before you build your tunnel. It is much easier to lay it before you have set up the ribs of the tunnel.

The plastic mulch will help the soil warm up and will then keep it warm. It also keeps down weeds and minimizes moisture

evaporation. I do not use my drip irrigation system in the early spring because I am wary of a quick freeze, but I do set up the drip system under the black plastic before I build my tunnel. The plastic is laid right over the drip irrigation tubing.

The trick with plastic film mulch is to cut holes in it that are big enough for the plants but not so big that the heating and weed protection value is reduced.

As you will see later in this chapter when I talk about how to use the tunnels in the spring and fall, it is handy to be able to put in holes for smaller plants such as spinach as well as for larger plants such as broccoli and cabbage. I designed a form for cutting holes in plastic that is easy to use and allows you to take maximum benefit offered by black or clear plastic mulch when used in a tunnel (see illustration 3–4).

Plastic mulch inside a tunnel is not so vulnerable to blowing around from the wind as is plastic just set out in the open garden. So, you don't have to worry so much about covering the edges with dirt to hold the mulch down. I use the "hairpin" hold-down pins (see illustration 5–5) while I'm setting up my tunnel. I'll talk more about black and clear plastic mulch in chapter 5.

VARIATIONS FOR THE TUNNELS

There are several additional applications for the tunnel system in the vegetable garden. The tunnel can be used to shade heat-sensitive plants and can be used to protect parts of the garden from small animals, birds, or insects. Using the tunnel to protect against pests is discussed in detail in chapter 8.

SHADING DEVICE

Lettuce, spinach, and Chinese cabbage are three vegetables that do not like the hot sun of summer. When the weather gets warm and the sun is high in the sky, they tend to bolt to seed and become bitter. One of the ways to protect against this problem, or at least to slow down its development, is to shade these crops from the direct rays of the sun. Some people rig special covers made of snow fence to accomplish this task, but for the tunnel system, a cheesecloth panel works very well. Using cheesecloth or commercial mosquito netting, you simply rig a panel in the same fashion as you build the panels with the polyethylene film. Mount the cheesecloth on two strips of wood using a staple gun. Then drape the cheesecloth panel over the ribs, and your lettuce, spinach, or Chinese cabbage will not bolt so quickly. You can grow lettuce under this device throughout the entire summer.

SET UP AND STORAGE

Once you have made all of the panels and tunnel ribs, and have attached the PVC foundations to your beds, setting up a tunnel takes a matter of minutes. I suggest you have two bricks or stones for each rib in your tunnel to hold down the plastic panels. My tunnels have withstood 40-mile-per-hour winds, so the bricks seem to be sufficient to hold down the panels in normal kinds of storm conditions.

It is important to find a place to safely store your polyethylene panels during the summer and in the dead of winter. I built a rack in a storage area to stack the panels that have been rolled up on their own sticks. This same storage area can be used to store the netting for the vertical trellises described in the next chapter. The PVC ribs don't need any special care, since they are virtually indestructible, but they can be unsightly just lying around the garden when not in use. I store my rib pieces behind a bush in the backyard.

HOW TO USE TUNNELS IN THE BACKYARD VEGETABLE GARDEN

Introducing tunnels into your vegetable garden, especially if you have been gardening for more than a few years, can be a bit complicated. Using tunnels creates a whole new set of scheduling and space allocation decisions that you didn't have to cope with in the past. So there is a small price for using this effective tool for extending your growing season. Actually, tunnels offer you two brand new growing seasons, which means you have to do some additional garden planning. I call these two new seasons the early spring season and the early winter season.

Normally, most folks look at their garden year as having three distinct seasons—spring, summer, and fall. Each season has its own distinctive gardening requirements and cultural practices. The fall season is planned differently from the spring season. In the spring the days are getting longer each week, while in the fall they are getting shorter. Therefore, we have to use different methods for calculating how long it will take any vegetable to grow to maturity. The fall crops take a bit longer than the spring crops.

Now, with tunnels in our garden, the two additional seasons (early spring season and early winter season) mean that we have a two-month period prior to the last frost in the spring and a two-month period after the first frost in the fall to work into our garden planning and management. Each of these extra seasons, while involving tunnels to a great extent, is handled quite differently from the other. Vegetable selection in the early spring is somewhat different from vegetable selection for the late fall production. Spinach is great when started in cold weather, but not so terrific when started in the heat of the summer. Tomatoes are not a part of the early spring plan but can be an integral part of the late fall plan.

Some consideration must also be given

TABLE 3–1

CROPS FOR FIVE GROWING SEASONS OF THE 60-MINUTE GARDEN

EARLY SPRING SEASON	SPRING SEASON	SUMMER SEASON	FALL SEASON	EARLY WINTER SEASON
Beets	Beans	Beets	Celery	Beets
Broccoli	Beets	Broccoli	Chinese cabbage	Broccoli
Cabbage	Broccoli	Brussels sprouts	Collards	Brussels sprouts
Carrots	Cabbage	Cabbage	Kale	Cabbage
Cauliflower	Carrots	Carrots	Leeks	Cauliflower
Celery	Celery	Cauliflower	Lettuce	Celery
Chinese cabbage	Cucumbers	Celery	Spinach	Chinese cabbage
Lettuce	Eggplant	Chinese cabbage		Collards
Peas	Lettuce	Collards		Kale
Spinach	Peppers	Lettuce		Lettuce
Swiss chard	Squash, summer	Melons		Spinach
	Tomatoes	Squash, winter		Squash, winter

to space allocation. Now that we are going to add up to four months to the normal growing period, we have to give some careful thought to where and when we will plant each vegetable, since the tunnels will be there in the early part of the garden year. And to complicate matters more, the tunnels will be reestablished in the garden a few weeks before the first frost and will stay in place for up to two more months. You shouldn't have a patch of corn in the bed where you expect to set up your tunnel. Tunnels can be fairly high, but that is ridiculous.

The rest of this chapter describes a typical 200-square-foot garden through all five seasons (early spring, spring, summer, fall, and early winter) from February through early December. I leave January for daydreaming and pouring over seed catalogs. The following, points out those planning issues that you have to consider for each season now that you are using tunnels in your garden. It's not really such a big deal, but a little planning ahead can help get maximum value from this easy-to-build season extender—the tunnel.

EARLY SPRING GROWING SEASON

For purposes of this discussion, the early spring growing season begins one to two months prior to the anticipated last frost and runs until that last frost. Frost dates are really only general guidelines anyway, since they can vary by two weeks on your very own property. You may have a low spot on your land that will get hit with frost two weeks before the elevated parts of your little kingdom. The last frost date is around April 15 where I live in southeastern Pennsylvania. That means I set up one of my tunnels as early as February 1. Most gardeners will have to experiment for a few years, to determine the best date for setting up tunnels.

One of the best tools to use during this phase of the garden year is a soil thermometer. I never used one before, having tunnels in my garden, but now it is as important to me as my trowel. As I pointed out earlier, it is the temperature of the soil that is most critical to the growth of vegetables in this early part of the season. Below a soil temperature of 40°F, vegetable plants, with the possible exception of Chinese cabbage, won't do much growing. So it is the soil temperature that should dictate much of your planting activity before the last frost.

While monitoring both the air and the soil temperature helps you to decide when to plant what vegetable, it is the soil temperature that you watch most closely. Soil temperature changes much more gradually than does air temperature. You should measure the soil temperature 1 to 3 inches below the surface of the soil. The best time to take a measurement is between noon and 3:00 P.M. Remember to shake the thermometer down before you use it. If you are curious about how cold the soil is getting, that measurement can be taken between 6:00 A.M. and 8:00 A.M. When you have set up your tunnel over black plastic mulch, measure the soil temperature under the mulch.

Table 3–2 lists those vegetables best suited for growing in a plastic tunnel in early spring. The germination temperature and the air and soil temperature for the best growing conditions are included to give you some guidance for when to plant each vegetable in your own area. Because the tunnel offers much more growing area than the traditional cold frame, I believe you can take a few more chances with planting some things earlier than other gardeners might advise. If you lose a few plants, it's no big deal because at this early stage in the garden year, you have all kinds of space to play with.

It is possible, if you desire, to devote up to half of your total garden to growing vegetables in tunnels during the early spring season before the first frost. In our model 200-square-foot garden, 100 square feet are used for tunnels two months before the last frost. Here we have such hardy vegetables

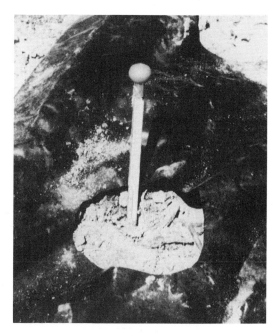

Photo 3–3: This soil thermometer, placed in the soil through a hole cut in black plastic mulch, measures the temperature of the soil 3 to 4 inches below the surface. Another type of soil thermometer has a flat gauge on the top and looks something like a meat thermometer.

as peas, onions, Chinese cabbage, lettuce, spinach, and kale. All of these hardy vegetables have instructions on their seed packets to "plant as soon as you can work the soil." Well, when you put up a tunnel with black or clear plastic mulch, the soil will warm up quite rapidly. As soon as it is thawed, you can begin to plant any of the vegetables listed in table 3–2 that are within the rising soil temperature ranges and that are not transplants. You start the transplants indoors, and you can put them in the tunnel after the soil temperature hits the appropriate growing range.

One of the new planning problems you didn't have to face in the past is how to lay out the holes or flaps in your plastic mulch. If you are planting your beds intensively,

TABLE 3–2

SOIL AND AIR TEMPERATURE RANGES FOR CROPS
(EARLY SPRING SEASON)

CROP	SOIL GERMINATION TEMPERATURE (°F)	IDEAL SOIL TEMPERATURE (°F)	IDEAL DAYTIME AIR TEMPERATURE (°F)
Beets	50–85	65–75	40–75
Broccoli	45–85	65–75	40–75
Cabbage	50–85	65–75	40–75
Carrots	60–80	65–75	45–75
Cauliflower	50–85	65–75	45–75
Celery	50–70	60–70	45–75
Chinese cabbage	40–85	60–70	45–75
Kale	40–70	60–70	40–75
Kohlrabi	50–85	65–75	40–75
Leeks	40–75	65–75	45–85
Lettuce	40–80	65–75	45–75
Onions	50–85	65–75	45–85
Parsley	50–85	65–75	45–75
Peas	40–85	65–75	45–75
Radishes	40–85	65–75	40–75
Spinach	40–85	60–70	40–75
Swiss chard	35–70	60–70	40–75

then you will have spinach that uses holes on 3-inch centers and broccoli with holes on 12- or 15-inch centers. One method is to make the whole piece of black or clear plastic with holes or flaps at 3-inch centers, knowing that you can fit anything anywhere on the plastic. Use a sharp knife to cut larger holes as you need them. Another method is to cut pieces of plastic mulch for the different crops. Because the tunnel protects the bed from the wind, you don't have to worry so much about anchoring the black plastic down on the soil, so smaller pieces fitted together will stay in place just fine.

Some gardeners have experimented with planting peas and spinach in the late fall after the ground has frozen, and then they used tunnels and black plastic to get an even earlier germination than would occur if they had waited until the soil could be worked in the spring. This is just one example of the many cultural practices that are being revised and adjusted with the availability of tunnels and black or clear plastic mulch.

Everyone in this country seems to love peas. Now that snap peas are a new favorite, let me give you some tips on them. Normally you plant peas about a month before the last frost. So if you follow my advice and plant your peas two months before the last frost, what do you do when they get big enough to be ready to climb a fence or some netting? You still have this tunnel, forcing the peas toward the center of the bed and preventing them from growing up. Well, the simple solution is to pull the ribs of the tunnel out of the PVC foundations and stick them into the ground a few inches inside the edge of the bed. Then you mount your trellis system, described in the next chapter, so the peas can begin to climb. By this time you are only two weeks away from the last frost, and peas at this stage can handle fairly heavy frosts. Your tunnel keeps on working for another three or four weeks, helping the broccoli and cabbages get a super good start. In other words, this system gives peas the best of both worlds—a very early start and vertical support when they need it.

In the second phase of the early spring growing season, you can put the hardy transplants or seedlings into the ground three to four weeks earlier than normal. Broccoli, cabbage, cauliflower, kohlrabi, and Swiss chard fall into this group. You can start these vegetables in the house under lights as early as 2½ months before the last frost. In six weeks they are ready to transplant out into the tunnel. You should take the same hardening-off precautions you took when you used a cold frame. The combination of the protection of the tunnel and the warming of the soil by the black plastic makes these hardy

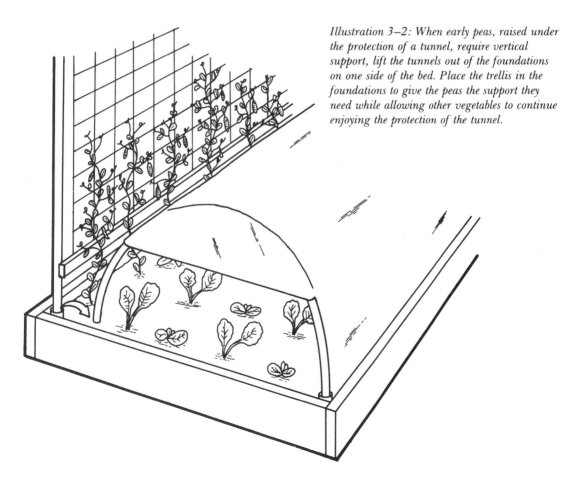

Illustration 3–2: When early peas, raised under the protection of a tunnel, require vertical support, lift the tunnels out of the foundations on one side of the bed. Place the trellis in the foundations to give the peas the support they need while allowing other vegetables to continue enjoying the protection of the tunnel.

vegetables really thrive.

The beds that are used for the early spring season will be pretty much harvested by the end of June, when you can then replant them and set out seedlings for harvest in the fall prior to the first frost.

Using this system of early planting, in my area I can be eating spinach and lettuce from my garden in March. Peas can be coming in late in April, only a few weeks after the last frost. Broccoli and cauliflower can be enjoyed in early May, and baby carrots can grace the table in early June.

There's another idea to consider in terms of the garden producing food for consumption in March, April, and May. If you set aside part of a bed with carrots, leeks, and parsnips that mature in October and November, you can leave them in the ground to be harvested during the early spring season to be enjoyed with your fresh spinach and lettuce. In late fall simply cover these vegetables with about a foot of straw or hay. Then in February rig a tunnel over the bed *without* using black plastic. You want to thaw the soil if it is frozen, but you don't want to heat things up too much and cause these plants to grow too much—the carrots and parsnips can lose some of their flavor after they begin to grow again. The leeks can begin growing without hurting their flavor. If you are not inclined to store many vegetables in your attic or root cellar (if you happen to have one) then this is a fine method for increasing your garden's productivity at a time of the year when most gardens are frozen solid.

I keep my tunnels up until the third or fourth week after the last frost in the spring. I watch the soil and air temperatures, and when the air temperatures are getting higher than 70°F even with good ventilation, I remove my tunnels. By then I've been eating fresh garden produce for almost two months, and my neighbors are just beginning to get their first scallions and leaf lettuce. Those tunnels make a tremendous difference!

SPRING GROWING SEASON

For our discussion here, the spring growing season begins with the last frost and runs roughly to the heat of the summer, around the first of July. For my garden, that is April 15 through June 30. This is the time for planting heat-loving vegetables that will usually be harvested in July and August. Do the tunnels help us with these crops? Most certainly they do.

The first thing you do is set up your tunnel for your spring crops at least a month ahead of time—perhaps six weeks prior to the predicted last frost. This allows the soil to warm up and stay warm. Black or clear plastic is again a critical component of this tunnel. Here you can have a piece with holes on 15-inch centers since most of the heat-loving plants, such as tomatoes and peppers, will require that amount of spacing.

While this is still a relatively new idea in backyard vegetable gardens, starting heat-loving plants at the last spring frost can give you significant benefits. Research at the University of New Hampshire has shown that tomatoes, peppers, and some other heat-loving plants produced two to three weeks earlier with 50 percent heavier yields when they are started under tunnels with black plastic mulch. The general rule of thumb is that you can put your heat-loving plants out in the tunnel when the soil temperature holds at or above 60°F.

Remember, you will be placing plants like tomatoes and muskmelons along the edge of your bed so that they can be trained onto the trellis system when they become tall enough. Peppers and eggplants can be placed in the middle of the bed and kept under the tunnel even longer than the trellis crops. When you have to set up the trellis device, you simply pull the ribs of the tunnels out of the PVC foundations and stick them into the ground 8 to 10 inches inside the edge of the bed. This will happen about two or three weeks after the last frost, the time when most neighbors are just putting their heat-loving plants out in the garden in the first place.

While corn is not a vegetable we would find in a garden with only 200 square feet of space, folks with larger gardens generally consider corn a favorite. The tunnel can help the corn grower become the neighborhood champion for having the earliest corn in the area. You will need to experiment a bit, but you can start sprouted corn under a tunnel at least at the last spring frost date. Some folks plant a few dozen seeds about three weeks before the last frost date and hope that there is no hard freeze so late in the season. That is a month and a half earlier than normal corn planting time. Again use the black plastic mulch with holes at 12-inch centers. Use special early varieties of corn for this trick. Silver Queen, a favorite white corn, for example, won't germinate below soil temperatures of 60°F. A cold-tolerant yellow corn is Goldust, and for early white corn try Pearl White, Stardust, Polar Vee, and Northern Vee.

Watering your garden during the spring growing seasons, especially in the early stages, can be a problem if you are not used to working with tunnels. The general mistake is to water too much. The soil in a tunnel with the plastic mulch will have much less evaporation than soil outside of the tunnel. Also, there is no wind in the tunnel to help take water away. In this situation the drip irrigation system is very helpful (see chapter 7). The drip irrigation lines are laid down under the plastic mulch as you build your tunnel. You can feed your plants and water them with this handy timesaving device. A general rule of thumb for spring watering, whether it be with a drip system or by any other means, is to water early in the morning on a sunny day. This practice helps keep down any problems that might develop from mildew and mold. Chapter 7 gives a detailed discussion about how much to water.

In our model 200-square-foot garden, the spring crops go into the two beds not used for the early spring planting. For the most part these crops will be harvested

TABLE 3–3

SOIL AND AIR TEMPERATURE RANGES FOR CROPS
(SPRING SEASON)

CROP	SOIL GERMINATION TEMPERATURE (°F)	IDEAL SOIL TEMPERATURE (°F)	IDEAL DAYTIME AIR TEMPERATURE (°F)
Beans	65–86	70–80	50–80
Corn	55–85	75–85	50–95
Cucumbers	65–85	70–80	60–80
Eggplant	65–85	75–85	65–95
Melons	65–85	70–80	60–80
Peppers	65–85	70–80	65–80
Squash, summer	65–85	75–85	50–90
Squash, winter	65–85	75–85	50–90
Sweet potatoes	60–85	75–85	65–95
Tomatoes	65–85	70–80	65–80

in the summer, leaving space for planting crops for an early winter harvest in November and December. A tunnel is erected over these plants as the first fall frost approaches. When you have five different growing seasons and a need to manipulate tunnels and vertical trellises, you have to give some thought as to which vegetables will go into which bed so there are no conflicts.

SUMMER GROWING SEASON

Summer is the time to be enjoying the highest volume of fruits and vegetables your garden will produce during the year. If you have been a bit careful in not planting too much of anything at any one time, you will have a fairly uniform level of production throughout the whole summer season. Of course zucchini is the exception to that rule—there is always too much zucchini!

During this period the tunnels are used to protect lettuce and Chinese cabbage from the searing rays of the summer sun. The bird netting is stretched over the strawberry patch, and mosquito netting is covering the bush cucumbers to protect them from the dreaded cucumber beetle. Of course if your cucumbers are on a trellis, that trick is not available to you.

July and August are important planting periods, however. You have two more growing seasons (fall and early winter) ahead before you put your garden to sleep in December. Late June and July is the time to plant for the fall season, and August is the time to plant for the early winter season. Also you have shifted from black plastic mulch to some kind of straw or grass mulch, which is discussed more fully in chapter 5.

Those beds, where we had our early spring crops last March and April, we can now replant with vegetables that will mature in September and October. Crops such as carrots, all of the brassicas, beets, Swiss chard, and some peas are all good candidates for fall picking.

FALL GROWING SEASON

Like the early spring planting season, the fall planting period will be new to most gardeners. Most of us figure that if we don't get our late crops in by the first of August, we are too late. But now we have tunnels to extend our growing season and need to plan our crop layout so that those tunnels can be installed sometime in late September.

For the fall growing season we are talking about the cold-hardy plants again—lettuce, kale, collards, spinach, celery, and Chinese cabbage. These vegetables will continue to grow under the tunnels one to two months past the first fall frost date. Remember that these crops need to be planted in black or clear plastic mulch, although when they are initially set out in the garden you will probably still have straw or hay mulch on top of the black plastic to keep the soil cool.

A week or two before the anticipated first fall frost in your area, take some of your tomato vines very carefully off their trellises and lay them gently down on the plastic mulch. If they are intertwined with the trellis netting, simply remove the whole trellis panel, very carefully, and lay it down on the bed. Then cover them with a tunnel, and they will continue to ripen fruit for a number of weeks after that first killing frost. Peppers and eggplants will also continue to ripen fruit if they are under tunnels a few weeks before that first frost. Cabbages, broccoli, and cauliflower prefer cool weather, so they will do very well under a tunnel for four to six weeks after the first frost.

EARLY WINTER GROWING SEASON

While some gardeners may experiment with planting peas, spinach, and some other very early crops in October, for harvest next year, most of us will not be doing any planting during the early winter growing season. This is the time for enjoying the tail end of the longest harvest period we have ever enjoyed.

When most of your vegetables have finally succumbed to the cold, you will still have Chinese cabbage, celery, carrots, leeks, spinach, and collards well into December in most parts of the country. Because this late growing season is still very new to most gardeners, there are a number of cultural practices that remain to be tested to further extend the season through December and into January. For example, how will the tunnel work throughout the entire winter if combined with a foot of straw mulch over a carrot bed? Can we set up the old hotbed scheme by burying fresh manure a few feet below the surface of the bed in October and have enough heat in the soil to take us through December? There are some exciting exper-iments for the vegetable gardeners in the next few years.

The tunnel system increases production of an average garden by over 25 percent. I believe that what is even more important is that the tunnels produce food when the fresh vegetable prices at the grocery store are approaching their highest. So not only do tunnels increase total garden production, but the food raised in tunnels is more valuable per square foot than your summer produce. Tunnels are easy to use and give your garden a totally new dimension by adding two additional growing seasons to your gardening year. Now that our discussion of the 60-Minute Garden has reached a point just past the last frost in the fall let's move on to the next component of the system—vertical gardening.

TUNNELS AND PANELS
FOR FOUR BOXED BEDS

PVC pipe is easily cut with a hacksaw. It comes in various lengths, so you may wish to have the material cut at the store. Flexible PVC comes in large coils so that you could buy your whole supply in one piece and bring it home to cut. Each rib will cost between three and four dollars, depending on length. In my design, the ribs are 8 feet long.

The PVC foundations of the boxed beds are 3 feet 9 inches apart. Consequently, the ribs are also 3 feet 9 inches apart. The panels covering these ribs need to overlap each other to maintain the integrity of the tunnel. I have found that at least a 6-inch overlap of panels is desirable. Therefore, most of my panels are 5 feet wide (that's 3 feet 9 inches with about a 7-inch overlap on each side). These panels have furring strips attached on the outside edges so that they can be held down by bricks or some other modestly heavy object.

The length of each panel of plastic is important, too. They must be long enough so that they touch the ground on the out-side of the bed on both sides of the tunnel. Your measurements will vary with the height of the ribs and how high you have made your raised beds. In my design this measurement is 8 feet 6 inches. Make your panels about 4 inches longer than they need to be, which gives you some extra to wrap around the stick on each end before you put in the staples with the staple gun.

The end panel is different in its design. You need the minimum 6-inch overlap on one side, but on the end you need an overlap that will be considerably greater to fully cover the ends of the tunnel. These measurements again will depend on how high your ribs and beds are. As you can see in illustration 3–3, that extra material is folded down and secured by bricks or blocks.

Remember, these tunnels do not have to be super airtight. In fact you must cut several slits in the plastic for ventilation, so the end pieces do not have to have a hermetically sealed fastener. Bricks work just fine.

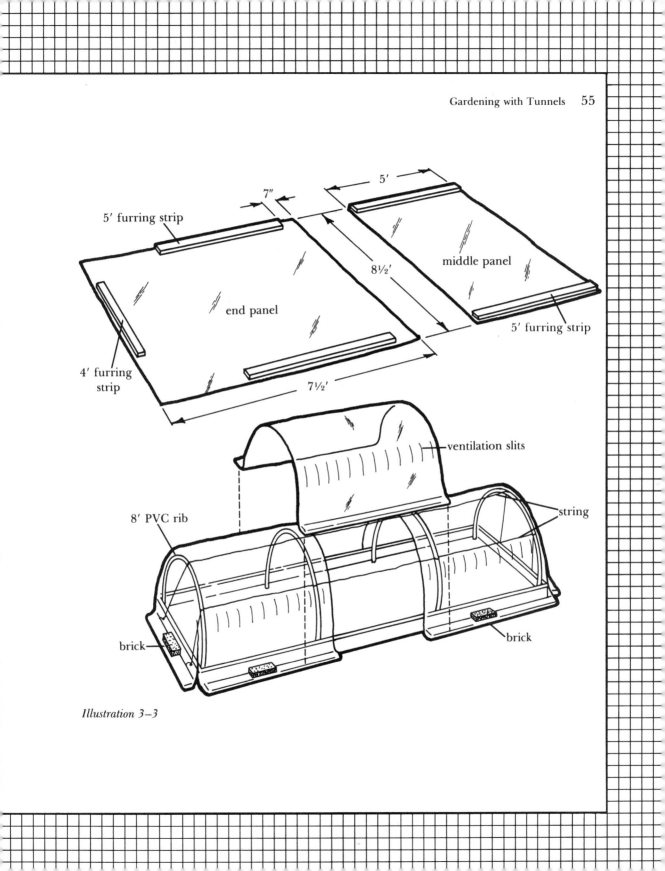

5' furring strip

5'

7"

end panel

middle panel

8½'

5' furring strip

4' furring
strip

7½'

ventilation slits

8' PVC rib

string

brick

brick

Illustration 3–3

———— SHOPPING LIST ————

Lumber
152 feet 1 × 2 furring strip
Hardware
128 feet flexible PVC pipe 1″
3 rolls clear 4-mil (or 6-) polyethylene film
    15′ × 25′
1 box staples ⅜″
1 ball nylon or synthetic string
a few small nails
        Total cost: $85
        Cost per square foot: $0.43

———— CUTTING LIST ————

Size	Piece	Quantity
8′	PVC tunnel ribs	16
5′	Hold-down middle strips	24
4′	Hold-down end strips	8
5′ × 8½′	Middle panels (polyethylene film)	4
8½′ × 7½′	End pieces (polyethylene film)	8

———— TOOLS ————

Hacksaw
Hammer
Measuring tape
Sharp, long-blade knife
Staple gun

CONSTRUCTION STEPS

1. Cut the PVC ribs to length.

2. Cut the polyethylene film according to illustration 3–3. Each boxed bed (12 feet by 3 feet 9 inches) has polyethylene panels of two different shapes. The one

middle panel is cut 5 feet by 8½ feet, which leaves enough film for wrapping around the furring strips for stapling. The two end panels are cut 8½ feet by 7½ feet.

The easiest way to cut this film, which comes in a roll, is to lay out the unrolled film on a flat surface. Cut the pieces to length first; then cut for width. This makes the best use of a roll that comes 15 feet wide. Cutting is done by folding the film along the line for cutting and using a long-blade knife to run smoothly down the fold.

3. Staple the middle pieces to 5-foot furring strips using a ⅜-inch staple gun. Wrap the film around the furring strip once before stapling. Staple film to both sides of the furring strip.

4. The end pieces are handled in the same way as the middle panels except that furring strips are stapled at the *same end* of the 7½-foot dimension (about 7 inches from the edge of the film), and a 4-foot furring strip will be attached in *the center* of the 8½-foot dimension at the other edge (see illustration 3–3).

5. Install the PVC ribs into the foundations, pushing the ribs down about 6 inches. To give the tunnel longitudinal stability, you need to attach string under moderate tension (see illustration 3–3). Wrap the string around each rib as you move down the tunnel. Secure the string on both ends to nails in the ends of the bed.

6. Lay the plastic panels over the ribs with about 7 inches overhang on each side, with the furring strips dropping to the ground on both sides of the bed. Secure the furring strips with a brick or stone, or however you wish. The end pieces require you to wrap the excess plastic back around the end of the bed much as you do when wrapping a gift package. Again, a brick or stone is sufficient to hold these in place.

7. With a pen knife or other sharp knife, cut vertical slits for ventilation on both sides of each panel according to illustration 3–3.

BLACK PLASTIC CUTTING FORM

The cutting form is used for two purposes. First, it is the form that is used to cut the holes in black plastic mulch prior to setting the mulch out into the garden. Secondly, it is used as a seeding board to allow careful and uniform direct seeding of such vegetables as beets, carrots, and parsnips.

The holes in the black plastic mulch are cut only partway around to form a flap. So, when you don't use a particular hole for a plant, the flap still gives the soil the cover needed to keep in heat and prevent weeds from growing. The whole exercise takes only a few minutes, and presto—you have uniform holes (or flaps) on 3-inch centers cut across the whole unfolded piece of black plastic mulch. Using the cutting form, you can prepare a piece of black plastic for a 48-square-foot bed in 10 minutes (see photos 3–4 through 3–7, which show how this is done). Obviously you can make a form with holes that are on 4-inch centers, 6-inch centers, and 12-inch centers. In any case, the technique described here works very well.

——— SHOPPING LIST ———

Plywood
2 square feet ½"
Hardware
1 roll 4-mil black polyethylene film (approximately 152 square feet)

——— TOOLS ———

Electric drill or drill press
Hole saw
Measuring tape
Sandpaper
Saw
Sharp knife

——— CUTTING LIST ———

Size	Piece	Quantity
12" × 12"	Cutting form	2
4' × 12'	Plastic film	4

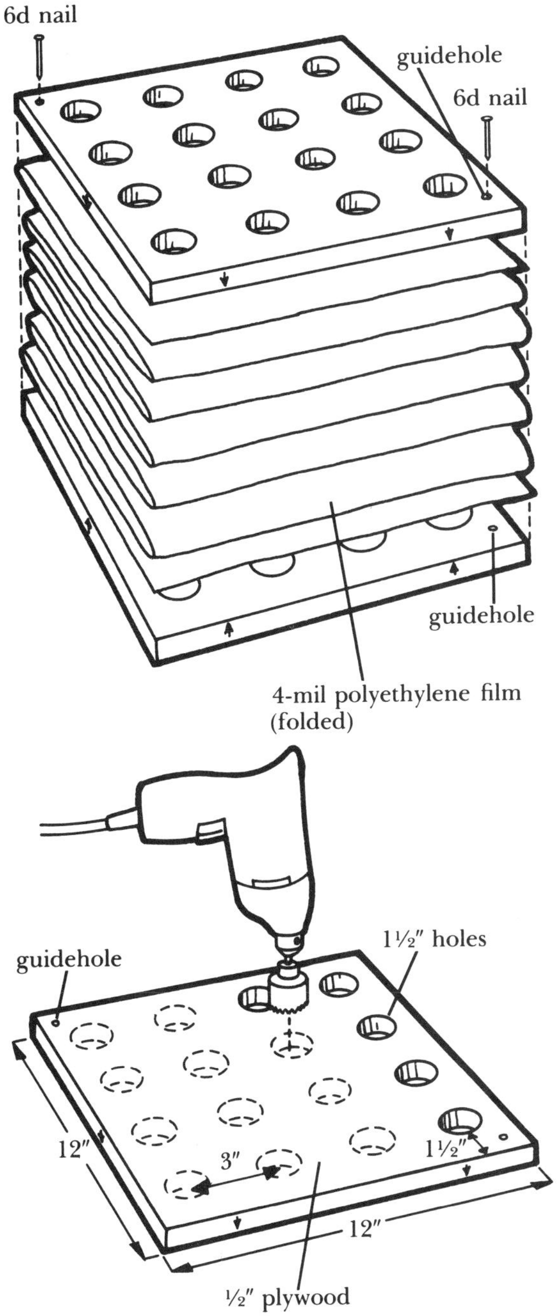

6d nail

guidehole

6d nail

guidehole

4-mil polyethylene film
(folded)

guidehole

1½″ holes

12″

3″

1½″

12″

½″ plywood

Illustration 3–4

CONSTRUCTION STEPS

1. To make the cutting form, use two pieces of ½-inch plywood cut 12 inches square. For each board, lay out a grid of 16 holes on 3-inch centers with the centers of the outside holes 1½ inches from the edge of the board, as in illustration 3–4.

2. In preparation for cutting the holes in the cutting form, drill two guide holes in the opposite corners of each board so that two 6-penny nails can be pushed through these holes. These nails will keep the two boards in perfect alignment, both for drilling the holes and for later cutting the black plastic.

3. To cut out the holes in the cutting form, use a 1½-inch hole saw, which you can find in any hardware store. You can use this saw in a hand electric drill or on a drill press. The best way to cut neat holes is to drill a guide hole through the form where each larger hole will be located. The two boards are held together by the two 6-penny nails. There are 2 kinds of guide holes in this construction exercise. To make the big holes in the form it is best to drill a little hole first so the wood doesn't split. The other guide holes are the ones in the corners. Now you can separate the boards for drilling the large holes. Use the hole saw to cut only halfway through the board on one side. Then turn the board over and finish cutting through. This produces a cleaner cut.

4. While every effort should be made to make these two forms identical, it is likely that there will be small differences if they are put together in a way other than the way they were drilled. To avoid any prob-

Photo 3–4: To cut the holes in the piece of black plastic, first cut the plastic to the length and width of your bed. Then, fold it lengthwise so that it is 1 foot wide.

lems, when the boards are held together with the nails, prior to drilling, mark each set of edges with some kind of code so you always join the forms together with exactly the same matching edges.

5. After sanding the edges lightly, you will have two identical forms to be used for cutting out the black plastic mulch and for intensive planting, which is described in chapter 6.

6. To fold the plastic so it will fit between the two forms, start with a strip of black plastic 4 feet wide and 12 feet long. Fold it lengthwise twice.

7. Fold the long piece accordian style to produce the final pack. Do this by folding over a 12-inch section at the end, and then alternately fold back and forth accor-

dian style until the pack is 12 inches by 12 inches (see photos 3–4 through 3–7 and illustration 3–4).

8. Take the folded pack of black plastic and place it between the two cutting forms. Hammer or push a 6-penny guide nail through one board and the pack of plastic film, so you can see to locate the nail hole on the other board. Otherwise, the boards will be very difficult to align. Then, place the second guide nail through the two boards and the plastic, giving you a firm pack for cutting holes in the black plastic.

9. Now you can cut out the holes in the black plastic, but cut them only three-fourths of the way around. A sharp knife with a stiff blade works better than one with a flexible blade.

Photo 3–5: Using the cutting board as a guide, fold the black plastic down its length so that you end up with a pile of folded black plastic that is 1 foot square.

Photo 3–6: Take the two cutting boards and clamp them together with the folded plastic in between them.

Photo 3–7: Using a stiff-blade knife, cut out three-fourths of each hole, which leaves the black plastic with hundreds of flaps through which you place seedlings into your bed.

CHAPTER 4

VERTICAL GROWING SYSTEM

Very few gardeners make use of vertical growing techniques except with the ubiquitous tomato, although the advantages of vertical gardening are no secret. The reason for this massive oversight is that putting up trellises, tepees, or poles every season is a great deal of trouble for most people. The 60-Minute Garden eliminates the bother of erecting trellises for vertical growing.

Simple mathematics demonstrates that when you install a 7-foot trellis along the length of two 4-by-12-foot raised beds you increase the growing area of that bed by nearly 175 percent! The trellis area is about 7 by 25 feet, which gives an area for vines to climb of nearly 175 square feet. With the nearly 100 square feet in the horizontal garden and the nearly 175 square feet on the vertical plane, you have roughly 275 square feet of growing area simply by setting up a trellis. This chapter will show you how to increase your garden's productivity by over 30 percent simply by using vertical space that is ignored by most vegetable gardeners. While you increase your growing space by nearly 175 percent, you don't have vegetables on every vertical square foot, so the net increase in productivity is 30 percent, which is still a respectable increase for only a little extra trouble.

The 60-Minute Garden includes a trellis for vertical plants on every bed in the garden. First let's look at how vertical growing works.

ADVANTAGES OF VERTICAL GROWING

The most important reason for using vertical space in the vegetable garden is to save space—space that can be used for growing additional vegetables that can't be grown on a trellis. Most folks don't realize that bush beans weren't developed because they taste better but simply because commercial farmers couldn't find a machine to harvest pole beans. Pole beans taste as good, freeze as well, and produce longer than bush beans. The disadvantage of growing pole beans is finding an easy way to set up some kind of device on which they can grow. Pole beans will produce twice as much as bush beans in the same space.

Tomatoes, as everyone knows, if left to sprawl will take up to 10 times as much space as those that are trained to grow vertically. Winter squash can take up to 20 times the space on the flat garden surface than is taken if it is trained up a trellis. Most backyard gardens don't include melons, vine cucumbers, and winter squash simply because of the space they take when grown flat on the ground. A vertical growing system allows these popular foods to be included even in a 200-square-foot garden.

A second advantage is that vertically grown vegetables are often healthier vegetables than ones grown on the ground. Fruits and vegetables that are grown off the ground are cleaner and avoid problems like soil rot and many crawling insects such as slugs and sow bugs. The leaves of vertical plants have more area exposed to the sun, and the improved air circulation around a vertical crop reduces the chances of disease. Vertical crops tend to dry off faster after a rain, and this further reduces disease problems.

Most trellised vegetables, except cucumbers, don't necessarily produce more per plant just because they grow vertically, but the production per square foot of the garden goes up 30 percent. Cucumbers are particularly happy when climbing on a trellis. They will actually grow longer because they are hanging from a support. Because of less danger of insect attack and disease, fruits and vegetables on a trellis usually are higher in quality than if they were grown flat on the soil.

One of the concerns with vertical growing is shading of other vegetables in the garden by the trellised plants. I have not found this to be a problem in a garden that has a north/south orientation. Even when the other plants are shaded in the early morning and late afternoon, they are still getting sufficient sunlight. One of the mistakes I made early on was to place two vertical trellises back-to-back on two adjacent beds. This created several problems. First, it was very hard to get down the path between the two beds when the plants had become full size, and secondly, the shading caused by two trellises so close together reduced

Photo 4–1: These cucumbers, growing vertically on a trellis, have more access to the sun, have better ventilation, and are not vulnerable to problems caused by sitting on the soil.

Photo 4–2: Gardeners who must have their trellises oriented in an east/west direction can install the trellises across the bed rather than along the edge of the bed. In this bed both inflexible and flexible PVC pipe form the trellises.

production in the bed on the west side. The best layout in a 60-Minute Garden is to put all the trellises on the same side of every bed, that is, all on the right sides or all on the left sides. The next year you simply switch sides, allowing for some crop rotation benefits (rotation is discussed in chapter 5).

There are some gardens that are laid out on an east/west orientation from necessity. You can still use this trellis system by simply installing your trellis across the beds rather than along the edge of the beds. Photo 4–2 shows a garden that has an east/west orientation because it is on a hill, and the slope of the hill faces south. The trellis installed across the bed works very well.

Finally, I think a trellised garden is a prettier garden. The blossoms show up better, and the bees have easier access to those blossoms. One gardener extolls vertical growing because it's easier for him to talk to his plants. In the final analysis, vertical growing makes enormous sense in a backyard vegetable garden, when it is not too much trouble to set up, which is the case with the 60-Minute Garden.

CONSTRUCTION OF THE TRELLIS SYSTEM

Building the trellis system in the 60-Minute Garden is a simple task. The design is based on the assumption that you have already installed the 1½-inch (or 2-inch) polyvinyl chloride (PVC) pipe foundations around your raised beds. These foundations hold the vertical poles on which the trellis panels are attached. The panels are made by attaching netting to two crosspieces of wood that are attached to the vertical poles with bolts and wing nuts. Installation of 50 feet of trellis, once all the parts are assembled, takes only about 15 minutes. Let's look at the components of the trellis—the poles and trellis panels.

POLES

You have two choices in selecting your poles for the trellis system—PVC pipe or wood. The best material, but the most expensive, is 1-inch PVC pipe. An 8-foot piece of 1-inch PVC pipe is about four dollars. The PVC won't warp, is extremely strong and very light, and will last forever. And, the PVC pipe is ready to install in the foundations when you bring it home. If you are using fewer than a dozen poles in your system, I strongly recommend that you use PVC pipe. They are worth the extra expense, and I think they are more attractive in the garden.

You can get pressure-treated 2 × 2 fir poles at most lumber yards for about $2.25 for an 8-foot pole. These poles will last for many years, but they have some limitations. They can split or warp when exposed to the weather. Since they come with a 2-inch diameter, they work best in gardens with foundations that use 2-inch PVC pipe. I use these wooden poles, but I have 1½-inch foundations. Consequently, I had to shave the ends down with a jointer to make them fit my system. This is not difficult but is a bit time-consuming.

I use 8-foot poles primarily because that is the length of the fir poles as I bought them. An 8-foot pole sits in the 12-inch foundation and therefore gives you a 7-foot trellis. While pole beans will grow to 10 feet, I

can't comfortably reach much past 8 feet, so I'm happy with 7-foot trellises. If you use PVC pipe for your poles, you can make your trellis any height you prefer because PVC can be cut to any length.

TRELLIS PANELS

For the crosspieces of the trellis panels, I use 1 × 2 furring strips. The length is determined by the distance between the foundations. My crosspieces are 4 feet long with holes 3 feet 10 inches apart, which is the distance between my foundations. I use three different designs on my trellises, which then determine how I use my crosspieces and netting. These include a short panel, a long panel, and string. I recommend using all three designs.

For vegetables such as peas, determinate tomatoes, and sweet potatoes, a 3-foot trellis is sufficient. I construct the panels by mounting netting on the crosspieces with staples, using a heavy-duty staple gun. I use two poles to hold the crosspieces in place so that the stapling process is quite simple. When these panels are not in use, they roll up neatly for easy storage.

For the taller plants such as snap peas, indeterminate tomatoes, cucumbers, pole beans, and winter squash, I use trellis panels that are 6½ feet long. Again I use the same procedure for mounting the netting. In some cases, these longer panels will be supporting some significant loads if you have a bumper crop of tomatoes or winter squash. While the heavy-duty staples are likely to hold, I like to reinforce these panels with some wire wrapped around the top crosspiece just to make sure. Another material for this purpose is nylon mason cord found in hardware stores.

The third trellis design uses twine or string instead of netting. I like this design for pole beans and cucumbers. The string is cheaper than the netting and for these two crops works very well. With this design I

Netting is relatively low cost and is made from twine, plastic, or nylon. Netting comes in several sizes, though I prefer the 5-inch or 6-inch mesh so that I can pick vegetables through it. Both the plastic netting and the nylon netting are strong enough for any load you'll put on it with this trellis system. Nylon trellis netting costs between $0.08 and $0.12 a square foot. It will last about three years with proper care. The string netting is cheaper, and the plastic netting will last longer. There are some sources for netting listed in the appendix at the end of the book.

Photo 4–3: Attach trellis netting to the furring strips with a staple gun. Strong enough to support the heaviest of vegetable or fruit vines, this nylon netting has large enough holes to permit easy picking, and it will last for several years.

simply mount two crosspieces, as before, and wrap the twine around as shown in photo 4–4. While it is not absolutely necessary, I notch the crosspieces to make the wrapping of string more uniform, giving it a neater appearance. The notches are 2 inches apart. I use a power saw to make the notches, but a pocket knife would serve the same function.

You have many choices in selecting the material for trellis panels. Some gardeners prefer to work with wire because of its strength and durability. I prefer the netting that is available in garden centers and from mail-order houses because it is so much easier to work with and is much easier to store.

Photo 4–4: One method for using the trellis on a raised boxed bed involves stretching string or twine between the two crosspieces on the vertical poles. Spaced at about 2 inches, this twine is an excellent support device for pole beans.

There are all kinds of string and twine on the market that will work in this system. Baler twine, found in farm supply stores or in some hardware stores, is among the best support for pole beans and the like. I use real cheap polyethylene twine that I buy on sale at the local home center and find that my beans don't seem to notice the difference. You will use 1,000 feet of string in just 12 feet of trellis, so price can be a consideration in a big garden.

SLINGS

One other device you will need if you make full use of your 60-Minute Garden trellis is a sling to hold the heavier fruits as they ripen. Melons and winter squash will need some extra support, especially as they get close to becoming ripe, a time when their stems weaken. Remember that vegetables grown vertically tend to be a bit larger than their cousins grown on the ground; even more reason to install a sling. The easiest way to rig a sling is to tie a hair net or any other small-mesh netting material to the trellis panel so that the fruit rests lightly in the mesh. A sling can be rigged when the fruit is the size of a softball. Rig it so the weight of the fruit is off the stem. Other materials that work are pantyhose and the net bags that onions come in.

USING THE TRELLIS SYSTEM

The trellis system in the 60-Minute Garden adds up to 30 percent additional production to the standard raised-bed garden. It allows you to grow vegetables that previously you just could not grow, or that you grew in the bush variety. Now that you have a strong and easily mounted trellis system, what can you grow? The following vegetables prefer growing on a trellis:

Photo 4–5: This butternut squash sits comfortably in a sling made from a pair of pantyhose. Large vegetables or fruit grown on trellises need enough support so that there is no strain on the stems.

Acorn squash
Butternut squash
Cucumbers
Garden peas
Pole lima beans
Pole snap beans
Snap peas
Sweet potatoes (some varieties)
Tomatoes

The vegetables above offer variety throughout the seasons. Peas can be started in the early spring, and the winter squashes can be harvested right around first frost in the fall. You can have vertical crops in your garden throughout most of the growing season.

PEAS

Peas have weak-kneed vines with skimpy roots and therefore grow best when they have support. They have strong clinging tendrils that hold on to netting very well as long as they make contact. Both the garden peas and the snap peas tend to grow away from the large 4-inch or 5-inch netting, so they need to be woven back into the trellis panel once a week or so. They grow extremely well on the finer chicken wire size netting, but you cannot pick through that netting, making it impractical for this system.

Garden peas can use the short 3-foot trellis panel, while the snap peas require the full-size 6- or 7-foot panel. Snap peas and tomatoes make an excellent succession combination in the 60-Minute Garden. You can start snap peas extra early under the plastic tunnel. When they are tall enough to begin needing support, pull the tunnel out of the foundations and stick the ribs into the soil about 4 inches in from the edge of the bed.

Then you can mount the trellis system with 6- or 7-foot panels to accommodate the snap peas. Assuming you have started your tomato plants inside to get an early jump on the season, they should be ready to transplant out into the garden about the same time the snap peas are finishing up. Actually, you can put the tomatoes in a few weeks before the peas are done because the tomato seedlings will not offer any serious competition to the snap peas. As the snap peas come down, the tomatoes are ready to be supported on the trellis, making intensive use of the vertical space.

Planting peas for a fall crop can be a bit tricky. The key is to start them in early August and load them up with at least 6 inches of straw mulch when they are tall enough. This cools the soil, which is important for peas. One trick is to interplant snap peas in the fall with cucumbers that have been planted a bit farther apart than normal.

Illustration 4–1: This setup allows you to grow garden peas later in the season than is normally feasible. Growing peas inside a tunnel creates a good growing environment for two to four weeks past the first frost, which is usually fatal to full-size pea plants left out in the open.

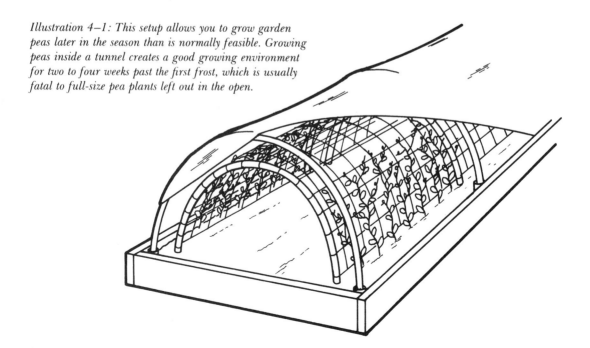

Photo 4–6: In the fall, you will often have crops such as pole beans and winter squash still on trellises when you want to install your tunnels for late fall and early winter crops. Here, the tunnels sit in PVC foundations on the right side of the bed, but on the left side they are stuck into the soil just in front of the trellis, which still has a crop of pole beans producing food.

The cucumber leaves tend to shade the peas from the hot August sun but not enough to hurt their growth.

One of the problems with peas is that the full-grown plants are not very frost tolerant, so your picking season has to be planned to be fairly well completed by the first fall frost. There is a way around this problem with the 60-Minute Garden tunnel system. This trick for successfully growing fall peas involves using two tunnels, one inside the other. The inside tunnel is made with the 4-inch trellis netting, and the second tunnel, covered with clear plastic, is set up later over the first tunnel. Garden peas are planted on both sides of the bed and are trained up and over the netting tunnel. Snap peas don't work very well with this scheme because they grow too tall. Before the first frost, cover the netting tunnel, which should be supporting full-size plants by now, with the clear plastic tunnel. This extends the pea harvest well past the first fall frost and allows you to plant your peas a bit later in August, avoiding the excessive heat. The peas hang down through the 4-inch netting and are very easy to pick.

BEANS

Beans grown on a trellis offer a number of advantages when compared to their bush cousins. While both pole snap beans and pole limas will begin to produce somewhat later in the season than bush varieties, they will then produce continuously for the rest of the season. The trick is to keep them picked. As soon as you leave some beans on the vine to get large and begin to dry, the plant will stop producing flowers.

TOMATOES

When you grow tomatoes on a trellis, you can plant them closer together than standard recommendations (12 to 18 inches instead of 24 inches). Tomatoes need to be tied to the trellis netting with some material.

I use the wire twistems that come in a big roll. And, I have used old rags and old nylon stockings with success as well. You have to be careful not to tie the stems too tightly, which would inhibit growth. Whenever I can, I weave the new shoots in and out of the netting so the plant is supported more by the netting than by the tie-ups.

The *determinate* tomato, a compact bushy tomato that produces its crop once in a season, only needs a 3-foot trellis. Determinate tomato varieties like Roma, Tiny Tim, and Floramerica do not respond well to pruning.

The *indeterminate* tomato grows and bears all season long—to exceed 20 feet in some cases. The indeterminate tomato needs regular pruning. Some gardeners will train two or three stems per plant, pruning all other side stems as they appear. I just let the side shoots fill up the trellis, and when I think a shoot is superfluous, I prune it. It is important to do some pruning of your to-

mato plants throughout the season, or all of the plant's energy will go to producing leaves and stems and not to producing tomatoes. When my indeterminate plants get up to 7 feet, at the top of the trellis, I cut the main stem to stop any further growth upward. Most of the suckers that grow out from the stem right above a leaf branch are plucked as soon as they appear. A few suckers are allowed to grow 4 or 5 inches and then are pruned at that point. This gives the plant a little more foliage, which helps reduce the problem of sunscald, a common occurrence with trellised tomatoes.

About six weeks before the projected first fall frost date, prune or break off all the growing tips of each plant. Also, you should pick all the blossoms at that point. This allows the plant to direct all of its energy, at a time of diminishing light and shorter days, to ripening fruit.

About four weeks before the first frost, you can carefully take your tomatoes, or at

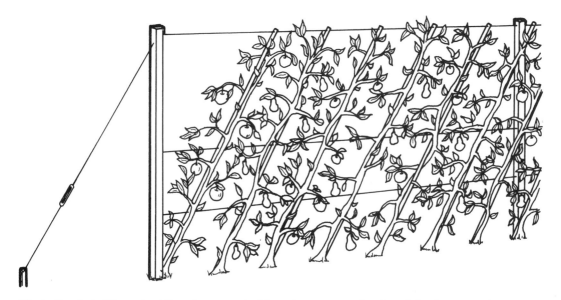

Illustration 4–2: The orchard fence is composed of 4 × 4 posts supporting 1 × 2 furring strips that are secured at 45-degree angles with wires attached to the posts. Each furring strip supports a single-cordon fruit tree.

least some of them, off the trellis and gently lay them on a bed of straw mulch. If they are all intertwined with the netting, remove the entire trellis panel and lay it down carefully. Remove the trellis and install a plastic covered tunnel. This will allow you to continue to have vine-ripened tomatoes for as much as a month past the first fall frost. Vine-ripened tomatoes not only have better flavor than those ripened on the windowsill or wrapped in newspaper, but they have a higher vitamin content as well.

CUCUMBERS

Cucumbers can take up a great deal of garden space if they are allowed to sprawl on the ground. They are natural climbers and are easily trained on a trellis. Research at North Carolina State University has demonstrated that cucumbers grown on a trellis will produce twice as much good fruit and have less disease than cucumbers grown on the ground. One of the reasons for this increase is that cucumbers grown on a trellis will produce fruit up to five weeks longer than the same variety on the ground.

Cucumbers have fairly strong tendrils, but you have to help them in the beginning with tie-ups of some sort. Once they are established they will grab on to the trellis netting by themselves. If there happens to be a particularly prolific crop of large cukes, you may have to reinforce the natural tendrils with some randomly located tie-ups just to be safe. When the vine is large enough to be placed on the trellis, you should prune the leaves from the bottom 12 to 18 inches of each vine. There may even be some blossoms down at this level, and they also should be removed. This procedure will delay fruit set somewhat, but it encourages vegetative growth, which increases yield later on. If you want a few early cukes, don't prune a couple of the plants.

Cucumbers require considerable water throughout the entire season. Research has indicated that foliar spray or leaf watering should be avoided with cucumbers because they are so susceptible to mildew and other moisture-related diseases. This is another good reason to use drip irrigation (see chapter 7).

A cucumber vine can grow to be over 20 feet long, so you should help the vine wander over the surface of the trellis rather than have it grow straight up. Another advantage of trellised cucumbers is that they are much easier to see when it is harvest time. It is very important to keep picking the cucumbers as they become ripe. As soon as you let a cucumber grow big and fat and yellow, the plant thinks it has produced the seed it needs to survive next year and stops producing blossoms. So if you go on vacation in the middle of the cucumber harvest, be sure to have a neighbor keep those vines picked.

SQUASH AND MELONS

Winter squash and melons can be grown with little difficulty on a trellis. While it is a good idea to use slings for all the fruit that is formed, some varieties of squash and melon have smaller fruits that can be held up nicely all alone by their own stems.

All varieties of acorn squash and butternut squash do very well on a trellis. All the cantaloupe or muskmelon varieties enjoy growing on a trellis. Two especially good varieties of melon for trellis growing are Saticoy Hybrid muskmelon and Sugar Baby watermelon.

A VERTICAL ORCHARD FENCE

No one thinks much about having fruit and berries in the city or in the suburbs. They take up much more space than most of us have to spare; however, that is only

Photo 4–7: Several 1 × 2 furring strips set at 45-degree angles to the ground support this single-cordon orchard fence. When these small trees grow to their full 7-foot height, the fence will be lush with green foliage and delectable fruit.

true if you think about growing fruit in the traditional manner—on a dwarf, semidwarf, or full-size tree. On the other hand, if you think about growing your fruit on a vertical system, you can have 10 or 20 separate trees of apples or pears growing in a single 50-foot row along side your 200-square-foot garden! That means you could have many different varieties of fruit producing 300 pieces of fresh fruit from July into November all from a 50-foot row along your property's fence line! Three hundred pieces of fruit for the season means about a dozen pieces of fruit each week—enough for most families in this country.

Like many other components of the 60-Minute Garden, the techniques for producing this productive fence orchard, as it is called, have been with us for centuries. *Espalier* is a growing and pruning technique that is usually thought of as a part of the formal gardens of royalty in Europe. This pruning technique simply cuts way back on the amount of vegetation a tree is allowed to have, giving more energy to the production of fruit. You get fewer pieces of fruit per tree, but you get an enormous increase in production of fruit per square foot of growing area. While many commercial orchards are using this method, espalier pruning techniques seem to have intimidated American backyard gardeners, including me. I always figured that you had to be a real professional horticulturist to know how to produce an espaliered apple or pear tree. It turns out that espalier is no more complicated than learning how to prune the suckers off of your tomato plants. A few simple rules, a good pruning tool, and any backyard farmer like I am can have a vertical orchard fence.

Just as with all the vegetables grown vertically, fruit trees (especially apple and pear) are easier to pick and maintain when they, too, are grown on a vertical system. Insect control is easier, disease control is easier, and the trees are healthier because of better air circulation and more access to the sun. The increased exposure to sunlight means larger and sweeter fruit. A recent study at Pennsylvania State University indicated that espalier systems produce more uniformly large fruit than a conventional tree or orchard system. Perhaps one of the greatest advantages of the orchard fence is that trees produce fruit two to three years *earlier* than normal planting and pruning techniques. The single-cordon pruning method with the trees trained at a 45-degree angle causes the trees to fruit within two or three years of planting, rather than the normal four to five years. For those of us that are a bit impatient to harvest our fruit trees, this system is ideal.

The first question you must answer is,

Which espalier design are you going to select in building this vertical orchard? As far as I am concerned, there is only one choice. The most practical design that I've seen was developed by Steve Frowine, a St. Louis, Missouri, gardener. Frowine uses the cordon method of espalier with a 45-degree angle on all his trees. A vertical cordon will also work, but there is evidence that the 45-degree angle allows fruit to ripen earlier. Some of the experienced gardeners using this method have fruit trees planted as close as 13 inches. I have set up my orchard with the trees on 18-inch centers, still very close together by normal orchard standards.

There are several concerns when using Steve Frowine's orchard fence system. In the first place, apples and pears are the only fruits that are adaptable to the single-cordon technique. Peaches, apricots, and plums cannot be cut back so severely. Not just any apple or pear tree grows well in the very close spacing of the orchard fence. You need to have a dwarf apple or pear that has a specific root stock. You need a tree with either an M9 or an M27 root stock for the single cordon to work well when placed extremely close together (12 to 18 inches). Other

Photo 4–8: As the trees of an orchard fence grow, they fill in the space between the furring strips. This process takes four to six years.

dwarf root stocks work well only if they are spaced at least 2 feet apart along the orchard fence line. The most common root stock for this purpose is the M9 stock. If your nursery can't give you M9 trees then you should plant your trees at 2-foot intervals instead of closer. When selecting trees for an orchard fence, the spur-type tree is far superior to the traditional dwarf apple tree. You can find the spur-type tree advertised separately from other trees.

Building a backyard vertical orchard may seem to be a bit expensive on first blush, but if you compute the value of the fruit produced by a cordon fence in the fourth or fifth year, you will see that your initial investment is generally covered in one full year's production. For discussion's sake, let's look at the costs and production of a 25-foot vertical orchard. Using 18-inch centers, you can have 16 trees in that space. That means you could have the following fruit trees:

Early apple—2 trees
Mid-season apple—2 trees
Late-season apple—2 trees
Storage apple—4 trees
Early pear—2 trees
Mid-season pear—2 trees
Late pear—2 trees

With each tree producing 25 to 30 pieces of fruit, this little orchard will give you roughly 300 pieces of fresh fruit from the trees and about 100 apples to store for use in December and January. You will have your own fresh fruit from July through January—seven months of the year! At 1984 prices, this orchard will cost $150 to build. The 400 pieces of quality fruit are worth about $110 wholesale (1984 prices).

CONSTRUCTING THE VERTICAL ORCHARD

The single-cordon trees need to be supported on some kind of vertical structure. I have seen dozens of designs for this structure and prefer the post and wire design because it seems to be the easiest and cheapest to build. For complete building instructions see illustration 4–5.

The key to espalier is to prune the tree so that energy is directed more to fruit production than to growing long branches and lots of leaves. Consequently, the pruning process is designed to regularly prune back branch growth so that fruiting buds are produced close to the main stem of the tree. Illustration 4–3 shows the basic pruning steps required in the first few years of tree growth. The basic principle is that you don't want the laterals or branches to be much more than 6 inches long, and you don't want the sublaterals, or branches of the branches, to be more than 2 inches long. Steve Frowine's advice is to prune the sublaterals just above the first group of leaves, which are usually about 2 inches up the branch.

The timing of your pruning is important as well. Traditional practice in this country has you pruning in the winter months. For your vertical orchard fence you should use the European technique of pruning in the summer. You will do about 75 percent of your pruning sometime in mid-June. Then you will prune a little more in mid-July and finally finish your pruning in mid-August. In each case, you simply prune back to the first set of leaves. Be sure the shoot has turned woody where you are going to cut it, so that a fruiting spur will form at that point. If you prune a stem when it is still soft and green, it will just turn into another stem—no harm done, but also no fruit at that spot next year.

You must be very careful with the material you use to tie the tree to the furring strip, or support strip. If you tie the tree too tightly, you can effectively choke it and kill it. One expert on espalier, Dr. Elwood Fischer, of Harrisonburg, Virginia, recommends using surveyors tape for ties. It is soft and pliable and won't choke the tree. Whatever you use, make sure it is loosely tied all year long.

Fertilizing an orchard fence can follow the same rules found in chapter 5 for the vegetable garden. If you must err in fertilizing the orchard fence, it is better to err on the side of underfertilizing. Too much nitrogen will greatly reduce the size and amount of fruit you harvest, while giving you tremendous green growth, which you must prune off anyway.

STORAGE OF THE TRELLIS PANELS AND POLES

One of the advantages to the panel design in the 60-Minute Garden trellis is that it is easily stored when not in use. I installed two cross beams in my little storage shed, which hold both the trellis panels and the plastic tunnel covers. I simply roll up the panel as tightly as I can get it on the crosspiece. Since I have two sizes of panels, I use some old paint to code the ends of each panel so I can tell which is a long panel or a short panel.

The wooden poles can be stored in a stack in some corner of the homestead. Those of mine that have developed slight curves from the weather are stored with a weight on them to straighten them out for next season. This is one of the reasons PVC is more attractive material for trellis poles—PVC poles don't warp.

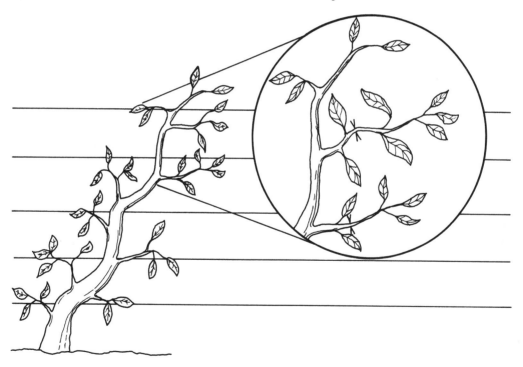

Illustration 4–3: Correct pruning is the key for successfully training trees for an orchard fence. Here the fruit tree is trained to a single cordon. The most important thing to remember is to prune the branches (or laterals) back to the first set of true leaves from the main stem. These branches should not grow to be more than 6 inches long. The sublaterals, or branches of branches, should also be pruned just above the first group of leaves so that they don't grow to be more than 2 inches long. There should be no pruning cuts made to the end of the main stem until the tree is 7 feet long. Then, you can prune the main stem to stop further vertical growth.

VERTICAL TRELLIS FOR FOUR BOXED BEDS

The biggest issue in the construction of the trellis system is the material you choose for your vertical poles. While rigid PVC pipe is definitely the best material, it is the most expensive. Wood will serve very well, but it has some limitations. It requires more time in construction, and it can warp after it is installed in the garden.

Holes must be drilled into the poles so that the crosspieces of the panels can be attached with carriage bolts and wing nuts. I have drilled all my poles to accommodate the two different setups I use—a short trellis and a long trellis. While that means drilling eight holes in every pole, I don't have to worry about keeping track of two different kinds of poles. I use a drill press to drill the 5/16-inch holes in the wooden and PVC poles. A hand drill will work just as well, but you must be careful to drill all the holes at the same angle.

You can mount the trellis panels two ways. You can use 4-inch carriage bolts and simply mount adjoining panels on top of each other. Another approach is to drill two sets of holes and stack the panels as they are mounted down the bed. This method uses shorter bolts, but you have to use twice as many. After trying both methods, I prefer the first, using the longer bolts, and requiring only one hole.

For the crosspieces of the trellis panels, I use 1 × 2 furring strips. The length is determined by the distance between your foundations. My crosspieces are 4 feet long with holes 3 feet 10 inches apart, which is the distance between my foundations. I use three different designs, which then determine how I use my crosspieces and netting. These include a short panel, a long panel, and string. I recommend using all three designs.

SHOPPING LIST

Lumber
16 poles 2 × 2 × 8'
or
16 poles 8' × 1" rigid PVC pipe
12 pcs. 1 × 2 × 8' furring strips
Hardware
32 wing nuts ¼"
32 bolts 4" × ¼"
netting and/or string to produce 12 panels
   4' × 6'
staples ⅜"
     Total cost (using wood): $75
        (using PVC): $100
     Cost per square foot (PVC): $0.50

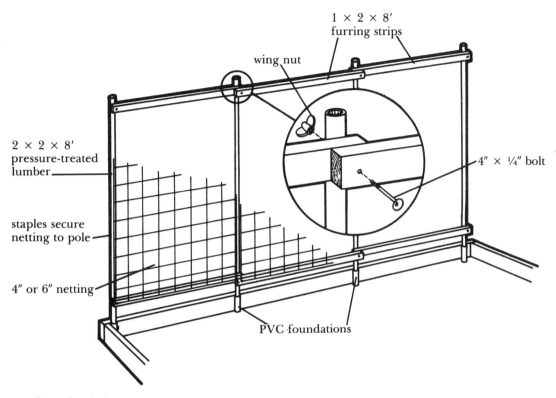

1 × 2 × 8′
furring strips

wing nut

2 × 2 × 8′
pressure-treated
lumber

4″ × ¼″ bolt

staples secure
netting to pole

4″ or 6″ netting

PVC foundations

Illustration 4–4

TOOLS

Coarse sandpaper
Draw knife or draw shave
Electric drill and ⁵⁄₁₆″ bit
Saw
Scissors for cutting netting
Staple gun

CUTTING LIST

Size	Piece	Quanity
4′	Panel strips	24
4′ × 6′	Panel netting	12

CONSTRUCTION STEPS

1. If wooden poles are used, clamp each one in a vise or to a bench top so that a draw knife can be used to trim the corners back about 12 inches down to an octagonal shape that will fit into the 1½-inch PVC foundations. Use coarse sandpaper to make it somewhat smooth.

2. In those same poles, drill ⁵⁄₁₆-inch holes, one 2 inches below the top end of the pole and the second down 6 feet near the bottom of the pole. If PVC pipe is used for poles instead of wood, this same hole-drilling process will take place, but great care must be taken to make sure that the two holes are in the same vertical plane. Otherwise the panels will not connect properly.

3. Cut furring strips to 4-foot lengths, and drill one ⁵⁄₁₆-inch hole in each end so that the distance between the holes is the same as the distance between centerlines of the PVC foundations in the beds (see illustration 4–4).

4. To assemble the panels, set two poles in a position leaning against a bench, a fence, or a porch rail. Attach the two furring strips to the two poles as they would be attached in the garden. This gives you a firm structure for stapling the netting to the furring strips. Cut and staple each piece of netting so that it is moderately tight on the frame (see photo 4–3).

5. After you have assembled the panel, put it in the garden. The middle panel in the bed will be mounted on the same bolts as are the outer panels (see illustration 4–4). I prefer placing the panels on the inside of the poles, to give me more room in the paths when those trellises are filled with plants.

ORCHARD FENCE

This orchard fence is not difficult to install. If you are careful to construct a good solid vertical frame in the beginning, you will have few problems later. Planting trees requires some patience but not as much for an orchard fence as is required for normal plantings. As I mentioned earlier, a single-cordoned tree that is trained to a 45-degree angle will produce fruit in two to three years from planting. At the same time, this fence is not only a wonderful source of high-quality fresh apples and pears; it becomes a very attractive border for any backyard.

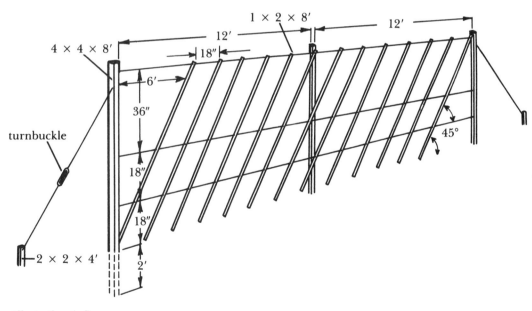

Illustration 4–5

SHOPPING LIST

Lumber
3 poles 4 × 4 × 8′ pressure-treated
13 pcs. 1 × 2 × 8′ furring strips
2 stakes 2 × 2 × 4′ furring strips
Hardware
2 turnbuckles
100 feet of wire heavy enough to support
    the trees
50 feet of light wire for attaching slats to
    the support wires
wire staples
surveyor's tape for attaching trees to slats
Other
13 trees
            Total cost: $150

TOOLS

Hammer
Heavy-duty pliers
Posthole digger
Staple gun
Wire cutters

CUTTING LIST

Size	Piece	Quantity
4 × 4 × 8′	Poles	3
1 × 2 × 8′	Slats	13
2 × 2 × 4′	Stakes	2

CONSTRUCTION STEPS

1. Dig three postholes 12 feet apart for the main vertical 4-by-4 timbers. These poles should be sunk into the ground so that they are very solid—probably about 2 feet deep. Attach the top wire to the three poles allowing enough left over on each end to attach to two turnbuckles (see illustration 4–5). Secure another shorter piece of wire to the other end of each turnbuckle and wrap it around the stakes. Tighten the turnbuckles so that the main timbers are vertical to the ground.

2. Starting at one end of the orchard fence, dig 13 holes along the fence line for the trees. It may be easier just to dig a trench 18 feet long from one end of the trellis structure to the other. The holes (or the trench) should be located a few inches in front of the fence line to leave room for the slats that will be attached after the trees are planted.

3. Plant the trees according to the instructions that come with the stock from the nursery. Remember to plant them at approximately a 45-degree angle so you don't have to bend the main stem too much in the next step when you attach them to the slats.

4. Attach the 13 slats at a 45-degree angle. The bottom of the first slat will be close to the bottom of the first trellis timber. The top of the slat will be connected to the top wire at a point about 6 feet from the top of the trellis timber. This will give you about a 45-degree angle. Then attach all the rest of the slats with 18-inch spacing. The slats are secured to the trellis wire with light wire, just wrapped around the slats a few times.

5. Attach the trees to the slats using surveyors tape, cloth strips, or any other wide material that will not dig into the trees as wire would.

CHAPTER 5
SOIL MANAGEMENT

When I first began gardening, I took my soil pretty much for granted, as I think many gardeners do. A common view of the soil is that it is simply a medium to hold the roots of plants. Many people tend to assume that the food needed by the plants comes from fertilizer, and the water for the plants comes from the garden hose. I believe that there are some serious problems with this approach to thinking about the soil in the garden. It fails to appreciate the relationship in nature between a healthy and live soil and the healthy and productive plants that grow in such a soil. The soil of your garden is much more than merely a support medium for your plants. While it is the primary vehicle for transmitting food and water for healthy plant growth, it is also the source of

that food and the storage area for that water. It is very complex stuff.

As I have said earlier, I believe in regenerative agriculture. At the end of the gardening season, I want my garden soil to be more fertile, have better structure, and have a more active microlife than it had when I started that gardening season. I want my soil, with some help from me, to regenerate itself with increasing value every year. In a sense, I feed my soil instead of feeding my plants. Then, in turn, my healthy soil feeds my plants.

I now approach my garden soil in much the same way that I deal with my vegetable plants. My soil needs tending just as my plants do. I look at soil management as having four components. A gardener needs to care for the content and structure of the soil, the moisture of the soil, the temperature of the soil, and the general health of the soil. The 60-Minute Garden incorporates devices and procedures to address all four of these concerns, without taking much time.

Briefly, the structure and content needs of the soil in the 60-Minute Garden are met by adding compost and/or manure and rock powders in large enough quantities so that regular fertilizing in the traditional manner of applying side-dressings is not needed. Moisture in the soil as well as soil temperature are managed with the drip irrigation system discussed in chapter 7 and by a combination of seasonal mulches. The soil's health is maintained by good garden hygiene, crop rotation, and a new technique called *soil solarization*.

MANAGING THE CONTENT AND STRUCTURE OF THE SOIL

The ideal garden soil is fertile, deep, friable, well-drained, and high in organic matter (5 percent humus is considered minimum). In the 60-Minute Garden, fertility is increased by adding to the soil the necessary materials that can be transformed into nutrients for the plants. The soil is deep because the beds are double-dug. The friable, crumbly soil is light and offers plenty of access for oxygen because the beds are planted intensively and have much organic material added, which also helps to keep the soil well drained; also because no one walks on the beds the soil is not compacted. In fact, over 5 percent organic matter is added *every year* to the top 12 inches of garden soil.

The ideal soil also has a very active population of microorganisms made up mostly of fungi and bacteria. Fungi are fairly flexible in terms of their needs, but bacteria want good aeration, a near-neutral pH, a moist but not wet environment, and warm temperatures. Soil temperatures between 65° and 80°F are about the ideal range for the microlife in a vegetable garden. Under those conditions there should be roughly 5,000 earthworms in the 60-Minute Garden, producing over 175 pounds of extremely valuable manure each year all by themselves! Let's look at how to get this ideal garden soil in more detail.

Vegetable plants have both major and minor mineral requirements to remain healthy and productive. The most common major nutrients are the nitrogen (N), phosphorus (P), and potassium (K) you read about on bags of fertilizer (for example, NPK 5-10-5). In an organic gardening system, the nitrogen and phosphorus availability is primarily dependent upon the activity of the soil microfauna and microflora that make these nutrients available to the plant's roots. To a lesser extent potassium is also dependent on these same biological processes that are at work in a healthy soil.

A gardener has two choices. The first approach is to use inorganic chemical fertilizers that give the vegetables all the nutrients necessary for healthy plants, while at the same time significantly reducing the microlife in the soil. The earthworms leave (there goes 175 pounds of manure produced by them), much of the bacteria and fungi die, and the plants become almost completely dependent on the continuing fertilizing efforts of the gardener to maintain their health and vigor. Another disadvantage is that regular fertilizing with inorganic chemical fertilizers takes time.

The 60-Minute Garden approach takes a somewhat longer view of the world. If all the materials needed for producing those nutrients are in the soil in sufficient quantities, and if conditions for a very active microlife are maintained, the vegetables will get all the food they need throughout the growing season, whether the gardener supplements the feeding process or not. With either approach the plants get fed; however, the 60-Minute Garden incorporates techniques that are designed to continually build the fertility of the soil while reducing the time required by the gardener to maintain that garden. The traditional approach does neither.

THE SOIL TEST

Before you can set up any soil management plan, you have to have an accurate understanding of your soil conditions right now. The only reliable way to assess your soil is with a soil test. Most garden books recommend a soil test every three or four years. For the 60-Minute Garden a soil test is a good idea every year. When you are planting a garden intensively, the relative quantities of nitrogen, phosphorus, and potassium become very important to ongoing health and productivity, and you can't properly manage that balance without regular test readings from your garden's soil.

While soil test kits for home use are available, I believe that, with some reservations, a more accurate soil test is available from the Cooperative Extension Service (CES) in each state. CES will provide information for a very modest fee, and the whole process takes less time than if you do the testing and analysis yourself. A soil test will give you data concerning the levels of phosphorus and potassium. The test will also give the pH of your soil and will often indicate the levels of those critical minerals calcium and magnesium. Soil tests will also give you a reading on nitrogen in your soil; however, these figures are often inaccurate. If you add 2 pounds of organic nitrogen to your 60-Minute Garden each year, your nitrogen needs will be met. The soil test report will also give you recommendations for how you should fertilize your soil. I ignore those recommendations because they are not based on the principles of organic agriculture. I use their data but not their recommendations.

The soil test report will tell you whether your individual nutrient levels are low, medium, high, or excessive. Vegetable crops do best in soils where the nutrients are in *balanced* amounts at the medium to high levels. The balance of the nutrients is almost more important than the level. Early on in my garden I had excessive potassium and medium nitrogen and phosphorus. While I had all the nutrients I needed in terms of quantity, they were out of balance, which meant that they were not as available to my plant's roots as they would have been if they had been balanced. In my case, I could not use any manure or wood ashes on my garden until I got the potassium level down to "high." I let the plants take the potassium out of the soil for a few years and just added nitrogen and phosphorous amendments to my soil. It is now in balance, and I can use modest amounts of manure and wood ashes.

The CES's soil test kits are usually available from your county agent for about two to three dollars. The kits will probably contain a cloth bag attached to a preaddressed envelope containing a questionnaire for you to fill out about your garden. You must take your soil sample properly for it to be of any practical value to you. It is not difficult to do, but there is a proper procedure for collecting the sample.

You should take a number of samples from 15 to 20 spots in your vegetable garden and mix them together to get an "average" sample of your soil. You want to take each of the 15 or more samples from a depth of about 6 to 8 inches below the surface. Stick a trowel down into the soil and twist out a plug of dirt and set it aside. Then take a spoon and reach down into the hole made by the trowel and scrape a spoonful of dirt from the 6-to-8-inch layer. That spoonful is added to the other 15 spoonfuls from which you get your sample to send to the laboratory.

If your soil is wet when you take the sample, don't bake it in the oven to dry. Simply spread it out on a newspaper and let it air dry for a day or so. Put all your 15 or more samples into a bag and mix them up thoroughly. Then take ½ cup of soil, or whatever the instructions tell you, and place it into the soil test mailer. This whole exer-

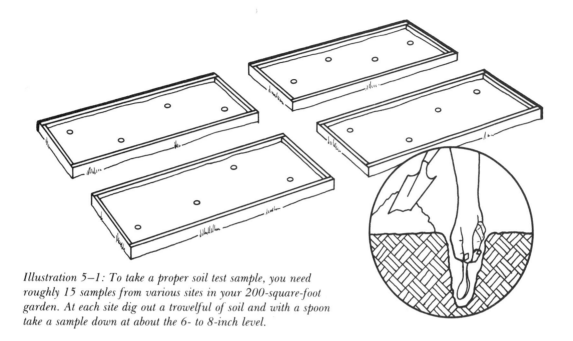

Illustration 5–1: To take a proper soil test sample, you need roughly 15 samples from various sites in your 200-square-foot garden. At each site dig out a trowelful of soil and with a spoon take a sample down at about the 6- to 8-inch level.

cise takes only about 20 minutes and will give you information that will be invaluable in planning your soil management activities. You can take this sample at any time during the year; however, the fall is a good time to complete your soil test. Then you have all winter to think about your soil management plans.

MANAGING pH

Your soil test will tell you the pH of the soil. This indicates whether your soil is more acidic or more alkaline. The pH scale goes from 0 (super acidic) to 14 (super alkaline) with 7 being considered neutral. The soil's pH is important because when it is at the proper level the microflora and microfauna are in the best environment for releasing nutrients, especially nitrogen, to the roots of the plants. Consequently, the gardener should try to keep the vegetable garden's pH between 6 and 6.8, a slightly acidic level. Below a pH of 6 there is a marked drop in the solubility of certain soil nutrients. Nitrogen, phosphorus, and other key nutrients are locked into more complex compounds that don't readily break down below a pH of 6.

The soil test report will often indicate how to raise or lower your actual pH reading to the preferred 6 to 6.8 level. Sulfur or acid peat moss is generally recommended to correct an alkaline soil condition, and lime is used to adjust soil that is too acid. The most common situation is one where your soil is a bit more acid than you need so you must add some lime. The fall is the best time to do this because it takes six months for lime to achieve its full effect. You will find that your pH will be affected over the years with the addition of the annual layer of compost to be discussed later in this chapter. Properly aged compost generally has a pH of 6.8 to 7. Even acidic oak leaves compost down to a material that is almost neutral. So if your soil is now acidic, you may have to add some lime for a year or two, but your soil tests may show that you don't need that step since the impact of the compost is eventually felt on the pH levels of your soil.

LONG-TERM AMENDMENTS

Your soil's need for phosphorus and potassium can be met by adding some rock powders to your garden every two or three years. Rock powders are long-term resources that provide important nutrients very slowly over time. For example, if you put rock phosphate in fairly high amounts on your garden this fall, you won't be getting phosphorus from this source to your plants' roots until next summer. At the same time, you will be getting a steady supply of phosphorus from this one application for over two years!

Rock phosphate is available in many garden centers and is an excellent source of phosphorus. If your soil test shows that your soil is deficient in phosphorus, you may want to add some rock phosphate to your compost pile for a year or two to speed up the availability of phosphorus from this particular source. Rock phosphate needs acid to break it down, and a garden with a good pH of 6.0 to 6.8 breaks down the rock phosphate very slowly. The compost pile is generally more acidic in the beginning of its decomposition, so it will release more phosphorus.

A good source of potassium is granite dust or greensand, also available from many garden centers. Again, if your soil test reflects a need for additional potassium, you might add some of these powders to your compost pile for a year or two to speed up the availability of this nutrient in your soil.

Because these rock powders (rock phosphorus, greensand, and granite dust) break down so slowly in the soil, it is difficult to put too much into your garden. At the same time, you don't need to waste your money by using more than you need. A good rule of thumb for these rock powders is to apply about 10 pounds of each kind to 100 square feet of your garden every two to three years. If you have a 200-square-foot garden, a 20-pound bag of rock phosphate and a 20-pound bag of greensand will take care of your phosphorus and potassium needs for two years. Again the fall is a good time to spread these long-term amendments. This gives them some time to begin breaking down for the next year's crop.

WINTER PROTECTION AND FEEDING

The freezing of the soil during a cold winter greatly reduces the microlife in the top 6-inch layer. While the soil bacteria and fungi come back the next spring, you can speed up that process by protecting the soil from the cold. Each year, if you follow the 60-Minute Garden schedule, you will cover the garden with a 6- to 10-inch layer of organic mulch, such as straw, when you are finished using the tunnels and are putting the garden to bed, as it were. This layer of mulch will not keep the soil from freezing, but it will protect it from the temperature shifts that occur throughout the winter. The rapid shift in temperature is more of a problem for the microlife in the soil than the cold temperature itself.

Straw is used throughout the season in the 60-Minute Garden for several purposes depending on the time of the year. This winter, straw mulch should be removed from the beds in the early spring when the tunnels are erected. It will be stored in a pile and used later in the summer garden as a cooling mulch. Finally in the fall season, this straw, combined with some weeds and leaves will be the primary source of compost material. At that time, in the fall, a new batch of straw is placed on the wintering garden, and the cycle continues.

COVER CROPPING

I should mention cover cropping at this point. A cover crop involves planting some kind of grass or other dense crop in a bed in the fall after the vegetable harvest is over. It is a common practice in commercial agriculture to prevent erosion. With a 200-square-foot garden however, cover crops must be treated a little differently. The entire garden space is used for food production throughout the entire season, so that there is never leftover space for cover crops in such a compact garden. The solution is to have an extra 4-by-12-foot bed. This bed allows for a rotation schedule among all your beds for both cover cropping and solarization of your soil, which is discussed in detail later in this chapter.

You must remember that in a healthy soil, at temperatures between 45° and 85°F, the microlife is constantly producing nutrients in a form useful to plants whether there are any plants actually in the soil or not. If there are no plants in the soil, those nutrients are simply leached away by the next rain. The point here is that if you have even part of a bed that is not being used for vegetables, you are wise to plant a cover crop that will later be dug into the soil, thus preserving those valuable nutrients for later use. Cover crops will add organic humus to the soil, will help control compaction problems, and will improve the soil's general tilth, or texture and structure.

You must be careful about what kind of cover crop you use. Commercial agriculture commonly uses oats, winter wheat, and winter rye as effective cover crops. These are not good cover crops for a vegetable garden. These plants have an *allelopathic* (negative) effect on certain vegetable plants. Allelopathy is the somewhat mysterious negative chemical communication that occurs between certain groups of plants. Wheat and rye, for example, will slow down the growth rate of peas in the spring. Oats have a bad effect on carrots. Perhaps the best cover crop for a vegetable garden is a plant called winter hairy vetch, which is available from some of the seed catalogs and is found in stores serving commercial agriculture. It is an ex-

cellent source of nitrogen for your soil.

In larger gardens, you would plant your cover crop in a bed after all vegetable production is over for the seasons. So you would roll up or remove the plastic mulch and sow the seeds in much the same way you seed your lawn. In the 60-Minute Garden, with its limited size and intensive planting schedule through five growing seasons, you would need an extra bed to take advantage of cover crops. This extra bed would be used for an early planting under tunnels in the early spring and spring seasons, and then in the summer season it would be set up for a solarization process described later. This process pasteurizes your soil. Then after the solarization process is over, you would plant a cover crop in that bed for the fall season, and cover it with straw mulch over the winter. That bed will be perfect for your tomato crop and other heat-loving vegetables next year. Next year another bed will be set aside for this same solarization and cover crop treatment. Ideally, your entire garden receives this special process every five years.

It takes about ¼ pound of seed to plant a cover crop in 100 square feet of garden. You can start a cover crop as early as late August, but September is the usual time for seeding. When it comes time in late October or early November to lay the protective layer of straw mulch, you can lay the mulch right over the cover crop. It will simply die and decompose in the soil. In the spring you may need to turn over the top 4 or 5 inches if it has not decomposed enough to be broken up with a rake.

SOIL MANAGEMENT IN THE SPRING

In chapter 2 I made my case for not digging your garden beds every spring. In the 60-Minute Garden there are all kinds of forces working to keep the soil in top condition for growing healthy plants. By not walking on the beds, compaction is greatly reduced. Intensive planting causes root systems to work their way throughout the entire top 12 to 24 inches of soil several times a season. Digging potatoes, pulling carrots and other root crops, and digging holes for transplants all are a form of digging. A healthy earthworm population and the other active microflora and microfauna are continuously making channels for oxygen access. All these actions eliminate or at least greatly reduce the need for digging the garden every spring.

On the other hand, if your soil is not yet in as good a condition as you might like, you may feel that you must still dig up the soil so you can get more humus down deeper into the top layer. If this is the case, your best tool is the spading fork rather than the spading shovel. To turn the top layer of soil under a layer of subsoil does more harm than good to your soil's ecosystem. The most important area for the critical microlife in the soil resides in the top 6 inches. A spading fork will just break up the clods of clay and aerate the soil without shifting the layers.

Even better tools for digging a bed, if you really must dig, are devices called U-bar Diggers or Double Diggers (see the Appendix for sources). This tool is not cheap, but it does an excellent job of loosening up the soil without disturbing the important layers of the soil. A U-bar digger is also very easy on the back, for those folks with bad backs.

ORGANIC SOIL SUPPLEMENTS

Your most important soil management activity occurs in the early spring after you have removed the winter mulch and set it aside for use later in the early summer. Every year you want to lay about an inch of finished compost or aged manure over the entire surface of the garden. This organic supplement is the critical source of nitrogen, some potassium, and the trace minerals needed by your garden for the entire season. Humus is generally low in phosphorus, so that is why we apply the rock powders. This layer of compost or manure performs several very important functions in our 60-Minute Garden. Researchers at the Connecticut Agricultural Experiment Station have demonstrated that 1 inch of compost on your garden will boost the yields of your vegetables by 10 to 75 percent. It contributes to the water-holding and draining capacity of your soil; it allows for more oxygen to enter the soil; it helps regulate soil temperatures; and it promotes the growth of the microorganisms so critical to the production of food for the plants.

But the most important role of this layer of compost or aged manure is to provide nitrogen to the plants throughout the growing season. You can think of compost or aged manure as having a half-life of fertility. About half of the nutrients that are present are released for plant use during the first year. Half of what nutrients are left are released the second year, and so on after that. Most vegetable crops require about $\frac{1}{2}$ pound of nitrogen per 100 square feet per crop. Since we have two and sometimes three crops in the 60-Minute Garden, we want to have at least a pound of nitrogen available per 100 square feet, or 2 pounds for our 200-square-foot model garden.

Determining how much manure is needed is easier than determining how much compost is needed because the nitrogen content of compost varies a great deal. If you have aged dairy cow manure available, then in the first year you should place a 1-inch layer of the stuff across the entire garden. This amounts to about 60 gallons of aged cow manure per 100 square feet. If you have aged chicken manure available, you should use only half as much. After that first year, you can then drop your layer down to only $\frac{1}{2}$ inch of aged manure or about 30 gallons per 100 square feet. This will produce about 1 pound of nitrogen per year. I think in terms of 5-gallon pails, so I would need twelve

Photo 5–1: This U-bar digger loosens the soil without disturbing its structure. It is also easy on the back. Use this tool for piercing the hardpan when double digging beds, as well as for loosening the soil and dressing the beds each spring.

5-gallon pails of aged manure for a 200-square-foot garden each year to give my plants their annual supply of nitrogen.

Most of us don't have a ready source of aged manure, especially a free source. So we must use compost—a lot of compost. While there is no uniformity in the amount of ni-

trogen found in finished compost, we must be conservative in estimating how much compost to spread in the spring. Compost made from hay is higher in nitrogen than compost made from straw. Leaves have about half the nitrogen that manure has. One of the ways to find out what you have if you generally use the same formula to make compost is to get a soil test of it. This will tell you how much nitrogen you have. For comparison, aged cow manure is about 1.4 percent nitrogen, and chicken manure is about 2.8 percent nitrogen. If your compost is 0.8 to 1 percent nitrogen, then you can supply your garden's need for nitrogen with a 1-inch layer each spring. This means about 120 gallons of compost for each 200 square feet. Another measure is that you'll need about 2 pounds of compost per square foot or about 400 pounds for 200 square feet. This adds up to about 16 cubic feet of compost, which is represented by a pile of finished compost that is at least 2 by 4 by 2 feet. This size pile can be produced in the compost bin described at the end of the chapter, using last year's straw mulch, garden waste, some leaves from around the yard, and some grass clippings. If you fill that 4-by-4-by-4-foot bin with all those materials, your finished compost pile will have decomposed down to a pile that is 4 by 4 feet around and somewhere between 1 foot and 2 feet tall. If you have more compost than that available, so much the better.

If you don't have enough compost, you can ensure sufficient nitrogen by buying a 20-pound bag of dried manure and spreading 10 pounds on top of the 1 inch of compost for every 100 square feet. If you have access to some free aged manure, then 15 gallons of aged manure and ½ inch of compost will give you your pound of nitrogen. There are a number of ways to get your nitrogen. The trick is to do it as cheaply as is possible.

The point of spreading this layer of organic material over your entire garden is to have available, in concert with the rock

TABLE 5–1

―――――――― VARIOUS SOURCES OF NITROGEN IN THE GARDEN ――――――――

FERTILIZERS THAT ARE ORGANIC
SOURCES OF NITROGEN

Blood meal (15%)
Coffee grounds (2%)
Compost (1–2%)
Cottonseed meal (6%)
Fish emulsion (10%)
Manure (0.5–1%)
Seaweed emulsion (2%)

COVER CROPS
THAT PRODUCE NITROGEN

Alfalfa (3–4%)
Red clover (2–3.2%)
Sweet clover (2–3%)
White Dutch clover (0.5%)

VEGETABLE CROPS
THAT LEAVE NITROGEN

Peas (amount varies with variety)
Pole beans (amount varies with variety)
Soybeans (amount varies with variety)

MICRO PALS
THAT PRODUCE NITROGEN

Azotobacter bacteria (½ lb in
    200 square feet)
Earthworms (180 lb of fertilizer with
    significant nitrogen content in 200
    square feet)
Rhizobium bacteria (amount varies
    with temperature)

powders, all the nutrients your garden will need for optimum production even if you do not do one more thing to supplement the feeding of your vegetables for the entire season! I talk about nutrient supplements with the drip irrigation system in chapter 7. These supplements will improve your crop, but they are *not* absolutely necessary to getting an optimum harvest. They move you toward getting closer to maximum productivity. This one application of a layer of organic material every spring is enough to do the job.

Note that I did not say "dig this material into the soil." You just lay it on top. If you have a desperate need to at least rake it in a little bit, go ahead if it makes you feel better. You don't really have to spend the energy or the time. After you spread your layer of compost and/or aged manure, you can then set down your drip irrigation tubing (see chapter 7), lay out your clear or black plastic mulch (see chapter 3), and erect

your plastic tunnel (chapter 3). For 200 square feet of garden, this whole project should take you about 2 hours, and you are ready to begin another productive vegetable garden.

MAKING COMPOST

The design for the compost bin found at the end of this chapter (see illustration 5–3) incorporates all of the principles for a good compost pile. You really don't need a bin to make good compost. The bin simply keeps things neat and helps you save some space. A good bin allows you to keep your backyard neat, produces the amount of compost you need, allows for easy turning of the pile, lasts a long time, and is generally attractive.

Making compost is a very simple process. Many books and articles make a big deal of using precise formulas and ratios of materials. All of those formulas produce compost, but they are much too complicated for my taste. The 60-Minute Garden needs a layer of organic material every year, and compost is the cheapest source of that material. If you use compost, you will probably need to use the active method for making your compost. The passive method is simple—you make a pile of stuff and let it sit for a few years. The active method requires that you turn the pile or mix up the pile a few times during the year so that the decomposition process works faster.

A compost pile needs carbon, nitrogen, oxygen, and water. The compost pile for the 60-Minute Garden gets its carbon and nitrogen from materials normally thrown away by gardeners in the suburbs and cities. The oxygen comes from turning the pile a few times, and the water comes from the rain absorbed by the leaves and other dried materials. You'll spend a few hours each year making enough compost for a 200-square-foot garden, but the price is right—it's free.

Great compost can be made from straw, leaves, grass clippings, garden waste, and kitchen garbage. That is all you need. Be especially careful never to use any meat products, bones, or grease in your compost pile, because they will attract rodents and cause the compost pile to smell bad. A compost pile should *never* smell bad. If it does you have probably put too much nitrogen material or green stuff in it. A compost pile needs to have much more carbon material

Photo 5–2: This three-section compost bin allows for easy turning of the pile from section to section until you get the final product—a pile of rich compost.

TABLE 5–2

COMMON COMPOSTING MATERIALS

CARBON MATERIALS	NITROGEN MATERIALS
Aged sawdust	Fresh grass clippings
Dry leaves	Kitchen scraps
Seaweed	Manure
Straw	Weeds and garden waste

(straw, leaves, and other dried organic material) than nitrogen material (grass clippings, fresh-picked weeds, kitchen garbage). Many gardening books recommend a ratio of about 30 to 1, carbon to nitrogen. My experience indicates that you can cut that ratio way down to even 10 to 1 if you turn the pile frequently. If the pile smells bad, add more carbon material. If the pile is not heating up, add more nitrogenous material. Some experimentation on your part will indicate that there is not much precision in the ratio.

My composting system is fairly simple. In the fall, I collect leaves that my neighbors have carefully raked up and bagged for trash collection. I pile those leaves in a back corner of the yard over the winter. If I have time I shred them with my shredder so they don't mat so badly when they get wet. You don't need a shredder for making good compost. If you don't have a shredder available, you should avoid putting sticks and fibrous stalks like cornstalks into your pile. The compost sifter, described at the end of this chapter, helps you screen out sticks and other materials that have not yet decomposed.

In the spring I build a pile, mixing leaves with grass clippings. I run the pile through my shredder every two to three weeks, and I have finished compost in a couple of months. I use that compost around the yard and garden as mulch and for setting seedlings. If you don't have a shredder, then you simply move your pile from one spot to another. This move will cause oxygen to be added to the pile, and it will mix up the ingredients for better decomposition. If you build two compost bins instead of just one, this exercise is accomplished by shifting the pile from one bin to the other every month or so. It takes about an hour.

In the late summer I build another pile with the remaining leaves and grass clippings, and that pile produces the compost I need in the spring. I do not cover the pile of leaves, so they get wet and stay wet from the rain. Then when I build a pile, I don't have to worry about moisture because the leaves and grass have sufficient moisture. I do cover my compost pile so the rain doesn't cool it down. My piles will heat up to about 140°F. You can tell if a pile is working well by sticking your fist into the pile about a foot. If it is real warm, the pile is decomposing nicely.

MANAGING THE TEMPERATURE OF THE SOIL

As I discussed at some length in chapter 3, the role of soil temperature in plant growth has not gotten the attention it deserves in most gardening books and magazines. We read about seed germination temperatures that are supposed to guide us in our spring plantings, but otherwise we read little about soil temperatures after that phase. Only a very few gardeners even own a soil thermometer so how do they know when to plant their seeds? Usually gardeners use the date to determine planting time, whether the soil temperature is at the proper level or not. The idea of actually *managing* soil temperature throughout the growing season is a concept new to everyone. Yet research has shown that the temperature of the soil around the roots of the plant is more important to the growth of the plant than the temperature of air around the leaves. This is a known fact among greenhouse managers, but it has not been discussed too much over the backyard fences of the vegetable gardeners.

Soil temperature is important because the microlife of the soil doesn't really begin to become active until the soil reaches about 45°F. On the other end of the season, the plant's growth mechanisms slow down considerably when the soil temperature exceeds 85°F. For example, the bacteria that make nitrogen available to plant roots in the form needed, do not begin to become active until the soil temperature is about 40°F, and they don't reach the height of their activity until the soil temperature reaches 80°F.

So for all intents and purposes, your gardening season doesn't start with the last spring frost and end with the first fall frost. It starts when the soil temperature reaches 45°F, and it ends when the soil temperature drops down again to 45°F. There is little correlation between air temperature and soil temperature. You can have a balmy spring day in terms of air temperature, but if the soil temperature hasn't reached 45°F, you shouldn't start to plant your seedlings.

Chapter 3 covers many of the issues involved in managing the soil temperature, especially in the spring season (see tables 3–2 and 3-3). Soil temperatures can be used to schedule much of your planting. A temperature of 40°F allows you to plant peas, leaf lettuce, spinach, and Chinese cabbage. You should wait until you have a soil temperature of 50°F to start your radishes, onions, onion sets, beets, and parsnips. A temperature of 60°F is needed for carrots and turnips. In

Photo 5–3: This compost tumbler holds 18 bushels of organic materials such as chopped leaves. With daily rotation of the drum, it produces compost in about two weeks.

all cases, germination increases when soil temperatures are up to 65°F. You need at least 65°F to seed beans, cucumbers, eggplant, muskmelons, peppers, squash, and tomatoes. Watermelon requires 75° to 80°F for good germination.

Once a seed is germinated, it has a preferred soil temperature for maximum growth. While seedlings and maturing plants won't grow very well when it's too cold, they won't grow very well when it's too hot either. For example, corn will grow, but very slowly, at a soil temperature of 60°F and will increase growth from 65° to 85°F. After 85°F corn stops growing. The ideal soil temperature for corn growth is 80° to 81°F, so that's

Photo 5–4: I staged this photo to show the layers in a bed in the 60-Minute Garden. First, cover the bare soil (as on the right) with a thin layer of rock powders, followed by an inch of compost. Next come the feeder lines of the drip irrigation system. Then, cover the whole bed with a piece of black plastic mulch. Later in the season, lay the straw mulch over the plastic mulch to help cool the soil.

where you should try to maintain the soil's temperature. How do you actually "manage" soil temperature? The answer is to use mulch and drip irrigation, but the temperature is mostly managed through the use of various kinds of mulch.

USING MULCH TO CONTROL SOIL TEMPERATURE

In the past, mulch was recommended for use in the vegetable garden because it held moisture in the soil by reducing evaporation, and it kept down weeds. The organic mulches were also valued because they decomposed over time and added humus to soil. These are still good reasons for using

mulch, but I don't believe they are the most important reasons. The primary reason for using mulch is to control the temperature of the soil. You want to warm up the soil early in the season, cool the soil during the hot summer, and warm the soil again as the first frost approaches. Research in the past decade has clearly demonstrated the value of mulch in controlling and managing soil temperature.

Clear plastic and black plastic film are excellent materials for warming the soil. Organic mulches, such as hay or straw, are excellent mulches for cooling the soil. Both types should be used during the growing season. Start off with a plastic film and then cover it with straw or hay when the summer arrives. When fall arrives, off comes the straw and the plastic film does its warming trick again.

BLACK VERSUS CLEAR
PLASTIC MULCH

Black plastic film is the most popular warming mulch. It will warm the soil from 6° to 8°F above unmulched soil; however, clear plastic film is a much better warming material because it transmits sunlight directly into the soil and holds the heat there, just like a greenhouse gets and holds heat. Black plastic film absorbs most of the solar radiation striking it and transmits heat to the soil much more slowly by radiation. The question for the 60-Minute Gardener is which one to use. The answer as usual is "it depends." The clear plastic can heat things up too much, and in fact, as you will see later in this chapter, can be used to sterilize the soil (see illustration 5–2). The decision on which to use is a function of how far north you live. In Wisconsin, experiments with clear plastic had soil temperatures going 20°F above the surrounding open soil. That same clear plastic might take the soil up 30° or 40°F in Virginia and do more harm than good.

My advice is to try both in your garden in the first season and watch the soil temperatures carefully. In Maine, the clear plastic is sure to be best, and in Kentucky the black plastic is probably best. Between those two latitudes experimentation must take place to determine the best choice.

Plastic mulch is often criticized for preventing the rain from moistening the soil evenly. This problem is solved by the method I use to cut flaps in the plastic on 2-inch centers (see the description of this in chapter 3). In addition, your drip irrigation system is placed on the bed *under* the mulch, giving

Photo 5–5: Put the straw or hay mulch on the bed as soon as the soil temperature approaches 80°F. This mulch should be 6 to 12 inches thick, depending on how warm your climate happens to be.

your plants free access to all the water they need. The clear plastic does not give off the radiant heat at night as the black plastic does, but when they are under a tunnel, the plants don't need that extra heat as much.

Clear plastic mulch, unlike the black plastic, does not prevent weed seeds from sprouting, but the physical barrier provided by the layer of plastic film prevents the weeds from becoming a significant competitor of your vegetables. In addition, when you add the layer of straw or hay in the early summer, those weeds will die.

ORGANIC MULCHES

Organic mulches, such as hay or straw, will cool the soil by 8° to 12°F, and chopped leaves will cool things down as much as 18°F. You should use only chopped leaves that have aged for a year or so because you might get some unwanted allelopathic effects between the leaves and the soil. The big advantage of leaves of course is that they are free. Use only chopped up leaves, since whole leaves mat down and reduce the even flow of rain into the soil. It is also important to place the organic mulch directly on top of the plastic mulch rather than directly on the open soil. The lower levels of that organic mulch are going to begin to decompose, and that process takes nitrogen from the top inch or so of soil that should be available to your plants. The layer of plastic mulch between the organic mulch and the soil reduces that problem greatly.

MULCHING CYCLE

So, let's review the mulching cycle in the 60-Minute Garden. In the late winter (in February) you will remove the protective winter mulch, spread a layer of compost, set out the drip irrigation hoses, lay out the clear or black plastic film, and erect the tunnel device. This allows the soil in the bed to warm up much faster than the surrounding soil outside the tunnel. When the soil temperature hits 40°F, for example, you can plant your peas. Young pea plants grow best at

TABLE 5–3

_____ MULCHING CYCLE _____

SEASON	ACTIVITY
Early spring	Remove winter straw mulch Spread a layer of compost Lay drip irrigation hoses Lay black or clear plastic mulch Erect tunnels
Spring	Begin using drip irrigation Remove tunnels
Summer	Lay straw mulch over plastic mulch Drip irrigation for moisture and cooling Erect tunnels again before first fall frost
Fall	Remove straw mulch to uncover plastic mulch
Early winter	Store tunnels for winter Lay winter straw mulch

soil temperatures between 59° and 68°F, so you use the plastic film to help the soil temperatures move up to that upper limit.

As soon as the soil temperatures around your pea plants average 65°F, you will add your 6 inches or more of organic mulch to the peas. I use straw. This new mulch in combination with using drip irrigation can keep the soil temperature around your peas from going above 68°F, giving you as much as a week or two of additional harvest from your peas. Other plants under the tunnel may prefer warmer soil temperatures, so you will hold off placing the straw around those plants until the soil temperature hits about 80°F.

In the summertime, the straw mulch, regular use of drip irrigation, and intensive planting all serve to keep your soil temperatures below the 85°F level where plants stop developing. By watching your soil temperatures carefully as the cooler fall season approaches, you will take the straw mulch off the beds when the average soil temperature is about 70°F. Now the plastic film is keeping the soil warmer, which extends the active growing period of many vegetables such as tomatoes, eggplant, and peppers. Before the first frost arrives, you will build your tunnels again, and plastic film will continue to keep the soil within them warm enough to continue to produce plant growth. When the soil temperature reaches 45°F sometime in late November or early December, you can take up the plastic mulch and lay out the protective winter mulch and end your growing season. In February, you start the cycle all over again.

PREVENTING DISEASE IN THE 60-MINUTE GARDEN

Just as with people, there are thousands of diseases that can attack particular vegetables in your garden. Fortunately, just as with people, if you take a few precautions, very few of those diseases ever occur. Never-

theless, a gardener must have some respect for the problems of disease. The virus carried by the squash beetle will quickly kill squash plants. Verticillium wilt will reduce your tomato crop considerably. Bean rust can reduce your bean crop.

By far, the most effective disease prevention measure in the garden is plain old hygiene. Keeping the garden free of rotting weeds or vegetable plants past harvest goes a long way to preventing the spread of disease. The compost pile is a great tool for eliminating many disease problems because of the heating process in the center of the pile, although vegetables that have rotted or have some disease are best disposed of in the trash. Certain vegetable plants with disease should be disposed of rather than composted. Those include tomatoes, potatoes, cucumbers, melons, strawberries, and raspberries. Cleaning up the garden at the end of the season is essential to minimizing disease problems in the following year.

ROTATING CROPS FOR DISEASE PREVENTION

Another important technique in preventing disease is crop rotation. Diseases often are found in spores that are transmitted over into the next season right in the soil; however, these germs or spores often do not travel very far from where their host plant was situated during the growing season. So by making sure that you never plant the same kind of vegetable in the same place two years in a row, you are preventing many disease problems. Crop rotation in a 200-square-foot garden may seem to be a bit difficult, considering how small the total garden is; however, if you have four beds, and you rotate your crops in different beds each year, then some crops will not be planted in the same place for three years. That is often sufficient time to control certain diseases. Even moving a crop from one side of a 4-foot-wide bed, 3 feet over to the other side of the bed

Photo 5–6: To solarize the soil in your beds, thoroughly soak the soil, and then lay clear plastic film over the entire bed. Seal the edges of the plastic with soil. The temperature under this clear plastic will reach 140°F, killing most of the disease spores, many of the nematodes, and other harmful microbiotic flora and fauna in the soil.

can be helpful in many cases.

One of the problems with crop rotation is keeping track of where you planted things the previous year. You probably think you will remember where you put the lettuce and the cabbage and the tomatoes, but sometimes it all seems the same and gets blurred as the years go by. I've tried a number of different schemes for labeling my garden so I could keep track. The best way of course, and the one guaranteed to work is to make a diagram of the garden on paper with the location of the different vegetables carefully labeled. Just because it is the best way doesn't mean I use it though. My garden is difficult to diagram because I am always sticking seedlings in spaces all over the place with no real concern for any orderly pattern. With two and sometimes three successions, my diagram is a mess halfway through the season.

The system I use now that seems to me the easiest and still effective is to keep track of which vegetables have been planted in each bed, without worrying about exactly where in the bed they were located. This means that my rotation plan will be set up to shift vegetables from bed to bed each year, trying to avoid planting a variety in a bed more than once every three years. Now my diagram is much simpler. I just list the vegetables by each bed, and it all fits onto one sheet of paper. In fact you can put three or four years of rotation records on one sheet of paper.

SOLARIZING YOUR SOIL

In the past, it has been assumed that if you had certain disease spores in the soil, such as verticillium wilt and fusarium wilt, you would always have that problem. Now there has been a development that may solve many of our vegetable garden disease problems. The technique, called *solarization* of the soil, was developed in Israel and has been tested in a number of universities across this country. It involves covering a portion of wetted garden with a sheet of clear plastic film in the middle of the summer during the heat of the season. The edges of the plastic film are sealed with soil so a greenhouse effect produces very high levels of heat in the soil. After a few days of continuous sunlight, the soil temperature begins to soar, reaching 140°F at the surface and as high as 100°F 18 inches down.

This heat creates nearly 100 percent humidity in the water-soaked soil. The effect of the heat and humidity over a period of four to six weeks causes the soil to be pasteurized. This process will destroy harmful bacteria, fungi, some nematodes, virtually every type of insect larvae, and the stock of weed seeds near the surface. Solarization has been found to be an effective control against such pesky disease problems as verticillium wilt in tomatoes, potatoes, and eggplant. It knocks out fusarium wilt in tomatoes and onions. It has been effective against pyrenochaeta in tomatoes and onions, rhizoctonia in potatoes and onions, and eliminates a variety of nematodes in potatoes and other crops.

What is truly amazing and an unexpected benefit of solarization is that it is also a soil enhancer. There is an unexplained increase in crop yield in beds that have been solarized. Jim DeVay, chairman of the plant pathology department at the University of California at Davis, is quoted as saying, "While many fungi, bacteria and other pathogens are killed, certain fungi that play an important role in utilization of plant nutrients and crop development withstand the heat and survive." Here we have a natural technique that knocks out the bad guys and helps the good guys in the soil, and again, the price of the sun's energy to do the job is free.

Solarization may not sound like a feasible technique in a garden as compact as 200 square feet. With that limited space, you would want to use every square inch for growing plants and would be unwilling to have part of it lost to production for six weeks at the peak of the growing season. That is why, earlier in the chapter, I suggested that an additional 4-by-12-foot bed would be an excellent addition to the 60-Minute Garden.

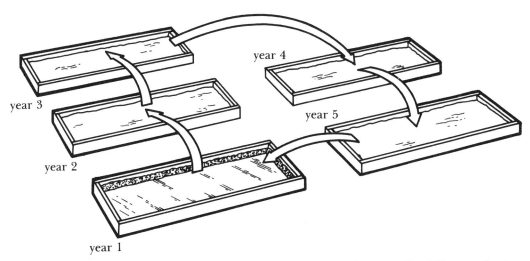

year 4

year 3

year 5

year 2

year 1

Illustration 5–2: The best way to take advantage of solarization in a garden as small as 200 square feet is to have an additional 50-foot bed, which allows you to rotate the solarization process throughout the entire garden every five years and still have 200 square feet of growing space each season.

With an additional bed, you can solarize an entire bed every year, pasteurizing your entire garden every five years. The extra bed can be used for an early spring crop under the tunnels, and then in the summer it can be solarized. In the fall it can grow a cover crop that will make it disease free and very high in nutrients for next year's crops.

This solarization process offers a wonderful opportunity to strike back at some of the soil diseases that have foiled us up to now. While research has not definitively determined how long the effects of solarization last, four to five years is a good estimate.

The best time to use this procedure is during July and August when you can be fairly sure of mostly sunny, hot days for four to six weeks. The procedure for solarizing all or part of a bed is fairly straightforward. You should loosen up the top foot or so of soil with a fork or U-bar Digger and water it heavily so that it is soaking wet—wetter than you would want it for watering the plants. Then, let the bed sit overnight. The next day cover the bed, or part of the bed, with 3- to 6-mil clear plastic film. Don't use black plastic because it will not produce the greenhouse effect.

You should seal the plastic film all around the edges with soil. I tuck the film down inside the boards surrounding the bed and then put soil all around the edge. You will likely get some rain during the four-to-six-week period that will leave some puddles in places on top of the clear plastic. You need to take a broom and wipe those puddles away because they reduce the effect of the sunlight striking the film. Do not punch holes in the plastic to drain the water because they will let the important heat escape.

After the solarization process is finished, you can put in a vegetable crop or a cover crop for late fall harvest. Try not to disturb the soil very much when you put in the new crop. The weed seeds near the surface have been killed, but the seeds down 4 or more inches could still germinate if they are brought to the surface.

Managing your garden's soil is not terribly difficult or time-consuming, but it is very important to the ultimate level of productivity of your vegetable plants. If you follow this soil management cycle of the 60-Minute Garden for a few years, your garden's soil will in fact be more fertile every year, even though you are producing an enormous amount of food in a relatively small piece of the good earth. In the next chapter we'll talk about some cultural techniques that also help improve our productivity while saving us some time.

GARDEN NOTES

COMPOST BIN

This compost bin is designed to be expanded with the size of the garden. For the 200-square-foot model garden, one bin will be sufficient to produce the 16 to 20 cubic feet of compost needed for a full year's supply of compost. The ideal compost pile is 3 by 3 by 4 feet, which fits into the dimensions of this bin. The bin is designed to be accessed from the front or the back, a feature that is convenient if the bin is located in or close to the garden. The sides of the bin are made of hardware cloth, and the front and back have air space between the enclosing sideboards. This design allows sufficient air to get to the pile.

The strips used in the guides for the sideboards require sizes not found in normal lumberyard stock. If you have a table saw, or if you have a friend who has one, these pieces can be made easily. If you don't have that tool, you can have the lumberyard cut these pieces for you.

There is no cover included in this design, to keep it as simple as possible. There are many ways to cover the pile, with the simplest being to lay a piece of plastic film over it. Any kind of material that will keep the rain off a working pile is satisfactory in this system.

The specifications below are for a compost bin with one section. A three-section bin would produce enough compost for a 600-square-foot garden. The design is laid out so that you can build one, two, or three

sections, depending on your needs and using essentially the same procedure described below. The only caution is to build the single section bin with at least one side having the double-sided guides so that you can expand the bin later if you desire.

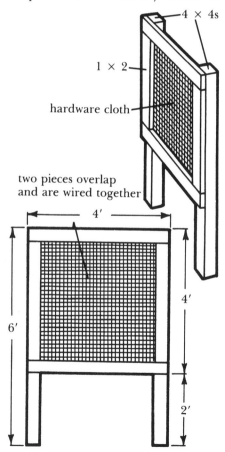

4 × 4s

1 × 2

hardware cloth

two pieces overlap and are wired together

4'

6'

4'

2'

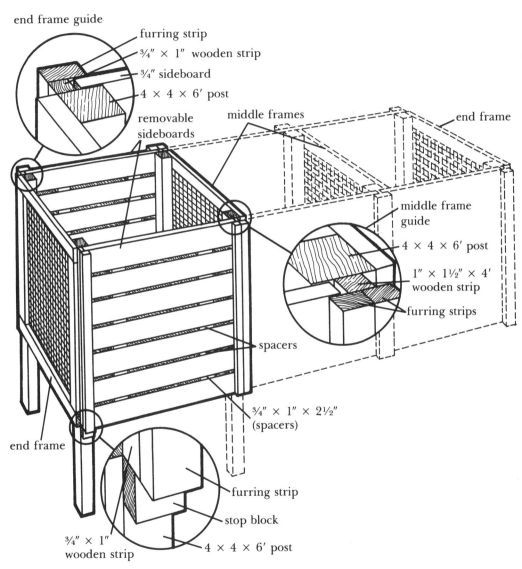

end frame guide

furring strip

¾" × 1" wooden strip

¾" sideboard

4 × 4 × 6' post

removable sideboards

middle frames

end frame

middle frame guide

4 × 4 × 6' post

1" × 1½" × 4' wooden strip

furring strips

spacers

¾" × 1" × 2½" (spacers)

end frame

furring strip

stop block

4 × 4 × 6' post

¾" × 1" wooden strip

Illustration 5–3

SHOPPING LIST

Lumber

2 pcs. 4 × 4 × 12′ pressure-treated
   timbers
8 pcs. 1 × 2 × 8′ furring strips
16 feet ¾″ × 1″, *actual dimension*, softwood
   board—4′ minimum length
8 feet 1″ × 1½″, *actual dimension*,
   softwood board—4′ minimum length
56 feet 1 × 6 low-grade planed boards in
   8-, 12-, or 16-foot lengths
Hardware
18′ × 24″ hardware cloth ½″ mesh
common nails 6d
finish nails 4d
galvanized nails for guides 8d
gun-type staples for hardware cloth ⁹⁄₁₆″
1 small roll of annealed iron wire
        Total cost: $80
        Cost per square foot: $0.40

CUTTING LIST

Size	Piece	Quantity
4 × 4 × 6′	Main vertical posts	4
1 × 2 × 4′	Top pieces of frame	4
1 × 2 × 3′8½″	Side pieces of frame	4
1 × 2 × 4′	Front and back guides	6
1 × 2 × 3′1½″	Bottom stop blocks	4
¾″ × 1″ × 4′	End post guides	2
¾″ × 1″ × 2½″	Spacer blocks	24
1″ × 1½″ × 4′	Center post guides	2
¾″ × 6″ × 4′	Sideboards	14
24″ × 51″	Hardware cloth divider panels	4

TOOLS

Awl
Hammer
Hand drill
Level
Measuring tape
Posthole digger
Saw
Shovel
Square
Staple gun
Tin shears for cutting hardware cloth

CONSTRUCTION STEPS

1. Note in illustration 5–3 that the end frame and the middle frame are different in their system of guides for the front and back boards. A three-section compost bin would have two end frames and two middle frames.

Fasten guides to the 4 × 4 posts. Illustration 5–3 shows that the end frame guides have right and left sides, while the sides of the middle frame guides are the same.

2. When constructing the end frame, remember to reverse the layout. The guide is constructed by tacking a ¾-by-1-inch wooden strip along the outer edge of two posts, according to the illustration. Make sure the 1-inch dimension is vertical to the post so that there is sufficient clearance for the ¾-inch sideboards to slide easily. Then nail a 4-foot piece of furring strip over the ¾-by-1-inch wooden strip and through into the post (use 8-penny galvanized nails). You may wish to drill guide holes for this procedure to ensure having the nails go in straight and prevent splitting.

3. Next construct the middle posts. With the 1-inch dimension vertical to the post, tack a 4-foot piece of 1-by-1½-inch down the center line of each post. Then nail two 4-foot pieces of furring strip to the first piece as shown in illustration 5–3, creating a guideway for the sideboards. You may wish to drill guide holes for accurate nailing.

Make the basic frames for the hardware cloth of 4 × 4s, two 4-foot furring strips, and two 3-foot 8½-inch furring strips, making sure they are square.

Then staple the hardware cloth on to this frame. The cloth will overlap in the center. For best results for this procedure, use an awl to stretch the hardware cloth diagonally after you staple the first side. This eliminates any bulges in the cloth.

Fasten a stop block at the bottom of the guides on each post so that the sideboards will all be even when they are installed (see illustration 5–3).

4. Erect the frames in the ground. The main concern is to ensure that the frames are at the proper distance from each other while being in line and level. This is easier said than done.

Install the frames one at a time from one end of the structure. Dig two postholes 2 feet deep and set the first frame into the holes, preferably on solid ground or even on rock. Make the frame level and vertical sideways and front to back and then fill in the holes with some rocks and soil, tamping as necessary.

Using two sideboards at ground level, locate the next two holes. Dig those two holes and install the second frame at the proper distance so that the sideboards have about ⅛-inch clearance at both ends. Again, make this frame level and vertical and then temporarily nail sideboards at the top and the bottom of both sides of the two frames. If you are building a three-section bin, continue with this procedure to install the last two sets of frames.

Leave the nailed boards at the top and bottom in place for two or three days to make sure that the posts have settled properly.

5. Using highly flexible soft wire, weave the wire between the two pieces of hardware cloth that are overlapped on each frame. This will keep the hardware cloth from separating and bulging when the bin is filled.

COMPOST SIFTER

Compost made without the benefit of a shredder will tend to have twigs and other chunks of matter that you may wish to sift out, especially if you are using your compost for potting soil. This sifter is designed to be used with the 60-Minute Garden compost bin (whether you build a bin with only one section or three sections).

—————————————————————

———— *SHOPPING LIST* ————

Lumber
24 feet 1 × 4 softwood boards
Hardware
6′ × 24″ hardware cloth ½″ mesh
finish nails 6d
staples ⁹⁄₁₆″
1 heavy-duty screw hook, ⅛″ wire
   minimum
1 carriage bolt 2″ × ¼″
1 washer and 1 wing nut
1 lag screw ¼″ × 3″
     Total cost: $20

—————————————————————

This sifter can be used inside the compost bin or on the side of the bin. If you use it inside the bin, hook it onto the top board of the bin on the back and rest the lower end on the ground or on one board as in illustration 5–4. If you use it on the side (especially if you have only a one-section bin), you will attach the sifter to the bin with the screw hook connected to the lag screw and with the support leg extended as far behind the sifter as is necessary to keep it level. A stone or brick under the support leg may help keep it steady.

—————————————————————

———————— *TOOLS* ————————

Hammer
Measuring tape
Electric drill
Saw
Staple gun

—————————————————————

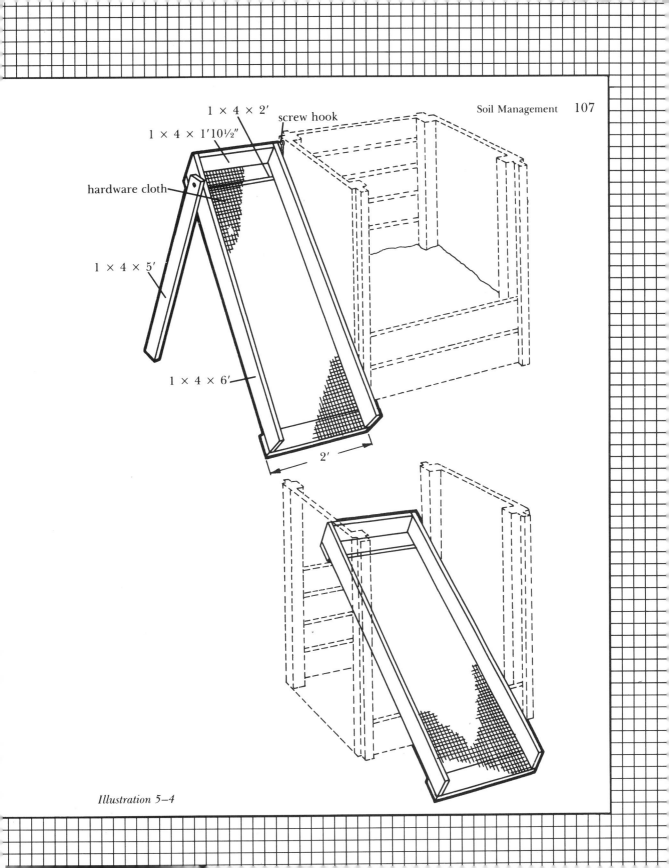

1 × 4 × 2'
1 × 4 × 1'10½"
screw hook
hardware cloth
1 × 4 × 5'
1 × 4 × 6'
2'

Illustration 5–4

———— CUTTING LIST ————

Size	Piece	Quantity
1 × 4 × 6′	Side pieces of frame	2
1 × 4 × 1′10½″	Upper end piece of frame	1
1 × 4 × 2′	Bottom end pieces	2
1 × 4 × 5′	Support leg	1

CONSTRUCTION STEPS

1. Nail the upper end piece between the two side pieces.

2. Staple hardware cloth to the bottom of the sides and upper end piece.

3. Nail the bottom end piece to side pieces so that hardware cloth is above the end piece, which allows compost material to roll out of the sifter. Staple the hardware cloth to the end piece.

4. Nail a 2-foot piece of 1 × 4 to the bottom of the upper end after the hardware cloth has been stapled. This is the hook for holding the sifter when used inside the compost bin.

5. Attach the screw hook to the upper end of the right-hand side piece at about the middle of the board's cross section so that it extends beyond the end of the sifter as in illustration 5–4.

6. Drill a ¼-inch hole close to the upper end of the frame through the middle of the left-hand side piece. Drill a ¼-inch hole 1 inch from the end of the support leg. Assemble the carriage bolt from the inside of the sifter through the side piece and the support leg. Secure with a washer and wing nut.

7. Drill a ³⁄₁₆-inch hole near the top of the back post on the left side of the compost bin. Assemble the lag screw to the point that only ¼ inch under the head remains visible.

8. You are now ready to sift some compost.

"HAIRPINS"

"Hairpins" made of wire coat hangers are easy to make and ideal for holding down plastic mulch or irrigation drip lines.

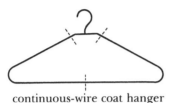

continuous-wire coat hanger

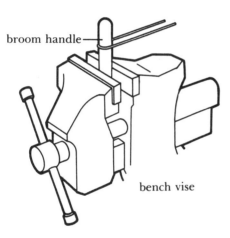

broom handle

bench vise

16" "hairpin"

Illustration 5–5

SHOPPING LIST

30 continuous-wire coat hangers
bright-colored spray paint

TOOLS

Bench vise or a 2″ C-clamp
Pair of heavy cutting pliers
Two pairs of regular pliers

CUTTING LIST

Size	Piece	Quantity
16″	Wires	60

CONSTRUCTION STEPS

1. Using the cutting pliers, cut the hooks off the coat hangers and discard the hooks.

2. Using the regular pliers, bend the wire to achieve reasonably straight pieces.

3. Using the cutting pliers, cut the wire to 16-inch lengths.

4. Using a bench vise, if available, clamp a broom handle so that 2 or 3 inches of the handle extend to the working side of the vise. If no vise is available, clamp the broom handle to a table top with a C-clamp.

5. Using the regular pliers, bend each length of wire tightly around the broom handle so that it forms a "hairpin" with the ends approximately even.

6. After forming all 60 "hairpins," bundle them together so that you can paint the tops of each hairpin with a bright-colored spray paint (for example, yellow, red, or white). Colorful hairpins enable you to find them when you are dismantling your garden at the end of the season.

CHAPTER 6

ADVANCED GROWING TECHNIQUES

It is often said that vegetable gardening, or any kind of gardening, is as much art as it is science. I generally support that old cliché, even while writing a book about the latest technical advances in producing vegetables in the backyard. Gardening as an art has particular application in this chapter about cultural practices. Why is it that with two anglers using exactly the same fishing reels and the same lures, fishing from the same boat in the same place in the lake, one can outfish the other 3 to 1? The answer is that one has more subtle skills as a fisherman. In the same manner, two neighbors can have similar soil in their gardens and the same amount of rain and sun, and they can use the same type of garden tools and have the same garden design, but one can produce

three times more vegetables than the other. Again, the more successful gardener often has more subtle cultural practices at work in the vegetable patch.

The subtleties of gardening are many and often elusive. There have been some real advances made in recent years in improving the growing techniques in a vegetable garden. These developments are often adaptations of techniques developed centuries ago. Most of them require no additional time. You are going to plant your garden somehow, so learning how to plant it for the most productive results is a value. The "art" will take care of itself.

The 60-Minute Garden uses two primary principles regarding cultural practice. First, for maximum production and variety, you should grow your own seedlings, and secondly, you should plant them as intensively as their growth limits will allow.

Succession planting, growing more than one crop in the same space during a season, is not a new idea. The 60-Minute Garden takes the concept and refines it to increase its impact on production, primarily by growing your own seedlings throughout the entire season. Intensive planting involves techniques for growing plants as closely as possible for increased productivity of your garden space. Intensive planting techniques, interplanting techniques, and companion planting techniques contribute to this increased productivity and have all been incorporated into this gardening system. I have included in the description of each the benefits of some exciting new research in the agricultural arena.

SUCCESSION PLANTING

Most simply, succession planting involves sowing a second crop in the place where an early crop has been harvested. Planting cabbage in the spot where you had early peas gives you two crops from the same piece of ground in one season. This technique effectively doubles your production from that single piece of garden. By itself, that is a value; however, this concept can be expanded to increase productivity even further.

Most of the time that a vegetable plant is in your garden is spent developing to the point when harvesting can begin. Vegetables such as cabbage and broccoli take three to four months to mature from seed. While those plants are growing, you are getting no food for the table from their particular niche in your garden. It is desirable then to reduce the amount of time a plant is physically taking up space in your garden before it is ready to harvest. By starting seedlings indoors and continuing them for a while in a seedling box, you delay taking up your garden's space

by almost two months!

If you plant that second crop of cabbage, following the peas, by seeding directly into your garden soil, you are going to have to wait six to eight weeks for those plants to be at the same size as they would have been had you had good-size cabbage seedlings ready to transplant as soon as the peas were finished. That means you actually waste two months of growing time in that part of your garden. In the 60-Minute Garden, you will start your peas early in the spring with tunnels so that using the cabbage seedlings will give you the opportunity for even a third crop to be planted after harvesting the cabbage. Three crops from the same piece of ground instead of only two gives succession planting some new value.

Succession planting definitely improves your garden's productivity, but is the timing of your crop's harvest really best for your family's needs? There is a "harvest time factor" involved with planning these successions. If you plant ten cabbages, dutifully filling your empty garden spaces, and they all become ripe at the same time, you have coleslaw for an army for 4 weeks and no fresh cabbage after that. The same problem occurs with celery, carrots, lettuce, and many other vegetables. Ideally, you want one or two cabbages to become ripe every 2 weeks, giving you ten fresh cabbages over a 10- to 20-week period. If you really plan your successions carefully, you can have a couple of cabbages available every few weeks from June until November!

While many vegetables like carrots and celery will keep well right in the garden, they are taking up growing space that could be producing some additional food for your family. Figuring out how to take advantage of this "harvest time factor" will be discussed in more detail later in this chapter and in chapter 9 when I talk about home computers. The primary point to make in this discussion is that for succession planting to work you should have good-size seedlings ready when a crop in the garden is harvested.

GROWING SEEDLINGS

Except for tomatoes and peppers, most gardeners don't grow their own seedlings, and I know why. It appears to many to be a complicated, time-consuming and frustrating business. It is much easier to go to the local nursery and buy perfectly good seedlings and save all that trouble; however, there are some serious limitations to depending on commercial nurseries for your vegetable seedlings. In the 60-Minute Garden you will need seedlings much earlier than they are usually available commercially. In the fall,

when you are ready to start your third crop, vegetable seedlings are hard, if not impossible, to find. Finally, while the commercial seedlings are usually top-quality plants, they generally represent only a few of the hundreds of varieties you might want to consider in your garden. Oh yes, it is also, in the long run, much cheaper to grow your own seedlings.

What we need then is a technique for growing seedlings that is not complicated, doesn't take much time, and produces healthy seedlings as we need them throughout the entire growing season. The 60-Minute Gar-

TABLE 6–1

MULTIPLE PLANTINGS BY SUCCESSION

CROP	EARLY SPRING	SPRING	SUMMER	FALL
Beets	X	X	X	
Broccoli	X	X	X	
Cabbage	X	X	X	
Carrots	X	X	X	
Cauliflower	X		X	
Celery	X	X	X	X
Chinese cabbage	X		X	X
Lettuce	X	X	X	X
Onions	X	X		X
Spinach	X			X

TABLE 6–2

CROPS THAT CAN BE STARTED INDOORS FROM SEED

Beans, lima	Eggplant	Peppers
Broccoli	Kale	Spinach
Brussels sprouts	Kohlrabi	Squash
Cabbage	Leeks	Sweet potatoes
Cauliflower	Lettuce	Tomatoes
Celery	Muskmelons	Watermelons
Chinese cabbage	Onions	
Cucumbers	Parsley	

Photo 6–1: This fluorescent fixture serves as an excellent source of light for young seedlings. Notice how close the bulbs are to the tops of the seedlings—3 to 4 inches is best for young plants.

den offers several options that are designed to respond to those requirements. The system is designed to produce seedlings every few weeks for the entire gardening season! This, of course, means starting seedlings every few weeks throughout the entire growing season, so the technique needs to be very convenient.

Not only do we need to have seedlings poised ready to plop into the soil, we need to be tough when it comes to deciding to pull up the former crop. You should pull up the plants when they have completed 80 percent of their production. To leave the peas in the soil for another two weeks to give those last few pods a chance to ripen is bad garden economics. Those two weeks could have given you a jump on the cabbage harvest and ensured a decent growing period for the third crop that goes in there after the cabbage is harvested. Gardeners are generally a bunch of softies—they hate to pull up plants with even one more piece of fruit on them, and they hate to throw away per-

fectly good seedlings. Sometimes, to get the most from our gardens, we have to be a little ruthless out there. Remember, too, that the nearly spent plants won't be wasted because they'll be added to your compost pile.

My seedling system involves growing seedlings in homemade soil blocks or in commercial peat blocks because they are easy to work with. They make transplanting very easy, and they avoid transplant shock that can cause the loss of two to three weeks of production time. In addition, they take little time each week to manage. Start seedlings under fluorescent lights throughout the entire season, not just during the cold months. The system includes a method for storing and organizing seeds so that your seeds are easily accessible and will last, in some cases, for years.

GROW LIGHTS

You can start seedlings on your windowsill or in a greenhouse, but you can't avoid the reality that in the late winter, there is not enough light to grow seedlings that are not spindly compared to those in a commercial garden center. Likewise, in the summer, growing seedlings outside is hazardous because they are so vulnerable to excessive sun and heat. I use fluorescent lights all year long to start seedlings. They give enough light to produce healthy strong seedlings with very little trouble. For most gardeners, I recommend setting up just one fixture with two 48-inch fluorescent tubes. Because you can use this device for almost the entire year, you should establish some kind of a permanent installation.

I locate my seedling nursery in my basement for several reasons. The temperature stays between 60° and 70°F all year round, so it is warm in the winter and cool in the summer—ideal for seedlings. I have water available in the basement, and I have space in the basement. For folks without basements, a seedling bench can be made to be very attractive and to harmonize comfortably in your living room with the other houseplants and people. The light fixture must be adjustable so that you can either move it up and down or move the plants up and down, because you must maintain the proper distance between plants and light as the plants get taller.

Photo 6–1 shows a fluorescent light installation for starting seedlings. You can have a setup that is either very simple, as in this case, or super fancy—either way you can grow healthy plants. You do not need special "grow-light" fluorescent bulbs for starting seedlings. Those special lights are more important in devices designed to support houseplants full-time.

The key to successfully growing seedlings under lights is the duration of light and the distance the light sits from the top leaf of the plant. Have your lights on for 14 to 16 hours a day, every day. Anything less and you are not going to get the best growth. When seedlings are just little sprouts, the lights should be no more than 3 inches away.

As the plants get their first true leaves, you can move the lights up to about 4 inches. I set the lights at 6 inches when the seedlings are a few inches tall so that I can disperse light evenly to all my plants, even those on the edge of the shelf. I use an automatic timer to turn my lights on and off. A timer costs about $10, and it eliminates one more thing I have to remember to do, which saves me more time.

If your garden is over 200 square feet, you, too, may find that only one fixture provides sufficient seedlings for your more extensive area. You can use the lights to produce those seedlings you need very early in the season, but then use commercial seedlings for your main crops. And, then use your lights to produce your successions later in the year. Once you have assembled the equipment for growing your own seedlings under lights, they take very little time to manage.

SOIL BLOCKS

Seedlings can be started in flats, Styrofoam coffee cups, egg cartons, or any other similar container. The considerations in choosing a container for your seedlings include convenience and how much damage occurs to the root system at transplant time. Transplanting seedlings from a flat actually causes you to lose growing time because half of the plant's feeder roots are severed when it is transferred from the flat to the garden. Coffee cups reduce this problem, but they take up a lot of space compared to other methods. In recent years, the soil block has become very popular with commercial growers. I recommend them for the 60-Minute Garden as well.

A soil block comes in many forms. Essentially, it is some form of growing medium (soil, peat moss, compost, or all of the above) that has been pressed into a compact form that is around 2 inches on a side. Photos 6–2 and 6–3 show different versions of the soil

Photos 6–2 and 6–3: Soil blocks can be round or square. A very light netting helps the soil blocks, as in the photo below, to keep their shapes.

Photo 6–4: This tool is helpful in making soil blocks.

block idea, and there are probably others. The soil block was designed primarily for its ease in initial planting and in the transplanting process. There is virtually no transplant shock to seedlings grown in soil blocks. The soil block is also convenient to use and produces healthy seedlings. You can make your own soil blocks, or you can purchase commercial versions at a very reasonable price, considering your needs for a 200-square-foot garden. I'll discuss three options—commercial soil blocks, homemade soil blocks, and a soil block container.

COMMERCIAL AND HOMEMADE SOIL BLOCKS

The easiest and most time-efficient way to grow seedlings is to use a commercial soil block. Usually, they are made of peat and are wrapped in some kind of netting. They come in small pellets, and when you add water, they expand into a block about 2 by 2 by 2 inches. You add the seed to the top of the block, and when the plant's first true leaves appear, it can be transplanted to another container or out into the garden. They cost about $0.08 a piece, and you would use about 300 in the five seasons of the 200-square-foot 60-Minute Garden.

You will need a special press to make your own soil blocks. Mix roughly equal amounts of peat moss, compost or soil, and sharp sand, and add water until the mix reaches the consistency of cooked oatmeal. Then compress this glop with a commercial soil block press and pop out a little block of soil that holds its shape even when it is watered. Place the seed in the center of the top, and the roots will grow well even in that obviously compressed medium. When the seedling has its first set of true leaves, the soil block is ready to transplant to another container or be placed out in the garden. Roots in this type of free-standing soil block avoid the sides of the block—they don't like to go past the surface of the soil in any direction—and wind throughout the space inside the cube. The advantage of this procedure is that you can make unlimited numbers of soil blocks at a very low cost, after you buy the press. The soil block press will last forever. The Appendix lists companies selling presses.

In both cases, whether you make your own or buy your soil blocks, the technique is to start your seedlings under the lights in the block. When the seedling gets to be 2 or 3 inches tall, after it's gotten its first true leaves, you have several choices depending on what season it is. In the early spring, I put my seedlings in Styrofoam coffee cups and add some potting soil so that I can keep the seedlings growing for another three or four weeks inside. Later in the season I still put the soil block with each seedling in a coffee cup, but I set them outside in a seed-

ling box and let them grow another few weeks before placing them in my garden. I happen to also have a greenhouse, where I get the best of both worlds—several sets of fluorescent lights for starting the seedlings and space in a warm environment for letting the seedlings increase in size before putting them into the garden. You don't need a greenhouse, however, to grow plenty of healthy seedlings all season long.

I have developed a variation of the soil block idea that I saw in a magazine article. Using Plexiglas and some old boards, my Dad and I built four seed-starting boxes that work on the soil block principle (see photos 6–5 and 6–6). There is no bottom to the box. It sits in a cafeteria tray I got at a secondhand restaurant supply store. I press

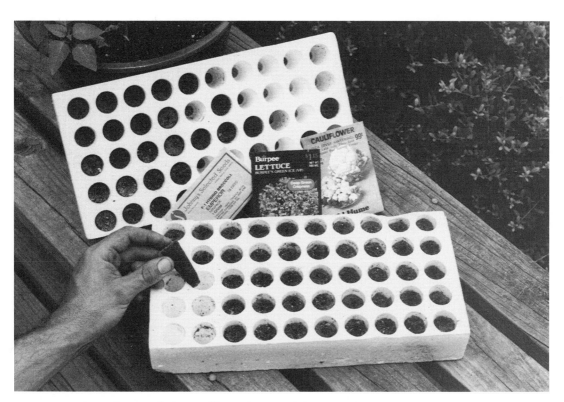

Photo 6–5: This seed starter device (see illustration 6–4) helps you make your own soil blocks for starting seedlings.

Photo 6–6: These seedlings in the starter box (see illustration 6–5) are ready for transplanting into the garden.

the soil, compost, and vermiculite down into the forms, creating the soil block; however, I leave the soil in the box and plant the seeds. I water from the bottom by just pouring some water into the tray, and I mist the seedlings with water and liquid fertilizer. When they are ready to transplant, I take a block of wood, which is cut to be just a hair smaller than the soil blocks, and I use this block to push the soil block and the seedling out of the container from the bottom. There is no root damage, I get fine seedlings, and I save the cost of the soil block maker since I use leftover materials in my basement, and I use my own potting soil mix. The compost sifter described in chapter 5 (see figure 5–4) is handy for giving me nice clean compost to mix with vermiculite and soil.

If you are just beginning to raise your own seedlings under lights, I recommend that you experiment with the commercial soil blocks for a year. Then you can decide whether you want to move into producing your own blocks either with a commercial block maker or with a homemade device.

KEEPING TRACK OF YOUR SEEDS

This whole succession planting process depends a great deal on how convenient it is to start a few seedlings every few weeks. One of the problems with gardens having more than just a few kinds of vegetables is keeping track of the seeds. After the season gets going, you find you've left seed packets opened but folded up in three different drawers in the kitchen and stashed out in the utility room. It takes more time to find the particular seed you want than it does to plant it. Then there is the problem of storing seeds in a place so that they're available for use again next year. If they sit in a warm drawer all winter, they are worthless. You'll have to buy all new seeds again. I've struggled with this problem for years and have tried a number of schemes, until I came upon my current very satisfactory method for keeping track of and storing my seeds.

Seeds are best stored in a cool, dry place. So I decided to store my seeds in the refrigerator all the time, from the first time I get the seed package; however, I didn't want them to take up too much space in the refrigerator. Having been a stamp collector as a youth, I knew that you could buy small glassine envelopes very cheaply that would be perfect for storing seeds in a compact space. Now I store all my seeds, except the big ones such as peas, corn, and beans, in glassine envelopes in a tight metal file box in the refrigerator (see photo 6–7). In the box, I have a little packet of dried milk wrapped up in a tissue and secured with a rubber band. That absorbs the moisture in the box to keep the seeds dry. Now here comes the important part.

The metal box is a 3-by-5-card file box

Photo 6–7: Soaking seeds in water overnight before planting them jump starts germination of those with hard coats such as parsley, celery, carrots, beets, and onions. Do not allow them to soak more than 12 hours, or to dry out before planting.

large enough to hold many seed envelopes. A set of 12 index cards, one for each month of the year, organizes the seed envelopes. When I am finished with an envelope of seeds, I file it in the next month I plan to use it. If it is lettuce, I file it in next month's section, because I plant lettuce almost every month. If it is eggplant, I file it in the month for next year's planting, since I usually have only one crop of each variety. Using this filing system, I know exactly where those seeds I want today are stored—in this month's section. The box is handy, being in the refrigerator, but it doesn't take up undue space either. My seeds are stored in a reasonably good environment so that I can expect to have some last two or three years, although these seeds would have a somewhat reduced germination rate.

When I use seeds for the first time from a newly opened seed envelope, I transfer all the seeds into the glassine envelope. I label the glassine envelope with the variety of the vegetable and the month and year I opened the packet. I store that glassine envelope in the month I expect to use those particular seeds again, and I throw away the original seed packet.

USING SUCCESSION PLANTING

Now we have all of our devices in place for taking advantage of the benefits of succession planting—a lighting device, a device for growing the seedlings, and a device for storing the seeds. Because the tunnels extend your growing season, you can start early seedlings under the lights 10 to 12 weeks before the last spring frost. You will then have nice-size seedlings out in the garden, under the tunnel, 4 or 5 weeks prior to your last frost or long before any seedlings are available from the garden center. As with all seedlings, you should not transfer them from the warm environment of the house out into the tunnels in just one day. They need to be *hardened off,* or slowly introduced to cooler days and nights over a period of 3 or 4 days. I set my seedlings outside during a sunny day and bring them in at night for a few days before I set them out in the tunnel permanently.

Remember, we are trying to grow sufficient plants to fill our garden space while at the same time trying to spread the harvest time by starting plants in small groups staggered over time. Here's where the soil blocks and the seed file become particularly handy. You can start a seedling by watering a soil block and placing one or two seeds just under the top surface and putting the block somewhere where the temperature is over 60°F (preferably 65°F). I place my block directly under the lights so when they germinate I don't have to worry about them. You can plant four varieties of 3 vegetables in 10 minutes. This way, you may be shooting for having 12 broccoli plants in your early

TABLE 6–3

INTENSIVE PLANTING DISTANCES

CROP	PLANTING DEPTH (INCHES)	INTENSIVE PLANTING DISTANCE FOR BEDS (INCHES)
Asparagus	6–8 (roots)	12–18
Beans		
Fava	2½	8
Kidney	1–2	4
Lima, bush	1½–2	4–6
Lima, pole	1½–2	6–8
Mung	1–2	4
Snap, bush	1–2 (deeper in hotter, drier weather)	4
Snap, pole	1–1½	6
Soybeans	1	10
Beets	1½–2	6
Broccoli	¼–½	12–14
Brussels sprouts	½	16–18
Cabbage	½	12–16
Carrots	¼	3
Cauliflower	¼	12–15
Celery	½	6–8
Chinese cabbage	½	10
Corn	2	12–18
Cress, garden	¼	3
Cucumbers	1	12 (when trellised)
Eggplant	¼–½	18–24
Garlic	1	2–3
Horseradish	Set top of root cutting 3 inches below surface	12–15

CROP	PLANTING DEPTH (INCHES)	INTENSIVE PLANTING DISTANCE FOR BEDS (INCHES)
Kale	½	15–18
Kohlrabi	½	4–5
Leeks	½–1	6
Lettuce		
Head	¼–½	10–12
Leaf	¼–½	6–8
Romaine	¼–½	10
Muskmelons	½–1	24 (when trellised)
Mustard	½	6–9
Onions		
Seeds	½	2–3
Sets	Plant so that tip of bulb is exposed	3
Parsley	¼	4
Parsnips	½	3
Peas		
Edible-podded	2	3–4
Garden	2	3–4
Snap	2	3–4
Peppers	¼	12–15
Potatoes	4	12–18
Pumpkins	1	24–30
Radishes	½	1
Rhubarb	2–3	24
Rutabagas	¼	6–9
Salsify	½	6
Shallots	1	2–3
Spinach	½	6
Squash		
Summer	1	12–18
Winter	1	24–30
Strawberries	¼	24
Sunflowers	1	24
Sweet potatoes	4–5	12
Swiss chard	½–1	9
Tomatoes	½	18–24
Turnips	½	6
Watermelons	½	18–24

Source: Adapted from Jeff Ball, The Self-Sufficient Suburban Gardener, *(Emmaus, Pa.: Rodale Press, 1983).*

garden, but you can start the seedlings in three groups of 4, ten days apart, spread over a month's time. This gives you a steady supply of broccoli for several months, instead of 12 heads of broccoli all in two weeks.

The 60-Minute Garden approach to succession planting means that those fluorescent lights will be used 16 hours a day for six or seven months, with the automatic timer turning them off and on each day. You will never have a lot of seedlings under the lights at any one time, but there will be a steady supply as you start new plants every other week or so throughout the five growing seasons.

You will be using liquid fertilizer in your drip irrigation system (see chapter 7), and that same liquid fertilizer can be used with your seedlings. I use it in very dilute solutions almost every time I water my seedlings, after they have gotten their first true leaves. Your seedlings will be healthy if they have abundant watering, regular fertilizing, and proper distancing from the lights. Healthy seedlings bear fruit earlier, have fewer pest and disease problems, and produce more food per plant. Assuming you use the commercial soil blocks, managing your seedlings will take about 10 or 15 minutes each week, spread over the week in 2- to 5-minute segments.

Your measure of success will be a steady, and not excessive, flow of fresh produce available from April through November. The types of vegetables will change throughout the season, but the amount of food available fresh from the garden for the eight-month period will be a function of your skills in using succession growing techniques.

INTENSIVE GROWING TECHNIQUES

Raised beds and intensive planting techniques have been used by the French for over a century. Intensive planting was introduced in this country by Alan Chadwick and was later refined by John Jeavons in just the last 20 years. They found that with very few exceptions, vegetables can be planted much

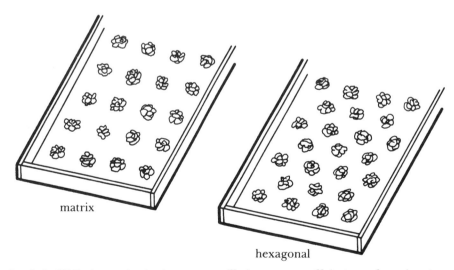

matrix

hexagonal

Illustration 6–1: While the matrix planting pattern will give you more efficient use of growing space than found in a row garden, the hexagonal pattern goes one step further toward packing in as many plants per square foot as is feasible for successful growing.

Photo 6–8: These seed-planting guides are the same boards used to cut the flaps in the black plastic mulch (see illustration 3–4). They are excellent planting guides for such root crops as carrots, parsnips, and beets.

planting techniques. The general results have shown that when you plant vegetables intensively, you will get less fruit from each individual vegetable, but you will get more produce per square foot of growing space. If you want the biggest eggplant at the county fair, don't plant intensively. If you want the most eggplant for your table from the available space in your garden, use intensive planting techniques. Onions are another example. Onions will grow larger with more space. If you plant onions at 2½-inch spacing, you will get onions that are about 1¼

Photo 6–9: A frame (above) or box covered with screening or netting will protect seedlings that are new to the outdoors. When they have outgrown the indoor grow light system, move them out into the garden to harden off prior to transplanting. The netting protects them from pest insects, wind, and bright sun during this period.

more closely than indicated on their seed packets. Seed packets still use planting distances that are overly conservative because they assume that vegetables will be planted in rows and need to be tilled to control weeds. Because you will be using beds in the 60-Minute Garden, you can plant everything more intensively than found in a row garden. Table 6–3 gives the planting distances for growing vegetables in beds.

Intensive planting means planting vegetables in beds at equal distances from each other so that when they are full grown, their leaves will just touch, and the entire bed will be covered by foliage. This creates a kind of roof or canopy over the garden that helps to keep the soil cooler. Because the 60-Minute Garden uses plastic and organic mulch during the entire season, weed suppression is not a concern, even though intensive planting also tends to suppress weeds. There has been extensive research done to determine the effects of intensive

Photo 6–10: This giant compass makes it easy to measure plant spacings in an intensively planted garden. All you do is adjust the arms to the spacing distance you need for a particular crop, and then tighten the wing nut to hold them in that position.

inch in diameter. If you expand that spacing to 4¼ inches, you get slightly larger onions at about a 1½-inch diameter; however, your total production of onions per square foot of garden will go down with the wider spacing.

There are two ways to lay out a bed for intensive planting—the matrix pattern and the hexagonal pattern. In illustration 6–1 you can see the difference. The matrix pattern is the easiest to lay out, but the hexagonal pattern actually packs more plants into the same space. Either way is effective. I use both approaches, depending on how much time I want to spend on being absolutely precise about my layout. There are two measuring devices that I find very helpful in the 60-Minute Garden: the seeding squares and the planting compass. I use them both in different situations, and they both help me to set my intensive planting patterns with little effort.

SEEDING SQUARES

If you remember from chapter 3, I use two templates with holes on 3-inch centers for cutting the flaps in the clear or black plastic that I use for mulch in each bed (see illustration 3–4). Those same templates make great seed-planting guides for things like carrots, onion sets, parsnips, and other veggies that need direct seeding. These templates use the matrix pattern because the hexagonal pattern doesn't work as well in laying out the holes in the plastic. While I may lose a little benefit from using the matrix pattern, I am still planting a lot more carrots per square foot than my neighbor with his row garden.

As you can see in photo 6–8, I can move the seeding template down the bed a foot at a time, and I've got my seeds placed on 3-inch centers, enormously reducing my need for thinning. Thinning takes time I don't have.

PLANTING COMPASS

One way to get equidistant planting (hexagonal pattern) is to use a planting compass, such as the one designed and built by my dad and shown in photo 6–10. It is nothing more than two sticks joined together with a threaded rod and two butterfly nuts. If I am putting out broccoli transplants and I want to set them at equal distances of 14 inches, I loosen the butterfly nut on my compass and spread the points to 14 inches. I tighten the bolt, and I have a tool to give me 14 inches on all sides of each of my transplants. The value of this device is that it can be set to any distance so easily. It is one of my handiest gardening tools.

As you might imagine, intensive planting can become almost an obsession as you try to squeeze one more plant into an already crowded bed. If you have six broccoli seedlings and room really only for five, what to do with that last seedling? My experience has been, after having stuck that last seedling in when I shouldn't have, that it is better to ease into intensive planting than to go all out in the first try. When plants are small seedlings, they don't look like they will fill up so much space. But they do need their own space, just like we do, so be conservative for a year or two until you are a good judge of how close you can plant and still have the neighboring plants just touching each other instead of overwhelming each other with overcrowding.

SHADING DEVICES

One of my favorite cultural techniques is using a shading device of some sort to shade lettuce in the dead heat of the summer. In the past, I had lettuce in the spring and the fall, but in the summer it was spindly and bolted almost immediately. Celery, spinach, cabbage, and other salad crops are also problems in the summer. The solution is a little shade.

Lettuce can be planted in among taller plants to get that shade, or you can cover it with a shading device. One method uses cheesecloth (see photo 6–11) or tobacco cloth to lay over two ribs of the tunnel device. Sew curtain rings or eyelets of some sort into the corners and along the sides to prevent tearing. Cheesecloth laid over the ribs of the tunnel device works well in a larger garden, but in a smaller garden, it takes up too much space. The umbrella cloche shading device works well, especially for small groups of plants (see illustration 6–7). Another method for shading your plants is to use one of the new materials designed to simply lie loosely on top of the plants. Such material is porous,

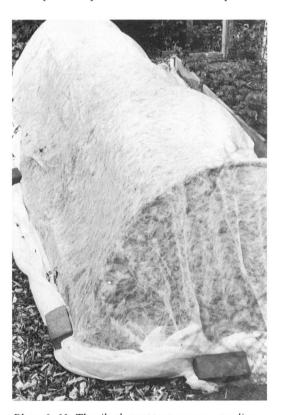

Photo 6–11: The ribs that support seasons extending tunnels will also support cheese cloth or polyspun garden fabric. This covering protects plants from pest insects, late frosts, winds, or excessive sun.

Illustration 6–2: Basically, there are five different ways to interplant a garden. First, plant sun-loving vegetables, such as peppers, next to those that need shade, such as lettuce.

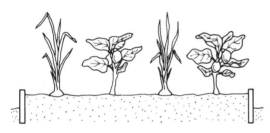

Second, plant tall vegetables, like onions, next to short ones, such as eggplant.

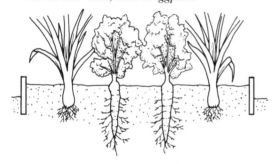

Third, plant vegetables with deep roots, such as carrots, next to ones with shallow roots, such as leeks.

Fourth, plant vegetables with long growing seasons, such as Brussels sprouts, next to ones with short growing seasons, such as spinach.

Finally, plant vegetables that help to build up the soil, such as peas, next to ones that take a lot out of the soil, such as lettuce.

allowing rain through, but it shades out the worst of the sun's rays. It is light enough so that the plants can support it without any damage. A source for this material is included in the Appendix.

Shading devices should probably not be used full time, if it is possible to avoid it. Most of the sun-sensitive vegetables still need the benefits of the sun, and the early morn-

ing sun is very good for them. If you have the opportunity to do so, apply the shading material at noon. If you have to leave it on all the time, you will still have lettuce, but it will be somewhat smaller. It's better to have small lettuce leaves in your salad than to have no lettuce leaves in your salad. The umbrella cloche shading device also serves as an excellent insect barrier for such plants as summer squash, eggplant, and spinach.

INTERPLANTING TECHNIQUES

This section is definitely not for the beginning gardener. Even advanced gardeners should have some respect for the complexity of using modern *interplanting* techniques. At the same time, however, these

TABLE 6–4

INSECT-CONTROLLING COMPANIONS

CROP	INSECT-CONTROLLING COMPANIONS
Asparagus	Tomatoes repel asparagus beetles
Beans	Catnip repels flea beetles
	Potatoes repel Mexican bean beetles
	Rosemary repels insects in general
Beets	Onion family repels insects in general
Cabbage family	Celery repels cabbageworms
	Onion family deters maggots
	Rosemary, sage, and thyme repel insects in general
Carrots	Onion family repels carrot flies
	Rosemary and sage repel insects in general
Celery	Cabbage repels insects in general
Corn	Potatoes repel insects in general
	Soybeans deter chinch bugs
Cucumbers	Radishes deter cucumber beetles
Eggplant	Green beans deter Colorado potato beetles
	Potatoes can be used as a trap plant
Lettuce	Carrots and radishes repel insects in general
Potatoes	Beans and corn repel insects in general
	Use eggplant as trap plant
Radishes	Cucumbers repel insects in general
Tomatoes	Asparagus and basil repel insects in general

techniques offer some benefits over simple intensive and succession planting schemes. True interplanting mixes different kinds of vegetables in an intensive planting pattern that considers the size and shape of the plant, the size and shape of the plant's root system, the plant's tolerance for shade, the plant's chemical relationship, if any, to its neighbors, and the plant's nutrient needs. I can't think of a more complicated set of variables, except perhaps for the variables for finding the perfect fishing hole.

Interplanting is definitely an art one learns over time with lots of experience. Why go to the trouble? Lots of reasons. Your garden's productivity increases with interplanting. Interplanted beds are less vulnerable to insect attack. Insects often find their target plant by means of their sense of smell. An interplanted bed has all kinds of mixed smells and odors confusing the insect and protecting its target plant. Interplanting allows even closer positioning of plants, making absolutely maximum use of the growing area available in any garden. Interplanting allows for sequential succession planting, which involves placing a few plants of many different kinds of vegetables into the garden each week throughout the seasons. And finally, interplanting allows the gardener to use allelopathic and beneficial chemical relationships between plants to protect against insects and to promote growth.

This is still a very new form of vegetable gardening, at least at this level of sophistication. I am just beginning to under-

TABLE 6–5

—— *BENEFICIAL COMPANIONS AND ALLELOPATHIC COMPANIONS* ——

CROP	BENEFICIAL COMPANIONS*	ALLELOPATHIC COMPANIONS
Asparagus	Basil, parsley	Onion family
Beans	Celery, corn	Fennel, gladiolus, onion family
Beets		Pole beans
Cabbage family		Pole beans, strawberries, tomatoes
Carrots	Peas add nutrients	Dill
Celery		Carrots, parsnips
Corn	Beans and peas add nutrients	Tomatoes
Cucumbers	Beans add nutrients	Potatoes, sage
Eggplant		None
Lettuce		None
Muskmelons	Corn	None
Onion family	Beets, carrots	Beans, peas
Peas	Carrots, turnips	Gladiolus, onions
Peppers	Carrots	Fennel, kohlrabi
Potatoes		Apples, pumpkins, raspberries, tomatoes
Radishes	Lettuce	Hyssop
Spinach	Strawberries	Potatoes
Squash	Corn	Potatoes
Swiss chard	Onion family	Pole beans
Tomatoes	Parsley	Corn, dill, kohlrabi, potatoes
Turnips	Peas	Potatoes

*All of the beneficial companions help with growth, whereas only some help with growth and add nutrients.
Note: For beets, cabbage, celery, eggplant, lettuce, and potatoes, research has not yet determined any beneficial companions.*

stand it, and I expect to take many years to acquire good interplanting skills. Interplanting requires that you know a substantial amount of information about all of your vegetable crops. Most of us know how tall or bushy a particular vegetable plant will get, but how many know the shape and size of the root structure? As you can see in illustration 6–2, if you know the shape of the root structure you can pack certain kinds of plants in closer together without their competing with each other for soil. In just a few years, you will be able to match root patterns on your home computer as you plan your interplanted garden.

Next you need to know the nutrient needs of each type of vegetable. A knowledge of which vegetables are heavy feeders and which are light feeders is not quickly acquired. Then we get into the mysteries of allelopathic and beneficial chemical relationships. Now things get interesting!

These terms are just the technical terms for what is commonly called *companion planting*—good companions have beneficial chemical relationships, and bad companions have allelopathic or bad chemical relationships. Allelopathy is any direct or indirect harmful effect by one plant on another through the production of chemical compounds that escape into the environment. Beneficial chemical relationships cause positive effects among plants in terms of growth and fruit production.

Allelopathy is a concern of commercial agriculture because it is a means of suppressing weed growth among crops. The release of toxic chemicals by certain plants and microbes causes one plant to dominate others whether in natural ecosystems, in 2,000-acre fields, or in backyard gardens. Scientists are just beginning to understand this relationship of attractants, stimulators, and inhibitors. You will be reading much on this subject over the next decade.

Since the 60-Minute Garden doesn't have any problems with weeds, the only allelopathic issues will come from one set of vegetables having a negative impact on the growth of another set of vegetables that are in proximity in the interplanted bed. These differences can vary by variety within the same kind of vegetable. We know that certain varieties of marigolds exude chemicals that kill tiny, wormlike soil parasites called nematodes. Certain varieties of cucumbers give off phytotoxins that inhibit nearby weed growth. Potatoes, tomatoes, and carrots have powerful chemicals that kill many kinds of soil bacteria and fungi. We also know that the ever-present quack grass has a serious negative effect on the productivity of most vegetables planted near it or planted in soil that grew quack grass the year before.

Looking at the opposite side of the coin, or plants with beneficial chemical relationships, we find longtime companions such as beans and corn. The beans provide nitrogen for the corn, and the corn provides a trellis for the beans. See table 6–5 for other beneficial companions.

Needless to say, interplanting is going to become a fascinating gardening technique as more knowledge is gained from research and as some of these tools like home computers are set up to help us with this high level of complexity. It is something like working with a three-dimensional crossword puzzle. Most gardeners may never go to that level of sophistication in vegetable gardening, but for some it will be an exciting and intriguing experience in the coming years.

SEEDLING GROW LIGHT DEVICE

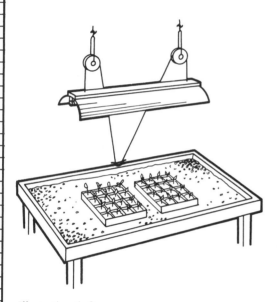

Illustration 6–3

If you watch for sales, you can get a light fixture and bulbs for about $15, or you can find a bargain at a yard sale. I have my lights rigged on pulleys so I can raise and lower them. I find that arrangement more convenient than using blocks to raise and lower the plants. A 48-inch fixture gives you enough light for growing from 75 to 120 seedlings, depending on their containers. I believe that's more than enough to start out with.

The shelf or table you use to hold your seedlings needs to be designed to withstand any potential damage from water. Ideally, you should have your seedlings sitting on white gravel in a shallow container that allows you to always keep a little water under the gravel to keep the humidity up.

SHOPPING LIST

48-inch twin-bulb fluorescent light fixture
chain or rope for hanging light
2 pulleys (2) at least 2 inches in diameter
gravel

Total cost: $20
Cost per square foot: $0.10

CONSTRUCTION STEPS

1. When setting up your grow light device, follow the directions that accompany the fixture and the pulleys.

2. Be certain that the table is protected from water damage.

SEEDLING STARTER BOX

Using Plexiglas and some old boards, my Dad and I built four seed-starting boxes that work on the soil block principle. There are no bottoms to the boxes. They sit in used cafeteria trays I got at a secondhand restaurant supply store. Using a block of wood, I press the soil mixture (soil, compost, and vermiculite) down into the forms to create the soil blocks. After a seedling has developed some roots, the soil block can be pushed out of the box and handled without it falling apart.

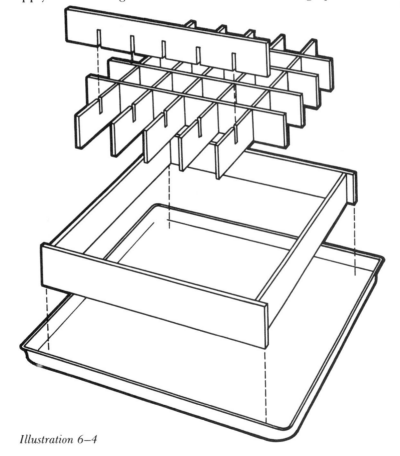

Illustration 6—4

SHOPPING LIST

Lumber
10 feet ⅜″ × 2¼″ softwood
1 block of wood 1¾″ square by 4 inches
Hardware
finish nails 4d
Other
1 sheet of Plexiglas approximately 2 square
    feet (any thickness from ⅛″ to ³⁄₁₆″)
1 cafeteria tray 14″ × 18″
        Total cost: $10

TOOLS

Circular saw or radial saw
Hammer

CUTTING LIST

Size	Piece	Quantity
2″ × 12″	Plexiglas dividers	10
2¼″ × 12″ × ⅜″	Side pieces of frame	2
2¼″ × 13¼″ × ⅜″	Side pieces of frame	2
1¾″ × 1¾″ × 4″	Block	1

CONSTRUCTION STEPS

1. Lay out and saw the sheet of Plexiglas into 2-inch-wide strips, whose lengths are multiples of 12 inches plus the saw cuts. Then cut 10 strips to 12-inch lengths.

2. In order to use the "egg crate" construction design, you must cut uniform slots along the edge of each of the Plexiglas strips. These slots must be slightly more than 1 inch in depth and slightly wider than the thickness of the Plexiglas sheet. It is essential that these slots all be exactly the same distance apart, or the "egg crate" will not assemble properly. The center of each slot should be 2 inches from the adjacent slot, and the end slots should be 2 inches from the end of the strip.

3. Assemble the "egg crate" of Plexiglas strips by fitting them together.

4. Nail a 13¼-inch side to a 12-inch side so that there is ¼ inch of the first strip outside the "egg crate" area. Place the assembled "egg crate" in the angle formed by the two sides and nail the other 12-inch strip in position. Finally, nail the last side piece.

5. Place the assembled seed starter box in the cafeteria tray because now it's ready for soil. The Plexiglas pieces do not have any adhesive or other means for attaching to the frame. The snug fit is sufficient to hold the "egg crate" form in place.

OUTDOOR SEEDLING BOX

This box serves as a holding pen for your seedlings when they are too big for your grow light device but still too small to be placed in the main garden. Seedlings left outside in pots or trays are very vulnerable to marauding insects, squirrels, and other pests, so the seedling box serves as a safe harbor until transplant time arrives. There is no bottom in this design because I simply place the box on the ground, so a bottom would just get wet and quickly rot away.

I did learn from experience that these boxes are vulnerable to an unexpected problem. They apparently represent just perfect perching platforms for cats and small dogs who want to be in position to comfortably survey the entire back 40 of their territory. My full-grown cat nearly destroyed my screen top 20 minutes after I installed it in my garden. He thought it was a great place to curl up. Thus, the hardware cloth got added to the design to protect the box itself from friendly pets.

The clear plastic film cover is used if you feel the seedlings need more direct sun. The screen cover is good for very young seedlings and for salad vegetables in the middle of the summer. While I have two covers, I use only one piece of hardware cloth, which just rests on the top of the box to support the rather large derriere of my cat buddy.

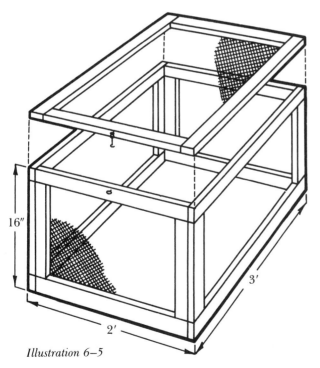

Illustration 6–5

———— SHOPPING LIST ————

Lumber
6 pcs. 1 × 2 × 8′ furring strips
Hardware
24 corrugated fasteners ⅝″
8 lineal feet 36″ wide aluminum fly
    screening
1 package aluminum tacks
1 pc. clear plastic polyethylene film 2′ × 3′
staples
finish nails (for box) 6d
common nails (for bottom) 2d
4 small hooks and eyes
1 pc. hardware cloth 23″
        Total cost: $10

———— TOOLS ————

Drill
Hammer
Measuring tape
Saw
Shears for cutting screening
Square
Staple gun
Tack hammer

———— CUTTING LIST ————

Size	Piece	Quantity
1 × 2 × 22½″	Frame	4
1 × 2 × 12¾″	Frame	8
1 × 2 × 36″	Frame	8
1 × 2 × 20½″	Frame	4
15″ × 22½″	Screening	2
15″ × 35″	Screening	2
23″ × 35″	Screening	1
23″ × 35″	Clear plastic film	1

CONSTRUCTION STEPS

1. Using two pieces of 22½-inch furring strips and two pieces of 12¾-inch furring strips, assemble a rectangular frame that will be 22½ by 16¾ inches, using corrugated fasteners (one in each joint).

2. Repeat the above step to make a second frame. These will become the front and back panels of the seed starter box.

3. The side panels are assembled in similar fashion with 36-inch and 12¾-inch pieces to make panels 36 by 16¾ inches.

4. Using 36-inch and 20½-inch lengths, make two tops in the same manner. The final dimensions will be 24½ by 36 inches.

5. Tack the appropriate pieces of screening in position on the rectangular frames. Also, staple the clear plastic film on one of the top frames.

6. Assemble two 36-by-16-inch frames to two 22½-by-16-inch frames, with the latter being on the inside of the larger frames. Use 6-penny finish nails, and support the frame being driven into with an axe head or other weight to absorb the shock. The screening should be on the inside of all frames.

7. Install the eyes in the center of the front and back of both the screen and plastic tops, while installing the hooks in the center of the front and back panels of the box at the top.

8. Install the seedling box in or around the garden with the piece of hardware cloth resting on the top to protect the cover from perching pets.

PLANTING COMPASS

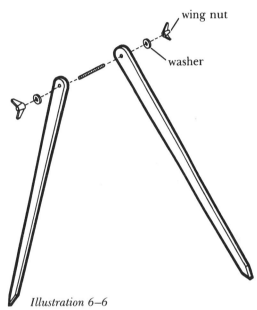

Illustration 6–6

This very handy device was designed and built by my father, Ed Ball. I wanted a device to help me get my seedlings more or less equidistant from each other in all directions, and so he invented the planting compass.

The reason for the two wing nuts (instead of just one on the end of a bolt) is to permit easy tightening of the compass so that it will not change its setting when you are using it.

SHOPPING LIST

Lumber
2 pcs. 1″ × 24″ × 5/16″ hardwood (maple, oak, so forth)
Hardware
1 machine bolt or screw 1/4″-20 × 2″
2 washers for 1/4″ bolt
2 wing nuts 1/4″-20

TOOLS

Drill
Saw

CONSTRUCTION STEPS

1. Drill a hole to clear the 1/4-inch screw at 1/2 inch from one end of each hardwood strip.

2. Cut the other end of each hardwood strip to approximately a 60-degree angle.

3. For aesthetic purposes only, the strips can be tapered to 1/2 inch at the pointed end and rounded to a 1/2-inch radius at the drilled end.

4. Cut the head of the threaded bolt so that you have a 1 1/2-inch threaded piece chamfered at both ends.

5. Assemble the threaded piece of the bolt through the two wood strips with a washer and wing nut on each side.

135

UMBRELLA CLOCHE SHADING DEVICE

This shading device is handy for covering only a portion of your garden bed, and it also serves as a very effective insect barrier as well. You can make umbrella cloches to fit several different size frames. The one described here fits a frame made up of crisscrossing ribs set in the existing foundations of my bed. Illustration 6–7 shows how you can use pieces of PVC pipe as portable foundations to erect umbrella cloches in any part of your garden over individual plants or small groups of plants.

SHOPPING LIST

Hardware
20 feet flexible PVC pipe 1″
string or wire
1 pc. of cheesecloth or tobacco cloth
  5′ × 20′
thread
binding tape

TOOLS

Hacksaw
Measuring tape
Scissors
Sewing machine

CUTTING LIST

Size	Piece	Quantity
10′	Ribs	2
4′2″ (base); 3′10″ (height)	Cheesecloth triangles	4

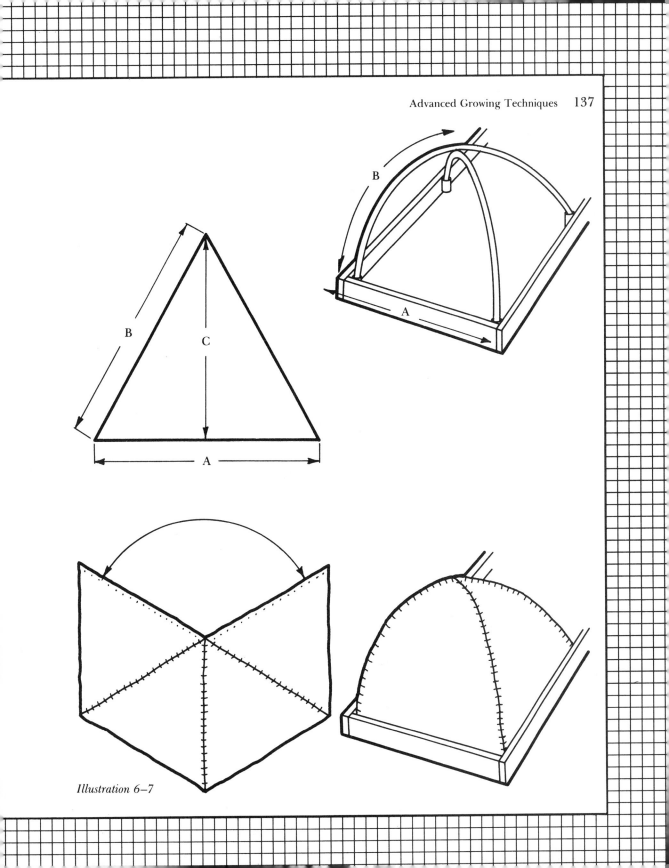

Illustration 6–7

CONSTRUCTION STEPS

1. Locate the ribs in the foundations of the bed as in illustration 6–7. With string or wire, secure the two ribs where they cross.

2. The umbrella cloche requires some calculations to get the correct size. When you cross two ribs, as in this design, you create four isosceles triangles. The measurements shown here have been calculated for a cloche to cover roughly 4 by 4 feet of my bed. The foundations are 3 feet 10 inches across from each other. I wanted the ribs to be roughly in the shape of a semicircle when they were installed. If the distances between foundations and/or the height of the cloche changes, the size of the triangles change. So, here is the formula to use.

A. The foundations must be in a square pattern for this formula to work so that the base of all four triangles will be roughly the same. You can measure that distance. That will be A in the formula.

B. Take a piece of string and lay it along the curve of one rib from the top of the foundation up to the peak or top of the cloche where the ribs cross. Then measure that string on a straight measuring tape. That will be a good estimate of the sides of your triangles. That will be B in the formula.

C. You need to calculate the height (call it C) of the triangle so that you can lay out a pattern to cut the cheesecloth. The formula for that calculation is the following:

C = the square root of B squared
plus half of A squared

Most calculators now have a function key for computing square roots, so this exercise becomes very easy.

D. Using this formula, I learned that the height of my triangle was 3.48 feet or 3 feet 6 inches. I want my cloche to overhang the soil with about 4 inches of cloth all around, so I added 4 inches to that figure, getting a final height of my cloche's triangle of 3 feet 10 inches.

3. Now I can make a paper pattern to use to cut my material. (It is a good idea to wash the fabric before making the cloche, or you will need to make the cloche a bit big to take shrinkage into consideration). I want the seams of the cloche to overlap a few inches, and I want it to be a bit large, so I add 4 inches to the length of the base

length as well. That allows me to lay out the base at 4 feet 2 inches, and I bisect that line with a vertical line 3 feet 10 inches. I then draw two lines connecting the ends of the base to the peak of the triangle, and I cut out my triangle. I repeat this operation three more times.

4. A sewing machine will create the neatest job. The cloche can certainly be stitched by hand, but the machine is faster and easier. Cut pieces of 2-inch bias tape the same length as the seams of the cloche. Then sew the cheesecloth to the binding tape, overlapping the tape just a bit with the cloth.

5. Drape the cheesecloth over the ribs to create an umbrella-shaped cloche to shade the plants and protect them from insects.

CHAPTER 7

WATERING AND FEEDING

Of all the aspects of vegetable gardening, I think watering and feeding activities are the most confusing and the least understood by a majority of gardeners. I know that these activities were a mystery to me for many years. I suspect garden writers must take some responsibility for this confusion. We tell you that the critical watering period for broccoli is during head development while for lima beans it is during pollination. Then we tell you to give the tomatoes nitrogen early in their growth and then reduce the nitrogen and increase the phosphorus as the fruit starts to form. When you add up all these very specific instructions for 15 or 20 vegetables, the result can be monumental confusion. There are two approaches to watering and feeding the gar-

den—the basic no-frills get-the-job-done approach that achieves optimum production and the more time-consuming and individual plant-oriented approach that seeks maximum production. I generally use the basic approach because I don't have the time to treat each vegetable separately in satisfying its feeding and watering needs. I know that the individual treatment will get better production in the end, but I am satisfied with the quality of my garden using the basic approach.

The key to my watering and feeding program is a drip irrigation system. The drip system offers the best method for watering and feeding a vegetable garden for gardeners who want to have a quality product but who are also pressed for time. When you install a drip system in your vegetable patch, you virtually eliminate the time it takes to water your garden and reduce the feeding time to almost nothing as well.

Drip irrigation is not all that new an idea. German farmers developed a kind of drip system over 100 years ago. They laid pipe for water underground in their fields in such a way that the joints did not quite connect, allowing water to seep into the earth and to the roots of their crops. Forty years ago, Symka Blass, an Israeli engineer, developed the idea of using special valves or emitters in a hose to release water one drop at a time. Since then drip irrigation has become a more and more popular watering method in commercial agriculture since it saves enormous amounts of water and in the long run is cheaper than traditional watering systems.

BENEFITS OF DRIP IRRIGATION SYSTEMS

Drip irrigation systems offer a number of important benefits to the backyard vegetable gardener.

First, a drip system uses much less water than the traditional sprinkler system. You can assume that you will save at least 30 percent, and in some cases 50 percent, of your water over the normal methods of watering, such as sprinklers. Water in a drip system has no chance to evaporate or run off because it is completely absorbed by the soil and never touches the leaves of the plants.

Second, you can water your garden with a drip system in 10 seconds, the time it takes to simply turn it on. Later, when the watering is finished, the system turns itself off. The best drip systems operate with a mechanical timer device that allows you to set the timer to a specified watering period and then it automatically shuts the water off. You can turn it on and go shopping.

Third, research has demonstrated that drip irrigation systems, especially those used in conjunction with mulch, increase the productivity of a garden. Plants have earlier blossoming, increased growth, and higher yields. Peppers grown with drip irrigation and black plastic mulch have produced more than twice the crop (120 percent) of peppers grown without drip irrigation and mulch. The same results have been shown in research with cantaloupes, tomatoes, okra, eggplant, and summer squash.

Fourth, because the water never touches the leaves of the vegetable plants, many moisture-related diseases are avoided with a drip system. Problems such as rust, mildew, and blossom damage are all reduced in gardens using a drip technique.

Photo 7–1: This drip irrigation system uses flexible PVC tubing with emitters spaced at 24-inch intervals. Particularly useful in beds with large plants, emitters deliver water directly to their root systems.

Fifth, an advantage just recently being appreciated is the cooling effect a drip system has on the soil. A properly managed drip irrigation system can be used to help keep down soil temperatures in the high heat of the summer, thereby increasing production because plants grow more effectively in a cooler soil.

Finally, a drip irrigation system reduces the problem of compaction of the soil in the beds. When the soil is saturated with large amounts of water, the structure of the soil is weakened somewhat and compaction occurs. Drip irrigation avoids this problem because the water is introduced into the soil so slowly that the structure of the soil is not affected.

A top-quality drip irrigation system will cost you about $0.25 to $0.40 a square foot, or $50 to $80 for a 200-square-foot garden. These systems will last for decades and take very little maintenance. On top of that you get a bonus—you can feed your garden with the same system.

Photo 7–2: Add liquid fertilizer to a drip irrigation system by using a siphon device that is attached to the head of the drip system. This device siphons fertilizer from a pail or container and mixes it with the water as it enters the drip irrigation system. The white device on the hose is the mechanical timer for turning the system on and off.

DRIP FEEDING

The better drip irrigation systems allow you to install a siphon device that draws liquid fertilizer from a pail into the drip hoses and mixes it with the water moving toward the plants. So as the plants are getting slowly watered one drip at a time, they are simultaneously being fertilized with liquid fertilizer. There are a number of advantages to feeding your garden in this manner.

First, liquid fertilizer is absorbed by the plant roots 20 times faster than dry fertilizer spread on the surface of the soil. More of the fertilizer applied is actually absorbed by the plants with the drip approach, reducing waste. Much of the dry fertilizer is leached by rain and misses the roots of the plants. Consequently, research has demonstrated that plants fed with regular applications of liquid fertilizer have better growth and production over plants fertilized in the traditional manner.

And, when used in conjunction with the soil management program described in chapter 5, the use of organic liquid fertilizer in a drip system is slightly cheaper than the traditional chemical fertilizer program used in most American vegetable gardens.

Finally, like the watering activities, feeding your vegetables through the drip irrigation system takes less time than fertilizing with traditional methods, such as side-dressing.

As you will see later in this chapter, a drip irrigation system allows you to provide all the necessary moisture and supplemental nutrients for a healthy and productive garden while taking much less time and while creating a better environment for more productive plant growth.

FOUR TYPES OF DRIP IRRIGATION SYSTEMS

The first task in developing a drip irrigation system is selecting the type of system best suited for the backyard. I believe that the emitter system is best, but let me review the other options, for the record. A major problem inhibiting vegetable gardeners from installing drip systems is the technical fog found in most catalogs and articles about drip irrigation. Most drip irrigation supply companies direct their efforts toward large commercial applications and consequently must offer a broad range of types of equipment and must get into fairly sophisticated technical calculations in designing those large systems. The backyard system, on the other hand, is pretty simple and is easy to understand if we sweep away some of that technical terminology and advanced mathematical calculations.

There are four types of drip systems available to the backyard gardener. They include the drip soaker lines, the porous soaker lines, the "spaghetti" type lines, and the emitter system.

DRIP SOAKERS

The drip soaker system is simply a hose with lots of holes punched in it that allow the water to drip out of the hose for its entire length. You simply lay the hose along the bed and turn on the water just a little bit so that the water doesn't squirt out of the holes but rather drips slowly into the ground. These hoses are found in most garden supply stores. They are used mostly for watering shrubs and flower gardens. They

have a number of disadvantages for vegetable gardens. Their most serious problem is that you can't control how much water is released into all parts of the garden uniformly. If you have more than one length of hose in a system, the pressure control along the length of the hose is difficult. Pressure is controlled by how much you turn the valve at the faucet. You will have more water coming out close to the faucet and much less water coming out at the far end of the system. These hoses are difficult to lay up and down a bed without having kinks develop at the bending points. I would not recommend these hoses for the 60-Minute Garden.

POROUS DRIP SOAKER SYSTEM

The earliest soaker hose was one made of canvas that simply sweated the water along its entire length. Again, it is difficult to control how much water is being released, and these canvas soakers should be dried out after every use to reduce deterioration. This makes them pretty impractical for a vegetable garden.

Technology has given us two other porous soakers. Du Pont has developed a white plastic tubing that feels something like paper. It is very light, and it sweats water along its whole length. There are several companies marketing this product, and it works very well for some watering applications. Its disadvantage is that it is very vulnerable to ultraviolet rays from the sun and therefore should be used under black plastic mulch. Even with that precaution, this tubing doesn't last more than two or three seasons before it breaks down with lots of leaks.

Another porous material, made from recycled automobile tires, is made into a hose with millions of little air spaces or holes in it. It sweats along its entire length and is very durable. Its biggest limitation is that it can't be used for fertilizing the garden because the organic liquid fertilizer, such as fish

Photos 7–3 and 7–4: The porous black drip hose (left) is made from recycled automobile tires. It oozes water all along its length. Another type of drip hose (below) is porous, feels like paper, and lets water seep out all along its length.

emulsion, will tend to clog the microscopic holes over time. This hose is also considerably more expensive per square foot than an emitter system.

"SPAGHETTI" DRIP SYSTEM

There is a drip system that uses spaghetti-like hoses attached to a main feeder line for dripping water into the soil. These systems were designed primarily for commercial greenhouse and nursery operations using thousands of pots to grow small plants. These "spaghetti" lines can be led to each potted plant, allowing very easy watering of a large number of pots at the same time. In the vegetable garden these "spaghetti" lines can get clogged and are also vulnerable to rodent damage. They are not very practical for the vegetable garden when compared to the standard emitter system.

EMITTER DRIP SYSTEM

It is the emitter drip system that I prefer for the 60-Minute Garden. The system is simply a series of hoses laid throughout the garden. Each hose has imbedded in it a number of evenly spaced nozzles or emitters that release water a drop at a time. These emitters come in several designs, making the system very flexible for almost all watering applications from a 20-acre orchard to our 200-square-foot 60-Minute Garden. There are at least four different types of emitters on the market today. The simplest, and the one that I recommend and use, is the orifice emitter, which is essentially a little valve with a small hole in it. The other emitter designs (long-path, vortex, and diaphragm) have features to reduce clogging and to deal with varying water pressures. They are more expensive than the orifice type emitter, and some of these features are of more interest to commercial growers, in my opinion. The rest of this chapter deals with the development and management of a drip system using the orifice type emitter. I like the emitter system because it is easy to maintain, at least in the backyard garden environment, and it is easy to use with liquid fertilizer.

You do not have to buy a complete packaged drip system kit, although there are some advantages in doing so. You can buy the emitters separately and install them yourself in a garden hose or in a piece of polyethylene hose. These homemade systems work just fine, but they can be a problem when you get into needing additional equipment such as a fertilizer applicator, filters, and such. Nevertheless, a homemade drip system will serve most vegetable garden watering and feeding needs and will be somewhat cheaper than the commercial packages.

One of the questions you need to resolve is whether you are going to start off with a kit, with all the basic parts included, or whether you will buy all the parts of your drip system and fabricate it yourself. The kits will cover a specified number of square feet, anywhere from 100 to 400 square feet. They sometimes do not include what I consider important parts such as pressure regulators, backflow valves, and filters. On the other hand, they give you the basics needed to try out drip irrigation in at least a part of your garden. My advice for a 200-square-foot 60-Minute Garden is don't start with a kit—start right off with a custom-designed system because it will work better and will cost only a little more than the kit. If you have a larger garden, you may want to start with a kit before you make a major investment.

DESIGNING THE DRIP IRRIGATION SYSTEM

It is very important, in designing a drip irrigation system, to work with a fairly accurate drawing of your garden layout. I use graph paper to lay out my paths and beds as close to scale as I can. You need this drawing to determine how much hose or tubing you need and how far apart you should place your emitters on the tubing. Most of the companies that sell drip irrigation equipment will help you with this planning. Usually if you send them a scale drawing of your garden, they will send you back a layout of the drip system and a recommendation for the spacing of the emitters and a complete parts list for your review.

Usually the company will want to know what your water pressure is and how many gallons of water you get per minute out of your faucet. If you tell them you are hooked up to a city water company, they will know that your pressure is between 50 and 80 pounds per square inch (psi) and that you get 6 to 7 gallons a minute out of your faucet. You can check the gallons per minute by timing the filling of a gallon pail. If it takes 10 seconds, you get 6 gallons a minute. If it takes 9 seconds, you get about 7 gallons a minute.

COMPONENTS OF THE SYSTEM

It is not very difficult to design a drip system for a backyard garden. There are four components of the design—the head (where you connect your system to your water source), the main supply line(s) that get the water to the garden itself, the laterals or feeder lines in the beds, and the emitters that are embedded in the feeder lines.

THE HEAD

The head is a term that covers all the pieces of equipment found at the head end of the system between the faucet and the main supply line. There are five items that I believe should be included in the head of a backyard drip system. They are a backflow preventer, a timer of some sort, a pressure control, a filtering device, and a fertilizer siphon. You will spend as much for these items as you do for the emitters and lines for the 200-square-foot garden, but the cost is well justified by the benefits.

TIMING DEVICE

There are three kinds of timing devices for a drip system. The simplest and least expensive is a mechanical timer connected to a valve that you attach to the head of your system. Whenever you want to water, you turn the timer to the desired length of time (usually up to an hour) and walk away. The timer device will turn off the system when the time has expired. There are other devices that are battery operated that allow you to schedule your watering over a period of time, such as weekly. This device will turn on the system and turn off the system automatically without your being in the area—perfect for when you are on vacation for a month. The most sophisticated device has

the capability to measure the moisture content of the soil, and when the moisture level gets below appropriate amounts, the system is turned on. The monitor then turns off the system when the desired moisture level is reached.

I use the simple mechanical timer in my garden, and it works very well. I think some kind of timer is valuable because it allows you to forget about keeping track of how long you wanted to water—it does that chore for you, saving you time and bother. Most gardeners in this country tend not to water their gardens enough. Anything you can do to make watering less of a chore will serve to improve your chances of getting to that task often enough to keep your garden thriving.

BACKFLOW PREVENTER

This little attachment is the first device to be attached to the faucet. It prevents water from entering the drip system and then backing up into the home's water system. This is especially important if you use your system for applying liquid fertilizer. You certainly do not want liquid fertilizer in your home's water supply because the fertilizer backed up into your water system for some reason. Most good fertilizing siphons also have a backflow preventer built in, giving you double protection.

PRESSURE CONTROL

A drip system works under a relatively low water pressure in order to discharge water drop by drop instead of in a stream or spray. Normal city water systems will have pressures from 50 to 80 psi (pounds per square inch). This pressure must be reduced in your drip system for the emitters to function properly. So you need a pressure reduction attachment that will take the pressure down to the 10 to 20 psi prescribed by the manufacturer of your system. In a home-made system, you accomplish this task by installing a washer with a small hole into the head end that will reduce the pressure for a drip system.

FILTER

Emitters have only one weakness: They can occasionally get clogged or blocked. This is not really a serious problem for systems tied to a city water supply, but precautions are still in order. You should have at least one filter device attached on the front end of your system to catch particles that can come through the water supply. This filter should always be attached after attaching a liquid fertilizing siphon to further protect your emitters from clogging. I have filters at the beginning of every feeder line as it enters each bed, just for double protection. My filters are fine wire mesh devices that are easy to clean out by rinsing them in water.

FERTILIZING SIPHON

For around $15 you can get a siphoning device that will allow you to introduce liquid fertilizer into the flow of the water in the drip system, which enables you to feed your plants while you are watering them. It doesn't make any sense to me to have a drip system without the ability to use it for feeding the garden as well.

MAIN SUPPLY LINE

You can use a standard garden hose to get water from your faucet to your garden and the beginning of the drip system. Usually, you would use 1/2-inch polyvinyl chloride (PVC) flexible tubing to take the water from the garden hose to each of the feeder lines in the beds. I put a "Y" fitting with two shutoff valves on my outside faucet and connect one side of the fitting to the 1/2-inch PVC tubing that I run underground to my drip system in the garden. It is always turned on so that I control my watering from a valve out in the garden in my garden sink (see photo 7–6). The other side of the "Y" fitting is used for the standard garden hose for washing the car, spritzing the dog, and doing other chores.

The primary issue in designing your main supply line is whether you need one or two sections to your drip system in order to maintain uniform pressure and a uniform water supply at all emitters. You must add up how many emitters you have planned for your entire garden. This number varies according to the emitter spacing. In my system, each emitter will give 2 gallons of water an hour, and the common city water system gives 6 or 7 gallons of water a minute or 360 to 420 gallons per hour. You can't have more emitters on line at one time that would release more than your total source of 360 to 420 gallons, or you will lose uniform pressure throughout the system. You won't hurt anything in the system if this happened, but the plants at the end of the system would be cheated.

For example, if you have 4-foot beds in a 200-square-foot garden, using 16-inch emitter spacing, you will have three lengths of feeder lines in each bed or about 150 feet of feeder line. If you use 16-inch spacing for your emitters, you would have 112 emitters, putting out about 224 gallons of water an hour. Using this calculation you can have up to approximately 400 square feet of garden, using 4-foot beds and 16-inch spacing on your emitters, before you will have to worry about splitting up your system into two separate sections. If you use 24-inch spacing, as I do, you can go up to 700 square feet of garden before you worry about having to split the system into two parts. You can play with the emitter spacing, and you can reduce the emitter size down to a gallon an hour and give yourself even more space, while staying with one main supply line. Most backyard gardeners don't have to worry about exceeding their water supply with a drip irrigation system using one main supply line.

LATERAL FEEDER TUBES

The spacing of your emitters affects the length of feeder tubing you will need. If you use 16- to 18-inch spacing, you will need two lengths for 3-foot beds and three lengths of feeder line for 4-foot beds.

Feeder lines are generally a smaller diameter hose than the main supply line. My feeder lines are ⅜-inch flexible PVC tubing. It takes emitter installation easily and is flexible enough to zigzag on a bed. My feeder lines have a shutoff valve and a screen filter on each bed, giving me a bit more flexibility in controlling my overall system. I can isolate a bed I'm not using or isolate a bed I don't want to receive liquid fertilizer. The extra filters just reduce the possibility of my emitters clogging.

EMITTERS

You want durable emitters that are easy to install, easy to take out, and easy to unclog. I use an orifice emitter in a ⅜-inch PVC tubing. The most important question in designing your system is how far apart to place your emitters on the feeder hose line. You will find that there is no consensus among designers of drip irrigation systems.

The two most important variables controlling emitter spacing are type of soil and what kind of plant you are watering. First let's talk about type of soil. As you can see in illustration 7–1, water from a drip emitter moves into the ground in different ways depending on the type of soil. In sandy soil, it seeps down fairly directly and in clay soil it spreads out more laterally than downward. Since the purpose of drip irrigation is to have uniform water available to all your root systems, you want the water pattern of each emitter to overlap. Therefore, in sandy soils you want your emitters to be closer together than if you had a very clayey soil. A nice loamy soil with lots of humus has a watering profile that is shaped somewhat like an onion—somewhere in between the sandy and clay configurations.

Therefore I recommend, for the 60-Minute Garden, placing emitters anywhere from 16 to 24 inches apart, depending on your type of soil. If you follow the soil management procedures outlined in chapter 5, you should soon have loamy soil in your beds and should use between 20- and 24-inch spacing for your emitters. I use 24-inch spacing for all the lines in my entire garden.

The way to test to be sure that you have the proper spacing is to run your system for about an hour. If your emitter spacing is right for your type of soil, the water profiles from each emitter should be overlapping at about 2 inches down in the soil at a midpoint between two emitters. If they are

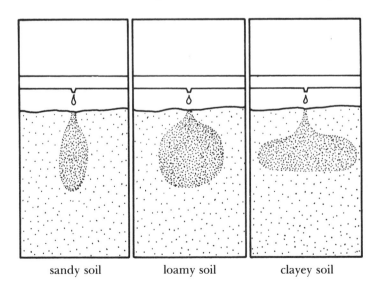

sandy soil   loamy soil   clayey soil

Illustration 7–1: Water enters soil with a different pattern depending on the type of soil. The distance between emitters in your drip irrigation system is controlled by the type of soil. Sandy soil requires emitters to be closer to each other than would be found with clayey soil.

Photo 7—5: Emitter types of drip irrigation permit spacing the water drops so that they are located near plant root systems.

not overlapping at that point, you might need to narrow down your emitter spacing the next winter when you are getting ready for the coming growing season. You don't want your emitters too close because you will waste water, and you will be giving the overlapping sections too much water for best plant growth.

Another variable found in catalogs listing emitters is the discharge rating or how much water is released by the emitter in 1 hour. Commercial emitters generally have either ½-gallon, 1-gallon, or 2-gallon discharge ratings. As a general rule, the 2-gallon per hour emitter is usually best for a vegetable garden application. If you have very, very clayey soil then the 1-gallon or even the ½-gallon emitter might be considered. Generally, if you follow the approach for soil management outlined in chapter 5, you should use a 2-gallon-per-hour emitter in your drip system.

HOW THE
DRIP EMITTER WORKS

The emitter releases water a drop at a time at a rate of 1 or 2 gallons an hour.

That slow release of water gives each of the droplets a chance to seep down and out into the soil in search of that soil particle that has lost most of its water film. It is important to understand that the water drips sideways as well as downward in the soil. It forms what is called the *water profile*, which will vary with the type of soil (see illustration 7–1). As noted earlier, in extremely sandy soil, the profile is much like a capsule, longer than it is wide. In a very clayey soil, the water profile is wider than it is deep. In a loamy soil the profile is shaped something like an onion. On top of the soil, you may only see a wet spot the size of a dinner plate, while 2 inches below the wet spot is an area of moist soil 2 feet in diameter with a varying depth, depending on how long you had the water on.

INSTALLING THE DRIP
SYSTEM IN THE GARDEN

The best time to install a drip system in the 60-Minute Garden is in the early spring when you are setting up your beds and tunnels. Normally, you would install your drip lines on top of the beds and then cover them with the black (or clear) plastic mulch that will stay in place for the duration of the season. You can install the lines long before last frost. Just don't use the drip system until the danger of freezing the lines is past.

If you are installing a system with flexible PVC tubing, it is easier to work with the tubing when it is warm. Let it sit out in the sun for a few hours or dip the ends in boiling water just before trying to attach pieces together.

Generally, you would begin installing your drip system at the head end and work out toward the garden. Usually, you will have some cutting and piecing together of various fittings to establish the whole system. The feeder lines are connected to the main supply line with various tee fittings or ell fittings to take the lines around corners. When

Photo 7–6: Drip irrigation systems can be run by mechanical timers or small computers. This computer can be programmed to turn the water on and off on specific days.

working with PVC tubing, a hacksaw and a measuring tape are about all you need to install the system. PVC fittings push into each other and lock, requiring no glue.

You can set up a drip system for a 200-square-foot garden in a few hours. Remember not to tighten plastic fittings with a wrench. Where you have plastic screw fittings, a piece of Teflon tape wrapped around the male fitting helps to keep leaks down with just hand tightening. You can buy emitter systems with the emitters already installed, or you can install them yourself. Emitter holes are easy to plug up if you make a mistake. While there are plier-like tools available for rapid insertion of emitters, the job can be done with an awl and a pair of pliers. If you are using a fertilizer injector or siphon, place it in the system before the final filter to catch any of the larger particles in the organic liquid fertilizers (fish emulsion or kelp emulsion) that could clog up the emitters.

I decided that since I was going to have a complete drip irrigation system in my garden, I might as well go the final step and build the garden sink I have always wanted as well. They seem to go together.

GARDEN SINK

With all our years of gardening, the only tension that has occurred between me and my good wife regarding the garden is the dirt left in the kitchen sink when I plunk a bunch of fresh picked carrots or turnips in the sink and don't get a chance to clean it up right away. I needed a garden sink to eliminate that minor tension in our relationship. A sink, located in or beside the garden, allows you to clean off the root vegetables, cut off the stalks, and wash your muddy hands after a transplanting session. I have gone a few steps farther and turned my garden sink into kind of a garden control center. Besides being a handy place to clean hands and veg-

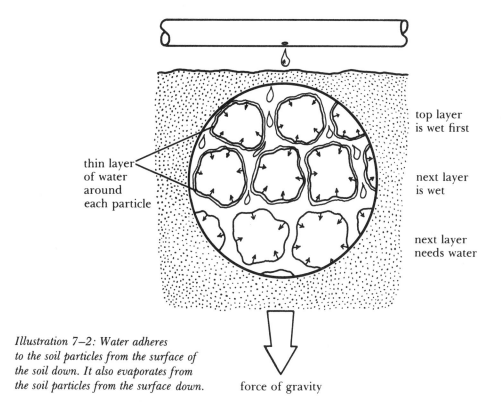

top layer
is wet first

next layer
is wet

next layer
needs water

thin layer
of water
around
each particle

*Illustration 7–2: Water adheres
to the soil particles from the surface of
the soil down. It also evaporates from
the soil particles from the surface down.*

force of gravity

etables, my drip irrigation system is controlled at the sink. My timer, which turns my system on and off, is inside the sink cupboard, protected from the weather. I also store my liquid fertilizers and my fertilizer siphon in the sink, making the feeding process very convenient. I have run electricity as well as water out to my sink so that I control my electric fence from that location (see chapter 8). My sink also stores my gardening gloves, several trowels, a sharp knife for cleaning vegetables, and a hand sprayer for those few times I use an organic spray to take on particularly pesky bugs. Finally, my garden sink is a godsend for cleaning those fish that I occasionally catch when I take a break from the rat race.

As you can see in photo 7–6, I have tried to make my garden sink as attractive as I could since it sits right out there in the middle of my garden in plain view to the world. I have it close to my compost pile so I can easily dispose of the vegetable stalks and cuttings. The sink drains into a 5-gallon bucket that also serves as the mixing pail for my liquid fertilizer concoctions. It has a spray attachment for rinsing things and a soap dish with a pure soap that doesn't harm the garden. Complete construction details can be found later in this chapter (see illustration 7–4).

WATERING THE 60-MINUTE GARDEN

Most gardeners in this country tend to underwater vegetable gardens. This occurs for many reasons. One common one is that during July and August, when gardens usually need the most watering, gardeners often find other demands on their time. Vegetables go through a dry/wet/dry cycle that has the net effect of stopping growth, starting growth, and stopping growth over and over again. This stop/start routine seriously reduces a garden's productivity. Of course, we can overwater our gardens just as easily. If we give our gardens too much water, the soil gets saturated, reducing the space for that critical oxygen. Again, plant growth suffers. Learning what is just the right amount of water often sounds like a mysterious code, known only to gardeners who have been at the task for at least 20 years or more.

In fact, watering is not all that complicated if you understand a few basic principles. Soil fills with water from the top down. The force of gravity causes the water to drop into the soil, but then it is exposed to the adhesion forces of the individual soil particles that makes a water droplet form a thin layer of water around each particle. As a particle is surrounded by a layer of water, the adhesion force diminishes, and gravity takes the next drop down or by adhesion over to the side to the next soil particle. Under good drainage conditions, soil will take up and hold a definite amount of water against the force of gravity—this is called its *field capacity*, which varies with differing texture and soil structures.

On the other side of the coin, the roots of the plants in that moist soil use the power of suction to take water away from those soil particles until the water film is so thin no more water can be sucked up by the plant. It is a regular war of the worlds down there with soil and roots fighting for droplets of water. The name of the gardener's game then is to find a way to make sure there is always enough water to satisfy the needs of the root systems but not too much water so that oxygen would be denied to those same roots.

The plant has a very simple reaction to too little or too much water—it stops growing. When it stops growing, you are losing production both in size of fruits and in

Photo 7–7: This rain gauge is right outside my back door, which allows me easily to keep track of the amount of rainfall on my garden each week. I use my drip irrigation system to make up the difference between the rainfall and approximately 1 inch of water per square foot per week.

yield. The problem is that when a plant starts to wilt from lack of water it has already stopped growing for as much as a day or more. Therefore, the task at hand is to anticipate a plant's water needs *before* it even slows down its growth, much less stops its growth. The secret to successful watering is *consistency*—try to keep the water supply as uniform as possible!

RAIN GAUGES

The task then is to give your garden enough water to maintain the proper amount

of moisture—not too much and not too little—after subtracting how much rainfall
you've recently had. If you get an inch of
rain, you should be able to wait a day or two
before worrying about watering your garden. Keeping track of rainfall helps you to
avoid overwatering your garden with a drip
system. The best way to do that is to mount
a rain gauge someplace in or around your
garden. You could put it on your garden
sink, for example. I have mine fairly close
to my back door so I can see it from inside
my kitchen. I can check it while it is still
raining, and because it is so close to the door,
I generally keep better track of what is hap-
pening than if it was located 50 feet out in
the backyard. The only thing you must avoid
with rain gauges is allowing water in them
to freeze. In early spring and late fall, you
must keep a watch out for possible overnight
freezes after a rain. The gauge is easily
cracked by ice.

I keep rough track of my rainfall on
a weekly basis and look for ½ to 1 inch a
week. If after a few days I have not gotten
that much, I know I should be thinking about
watering. I don't keep precise records on
paper. Just keeping rough track in your head
makes good use of this handy measuring
device.

HOW MUCH
SHOULD YOU WATER?

While the soil fills with water from the
top down, it also loses water from the top
down. The soil loses water in two ways—
transpiration by the leaves of the plants and
evaporation from the soil surface. In the 60-
Minute Garden, with its plastic and straw
mulch, there is little or no evaporation. Thus,
our need for watering is already reduced,
compared to our neighbors with traditional
gardens. The amount of water lost by plants
through the transpiration process varies with
weather conditions. Transpiration increases

with a rise in temperature and with an increase in wind velocity. Research has shown
that the ideal water level in the soil is between 40 and 80 percent of field capacity. A
full field capacity limits oxygen flow. Our
objective then is to guess how much water
has been lost by plant transpiration so that
we can avoid the soil's moisture content falling below 40 percent of its field capacity,
while not giving it too much water so it doesn't
exceed 80 percent of its field capacity. I don't
know about you, but that sounds like an impossible task to me. I need an easier way to
figure out this watering scheme, though it
helps me to understand generally how Mother
Nature has worked out her system for watering plants.

The rule of thumb, generally accepted by master gardeners, is to try to give
your garden an inch of water a week from
the rain and from watering systems. In arid
areas, 2 inches a week is the target. This is
probably too much water for the 60-Minute
Garden. Since the 60-Minute Garden loses
little or no water from evaporation, the weekly
need will be something less than an inch a
week, probably between ½ inch and ¾ inch,
depending on the season. An inch of water
puts ½ gallon of water on each square foot
of your garden. Likewise, ½ inch will then
put one fourth of a gallon or a quart of water
on each square foot of your garden. In a
200-square-foot garden, that means you need
about 50 to 75 gallons of water a week, less
any rain that falls.

If you have a drip irrigation system
with emitters that release 2 gallons of water
per hour and you place them 24 inches apart,
each emitter covers approximately 4 square
feet. Therefore, if you run your system for
one hour, you will get sufficient water for
your 60-Minute Garden for a week. Now,
watering the garden only once a week is not
necessarily a good idea. Remember, consistency is more important than quantity in this
case. You don't want the plants to go dry/
wet/dry over and over again. So if it does
not rain, you could water your garden three

times a week for 20 minutes each time and get sufficient water and maintain a more consistent level of moisture. Some people water their gardens daily, and that means a 10-minute watering session with the drip system. I prefer to water two or three times a week, keeping track of how much rain I get. If I get ½ inch of rain, I'll wait two days and start my 20-minute watering cycle again.

The objective of this approach is to replace the moisture that is lost from transpiration. We know that this loss begins at the top of the soil and works its way down. How deep does the water need to go? Another general rule of thumb is that a plant's root system is generally as deep in the soil as the plant is tall in the air. A 2-foot broccoli plant would have roots going 24 inches into the soil. Research on watering has indicated that when field capacity is about 50, 1 inch of water will wet soil to varying depths depending on it's structure. One inch of water will go down 24 inches in sandy soil, 16 inches in loamy soil, and only 11 inches in a clayey soil. So when you water for only 20 minutes, you still may be getting new water down fairly deeply because the water will seep down toward that soil needing replenishment. If the roots at 10 inches are taking water more than the roots at 2 inches, the new water will pass down past the 2-inch level and head for the 10-inch level where the adhesion forces are strongest to overcome the force of gravity that is pulling the water down in the first place.

If you are not sure whether your emitters release 2 gallons per hour or 1 gallon per hour, simply place a coffee can under one and time how long it takes to fill it so you can then compute how much would have been released in an hour.

The general rule, to water about 20 minutes two or three times a week, less the rainfall, should not be followed blindly throughout the entire season. In the summer months, during very hot periods with little rain and any kind of breeze, you can go up to a half an hour or more two or three times a week. August is the time for maximum production in the garden, so it is not the time to overlook the water needs of your plants. Feel under the mulch to double-check. It should always feel moist. It should never feel dry. In the spring time you may need to water new seed beds by hand for a week or two until their root systems get down past the 2- or 3-inch mark, where they can reach the water from the drip system. In the fall, you can probably cut watering back to only 10 or 15 minutes twice a week, since plant transpiration slows down as the days get shorter.

For master gardeners who know which plants need extra water at certain times in their life cycles, this approach to watering can serve as the base. Individual water supplements to certain crops can easily be done by hand in a relatively short period of time. For most of us, if we get our basic watering program going, our gardens will look better than they ever have in the past.

FEEDING THE 60-MINUTE GARDEN

The discussion in chapter 5 presents my general approach to soil management for the 60-Minute Garden. The major nutrient material for vegetable plant growth is put into the beds in the spring in the form of compost and/or aged manure. The slow breakdown of that material, along with biennial applications of rock powders, provides most of the nutrients the vegetables need to be healthy and productive.

Consequently, any feeding done during the growing season is providing a supplement to that primary nutrient resource. Most garden books talk about *side-dressing* the plants with a dry fertilizer of some sort at various key times during the growing season. You must be careful with commercial dry fertilizers not to put too much on the garden and to keep it from touching the plants for fear of "burning" the roots and leaves.

I prefer to use my drip irrigation system to provide the supplemental side-dressing in liquid form. This approach takes much less time, and it completely avoids any worry about "burning" the roots or leaves of the plants because the liquid organic fertilizer is very dilute when it gets to its destination.

There has been, in recent years, an increasing interest in *foliar feeding* of vegetables, even on a commercial scale. This involves spraying diluted liquid fertilizer on the leaves of plants. Research has shown that plants take up the nutrients very rapidly using this method and that the plant shows significant gains. I believe that feeding plants liquid fertilizer through a drip system is almost the same as feeding them through a spray method, and it takes a whole lot less time and trouble. With one exception, whenever I read an article about the benefits of foliar feeding, I simply change *foliar* to *drip* in my mind and assume that the two approaches are synonymous.

The exception, where foliar feeding is superior to drip feeding, involves the use of liquid seaweed emulsion. There has been a great deal of research in the past 20 years about the effect of liquid seaweed sprayed on to plants with some device. There is very strong evidence that liquid seaweed, when applied as a foliar spray, helps the plant in ways not possible from dry fertilizing or even by drip fertilizing. Liquid seaweed emulsion has virtually the complete range of micronutrients or trace minerals so essential to proper plant growth. One hypothesis is that

TABLE 7–1

FOLIAR FEEDING TIMES

CROP*	WHEN TO USE FOLIAR SPRAY
Apples	At flowering time
	When buds form for following year
	At fruit set
	3 weeks after fruit set
Cucumbers	First bloom
Melons	First bloom
Potatoes	Before first flowering
	3 weeks later
Soybeans	First bloom
Strawberries	At transplant
	At bud formation
	At petal fall
	After harvest
Tomatoes	At transplant
	At fifth leaf stage
	At first bloom
	At fruit set
	3 weeks later

*The crops listed here are those most commonly fed by foliar sprays.

foliar spraying with liquid seaweed emulsion causes the plant to produce additional enzymes and vitamins that are beneficial to the plant's growth and that are not produced by any feeding process through the roots of the plant. Research indicates that just two or three applications of very dilute liquid seaweed emulsion, applied as a foliar spray, will improve plant growth, increase its capacity to withstand drought, and reduce incidence of disease. For the 60-Minute Garden, a few ounces of seaweed emulsion will last for the whole season.

Plants take up nutrients 20 to 30 times faster in liquid form than when offered in powdered form. Remember, however, that the soil fills with water from the top down. Not until the top layer is saturated will the lower reaches be replenished. Therefore, if we were to feed our plants with a drip system right after a rain, the liquid nutrients would move right on down past the main root area and be wasted.

Because I want to encourage the growth of microbiotic life in the top 6 inches of my garden's soil, I use only organic liquid fertilizers. While there are others, I alternate between the standard fish emulsion and a kelp or seaweed emulsion as my supplemental nutrient sources. As I just mentioned, seaweed emulsion contains all the major and minor plant elements, all of the trace elements, vitamins, antibiotics, and other valuable chemicals a vegetable plant needs for a nutrient supplement. As an added benefit, research in South Africa has revealed that using kelp or seaweed emulsion as a liquid fertilizer significantly reduces nematode problems.

You can use homemade manure or compost tea in your drip system. It should be well strained, but it will be a good source of nitrogen. Manure tea offers the added benefit of containing just enough acid so that it tends to keep the drip lines and emitters free from any residue buildup.

When you use a drip system to apply liquid fertilizer, you are working with very dilute solutions, much more dilute than those used in foliar feeding. While different drip systems will vary, my drip system takes my liquid fertilizer mix and adds it to the water flowing in the drip lines at a ratio of 16 parts of water to 1 part of fertilizer. I mix my fertilizer with water at a ratio of about 1 cup of fertilizer to 1 gallon of water, or about a 6 percent solution. When you spread that over 200 square feet of soil, you are not in danger of overfeeding your plants. On the other hand, you are giving them a readily absorbed tonic or nutrient supplement that will make a definite improvement in their health and productivity.

There are no clear rules for determining the best frequency for drip feeding. Some gardeners give their plants a shot of liquid fertilizer every time they water. I use my fertilizer about once every two weeks. Then two or three times during the season, I give the garden a stronger solution (about three cups of fertilizer per gallon of water for 200 square feet). This is still pretty dilute after it is mixed with the water in the drip system, but plants can use an extra shot at times such as at bloom, crop setting, and maturing. I can't keep track of those stages for every vegetable I have in the garden, so I try to cover the whole group with periodic feedings. Because my liquid fertilizer is so dilute, it is not being wasted.

Feeding through a drip system is most effective if you apply the nutrients in the early part of the day. This gives the plants the whole day to absorb what they need. The exception is in the heat of the summer, when it is more important to water at noon or so to help keep soil temperatures down.

For the master gardener, drip feeding offers excellent opportunities to address the individual needs of plants at various times of the season. Research has shown that certain liquid nutrients are important in certain seasons.

Phosphorus is needed by plants in their early growth, but it is a difficult element for roots to extract from the cold soil in the spring.

In the summer, potassium and sometimes calcium are not taken up in sufficient quantities. All plants need the micronutrients that can be supplied with a liquid fertilizer through a drip system. At the same time, foliar feeding can be useful for applying nutrient supplements in stronger dosages to particular plants, such as tomatoes when they are in blossom. For general supplemental feeding though, the drip system is much more efficient than foliar feeding from the perspective of the gardener's time.

MAINTAINING THE DRIP IRRIGATION SYSTEM

Maintaining an emitter-type drip system is relatively simple. While emitters can get clogged for lots of reasons in large commercial settings, the backyard garden with a mulching system offers fewer opportunities for emitter clogging. One of the problems with the 60-Minute Garden design is that when the drip system is under black plastic and straw mulch, you can't easily see whether an emitter is clogged or not.

One of the reasons I have shutoff valves on every bed is so that when I am replanting a bed, or part of a bed, I can turn off all the other beds in my garden and run water just through the one drip line I am inspecting. I will look under the mulch, since I'm not disturbing any plants at that time, to check for clogged emitters. I find very few. I also use this opportunity to check the filter at the beginning of the feeder line as it enters the bed, to make sure there are no particles to be removed.

There are two ways to deal with a clogged emitter. You can unfasten the end clamp of the feeder line and run water through the line at normal 50 psi pressure. This flushing action will generally cure most clogged emitters. If you have a stubborn clog, you can simply remove the emitter, boil it in a pan of water for 10 minutes or so, and then replace it in the line, or you can remove

it and replace it with a new one for the cost of about five cents.

The drip system will have less problems with clogged emitters if it is used frequently. Even if you have a few weeks of lots of rain, eliminating the need for watering, it is a good idea to turn on your drip system every few days for a minute or two just to keep the lines from drying out too much around the emitters.

If you use a system that is made of flexible PVC tubing, you can leave your system installed permanently. You don't have to bring it in for the winter, even in the coldest parts of the country. The feeder lines will drain naturally through the emitters so that what little water is left in them will not be enough to swell and crack your tubing. The main supply line may need to be lifted so that it drains the majority of residual water before a serious freeze.

In the spring, you will want to flush all of your drip lines before setting them up for the next growing season. Again, this is done by removing the end piece of each feeder line. This step eliminates the low pressure control in the system and allows water to flow through the system at the normal 50 or 60 psi found in most city water systems. Check all your emitters to make sure they have not gotten clogged over the winter, and you are ready to start another growing season.

LOOKING TO THE FUTURE

Most Americans have been able to assume that, while taxes may go up and life seems to get more and more complicated, there will always be safe, clean water available every time we turn on the tap. In many parts of our country, that is no longer the case, and the future does not bode well for the water supply across the entire country. As water problems increase, drip irrigation should become more and more attractive to many vegetable gardeners as a good method for conserving increasingly scarce fresh water.

Some other developments in the future can be predicted. *Greywater,* already used in the washing machine and sink, is still an unproven resource for the vegetable garden because of the pathogens it can contain; however, this water coming from the kitchen and washroom is likely to become an important resource as fresh water becomes more expensive and scarce. The old rain cistern our grandparents used in the country may very well serve to provide us with an excellent source of water for our drip irrigation systems in the future.

Monitoring devices are already giving us tremendous help in managing the water needs of our gardens, yet there are improvements expected. There are devices to measure the moisture of the soil and devices to turn on and turn off the drip irrigation system. You can buy a rather expensive electronic rain gauge that gives you a remote reading in your kitchen of the last rainfall and tells how much rain has fallen in the past week or month. It is not very difficult to imagine putting all these components together and to be able to expect in the next few years a device that monitors the soil temperature, the air temperature, the wind velocity, and the amount of rain that has fallen in the past three days. The device will take that data and determine whether the garden needs to be watered, and if so, turn on the drip system for the necessary amount of time and then turn it off—all without your having to even be at home. This new device will not be exorbitantly expensive either. Technology will continue to find better ways to help those of us interested in achieving more self-reliance and in saving time.

GARDEN NOTES

DRIP IRRIGATION SYSTEM

There is not a whole lot of complexity in installing a drip irrigation system. If you use the PVC tubing with orifice emitters, then I strongly advise you to install your system when it is warm outside. The PVC is difficult to work with at temperatures below 40°F. Even in warm weather, a pot of hot water is a helpful aid for soaking the ends of the PVC parts to make them more pliable.

When you lay out your design, don't forget to take into consideration how the laterals in the beds will be attached to the main supply line. Will they stick out into the path? Will they go through the boards of the boxed beds or be installed over the edge of the boards? Make your measurements fairly carefully, taking into consideration overlap of the pieces. Otherwise you may have a part that doesn't quite reach to the next part. PVC is easy to cut and difficult to fix if it is cut too short.

CONSTRUCTION STEPS

1. Always begin laying out your drip system at the head. Assemble the various parts in the proper order: timer, backflow valve, pressure control valve, and filter.

2. Lay out all of your main supply lines, connecting the water supply to your garden with some extra at the end to be sure you have enough. Do not cut the supply line into all of its parts until you begin installing the laterals one by one.

3. Beginning with the bed closest to the head, install the laterals one by one so that the measurements of the lines between the connecting beds can be as accurate as possible.

4. Turn on your system to check for leaks.

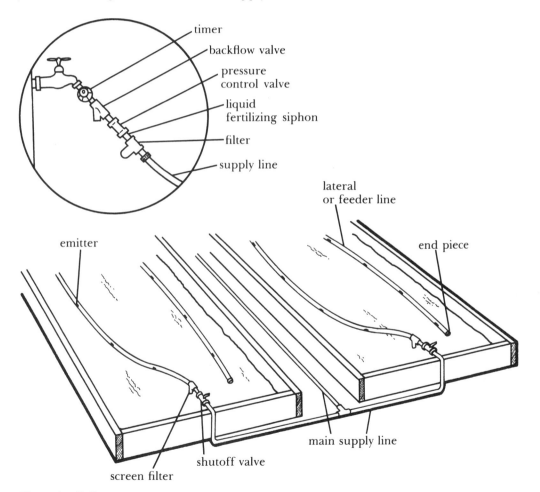

Illustration 7–3

GARDEN SINK

Building a garden sink is a project requiring some experience in working with wood. This design is functional while also being attractive, and you can add to this design if you wish. My garden sink incorporates as much practical storage space as possible, while still remaining relatively small and unobtrusive. You may wish to hang your trowels on the inside of the door or not have the back extending above the sink counter. I use my sink to store the electric fence controller, liquid fish emulsion, an extra soil thermometer, an air thermometer, a flashlight, twistums for the tomato vines, and a few other odds and ends. I have a rain gauge installed on the side, and my trowels hang from a covered rack on the back.

SHOPPING LIST

Lumber
1 pc. 1 × 8 × 8' clear pine board
16 lineal feet 2 × 2 pine (should be straight)
1 pc. 1½" × 8" × 8' pressure-treated plank
1 pc. 1 × 2 × 4' furring strip (for door jam)

Plywood
1 pc. 4' × 8' × ¾" outside-quality plywood (one surface good)

Hardware
1 small sink (including necessary faucets, drain, mounting devices)
50 flathead wood screws #10 or #12 × 1¾"
12 flathead wood screws #10 × 2½"
12 flathead wood screws #8 × 1¼"
2 hinges
door handle and a catch of some sort
	Total cost: $75

TOOLS

Drill with bits
Measuring tape
Saw
Screwdriver
Several wrenches

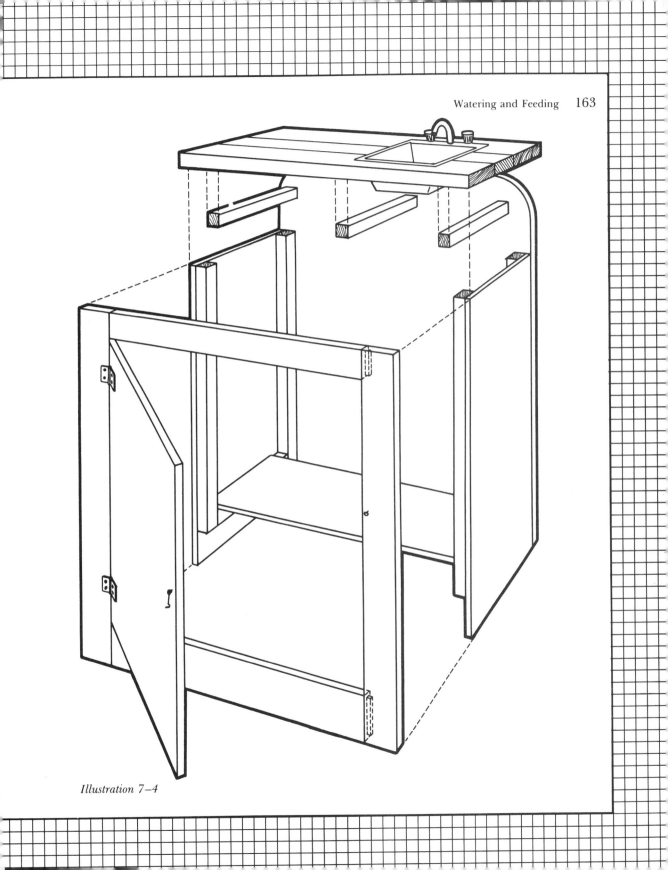

Illustration 7–4

CUTTING LIST

Size	Piece	Quantity
Plank		
2 × 8 × 3'	Countertop	2
2 × 5 × 2'	Countertop	1
Plywood		
2'8" × 3'6" (grain crosswise)	Back	1
1'4½" × 2'10½" (grain lengthwise)	Sides of sink	2
2'1¾" × 2'3¼" (grain lengthwise)	Door	1
1'1½" × 2'6½" (grain lengthwise)	Bottom	1
Misc.		
2 × 2 × 2'6½"	Inner posts	4
2 × 2 × 1'1½"	Countertop cleats	3
1 × 2 × 2'3½"	Door jam	1
1 × 2 × 1'1½"	Bottom cleats	2
Door frame		
1" × 2'10½" × 3" (finished width)	Sides of frame	2
1" × 2'3½" × 3" (finished width)	Top of frame	1
1" × 2'3½" × 4" (finished width)	Bottom of frame	1

CONSTRUCTION STEPS

1. Make the door frame using the mortise and tenon method for joining the corners. This gives you a door frame with an outside dimension that is 2 feet 8 inches wide and 2 feet 10½ inches high. The inside dimension will be 2 feet 2 inches wide and 2 feet 3½ inches high.

2. Attach the inner posts to the sink's plywood sideboards. Use five 1¾-inch wood screws to secure each inner post flush with the top and sides of the sideboards.

3. Attach bottom cleats to the sideboards. Using four 1¼-inch number 8 wood screws on each cleat, attach them to the sideboards, between the two inner posts and flush with the bottom of each inner post.

4. Attach the back to the two sides. Using five 1¾-inch screws in each inner post, attach the back to the two side pieces so that the back is flush with the bottoms of each of the side pieces.

5. Attach the door frame to two side pieces using five 1¾-inch screws in each inner post.

6. Attach the door jam. Rip the 1 × 2 × 2'3½" piece to be 1¼ inch wide, finished dimension. With four 1¼-inch screws,

fasten this piece to the inside of the door frame flush with the door opening to provide a jam for the door to rest against. This jam will be opposite the side where the hinges will be attached.

7.   Mount the door with a clearance of ⅛ inch all around by fastening the hinges at the desired locations on the door. Then install the handle and the door catch of your choice.

8.   With a saber saw round off the top corners of the back of the sink if you desire.

9.   For the sink countertop, cut the two 3-foot long planks. If you have a jointer available, you should joint the edges to make sure they will fit together tightly. Rip the remaining piece of plank to a width of 5 inches and joint the edges.

10.   Assemble the three pieces of countertop, as in illustration 7–4, after determining the location of the sink hole. This procedure allows you to determine the dimensions of the two pieces to be cut from the plank that is 5 inches wide.

11.   Reassemble the four pieces of the countertop, upside down so that they can be fastened together. Set the three countertop cleats according to illustration 7–4 so that the two outer cleats will fit between the inner posts and the side pieces of the sink. Fasten the cleats to the four pieces of the countertop with 12 2½-inch number 10 screws.

12.   Trace out the exact dimensions of the sink hole and cut it out with a saber saw.

13.   Assemble the sink countertop on to the sink cabinet with two sets of three 1¾-inch screws through the sideboards into the countertop cleats and with four screws into the countertop itself from the back of the sink.

14.   Place the bottom of the cabinet on to the bottom cleats. I did not screw this down so that I could get pipes and electrical wires in and out of the sink easily.

15.   Attach your sink to a water system and, if desired, hook it up to electricity.

CHAPTER 8

BACKYARD INTEGRATED
PEST MANAGEMENT

There is nothing in the gardener's world that is more discouraging and frustrating than to come out one morning and find that the whole crop of beans or cabbage has been seriously damaged by insects or rabbits or some other dastardly pest that has invaded the sanctity of the vegetable patch. First, there is a feeling of helplessness in preventing such an attack, and that is followed by a feeling of anger and a deep desire to wipe out that pest from the face of the earth if not at least from your garden. Insect and four-legged pests can be a major problem in any backyard vegetable garden, even to the point of discouraging you from having a garden at all. Pest problems don't have to be so catastrophic and destructive. In the 60-Minute Garden, pests are viewed from a slightly different perspective than pests found in the traditional vegetable garden.

With regard to personal health, we are discovering that it is cheaper to spend some money to keep well (by exercising properly and by eating well) than it is to wait to get sick and then spend money to treat the sickness. Likewise, in the 60-Minute Garden, it is cheaper and more effective to prevent insect and other pest problems than it is to wait until disaster has struck. The first challenge for the gardener is to get rid of the idea that there should be *no* pest damage in the garden whatsoever. A few holes in the bean plant leaves don't hurt a thing. It's when there are no leaves left because of insect attack that one should worry. In fact, research has shown that vegetable plants with moderate insect damage tend to produce higher yields than plants with no damage at all. The plants apparently compensate for the mild damage by shooting more energy into their systems as a defense. This reaction tends to increase the plant's productivity.

The point is, the healthy vegetable garden has both good guys and bad guys living in balance in your backyard ecosystem. The bad guys are kept in control by the predators or good guys. Traditional attitudes about insects are that any insect pest in the garden is one pest too many. The approach was to eradicate the entire population of insect pests rather than simply control them. By eradicating the pests, the predators, or good guys, were also eradicated. The garden was made defenseless from new attacks because of the gardener's lack of understanding of how nature works. Backyard *integrated pest management* (IPM) is a combination of biological, physical, and natural chemical insect control methods appropriate to the problem at hand. Backyard IPM is concerned with *controlling* pests rather than *eradicating* or *exterminating* pests—a very different approach from the traditional one.

You need to have some aphids in the garden at all times, or the lady beetles would have nothing to eat. We simply want to keep the aphid population down to a level that causes only an allowable level of damage to our vegetables, while keeping a healthy balance of pests and predators existing in our garden's ecosystem.

Backyard IPM is a process that takes very little time because it takes advantage of naturally occurring pest controls such as the weather, disease agents, predators, and parasites. It utilizes various biological, physical, and natural chemical methods to control rather than eradicate pest problems in the garden. IPM uses three broad steps to control pests: identifying your particular pest problem, establishing some ability to monitor those problems, and using control measures specific to those particular problems in your very own garden.

TEN STEPS TO INTEGRATED PEST MANAGEMENT

The 60-Minute Garden IPM system involves ten steps a gardener can take. They are listed below in the order of priority from the best prevention activities to the steps of last resort to save the crop. The philosophy is that it is better to prevent insect damage than to have to fight it after the pests have arrived. The last two steps then are taken only when the other steps have failed. My experience has shown that after a few years of this approach, the last two steps of using sprays and botanical poisons are seldom necessary. The ten steps are:

1. Maintain garden hygiene
2. Rotate crops
3. Build soil health
4. Use interplanting and companion planting
5. Learn pest emergence times and habits
6. Use pest- and disease-resistant varieties
7. Use biological controls
8. Use physical controls
9. Use natural sprays
10. Use botanical poisons

Don't be alarmed at the length of this list. It is not as complicated as it may sound. Becoming comfortable and skillful in using all these steps effectively will take a number of years, and that is okay. Most beginning gardeners start with step 11, which is not even on my list. This step is to use chemical insecticides designed to wipe out *all* of the bugs within striking distance. In my opinion, steps 1 through 8 yield far better results in the long run, but they take a number of years to begin to have their full impact. In addition, these steps take less time every year as their impact is felt. The first four steps have been discussed in some detail earlier in this book, so I'll just summarize their role in pest control and management.

TABLE 8–1

──────────── *INSECT PESTS AND DETERRENT PLANTINGS* ────────────

INSECT PEST	DETERRENT PLANTING
Cabbage looper	Garlic
	Onions
	Rosemary
	Sage
Cucumber beetle	Marigolds
	Nasturtiums
	Radishes
Cutworm	Onions
Corn borer	Sunflowers as trap
Flea beetle	Mint
Leafhopper	Geraniums
	Petunias
Mexican bean beetle	French marigolds
Squash bug	Marigolds
	Radishes
	Tansies

GARDEN HYGIENE

As discussed in chapter 5, garden hygiene means simply keeping the garden in a condition that minimizes the opportunities for insects to breed and multiply. No piles of rotting weeds or vegetable refuse should be allowed to lie around the garden; no stagnant water or piles of rotting wood or objects that can harbor insects underneath should be allowed. Some insects will dwell under mulch, but most of them are harmless, and those particular pests can be controlled in other ways.

CROP ROTATION

Also discussed in chapter 5, crop rotation helps in pest control even in a small garden. Moving the crops around not only discourages disease, but it also confuses the insects and keeps concentrations of insect pest populations from building up.

GOOD SOIL HEALTH

Good healthy soil produces healthy plants, and healthy plants are a form of insect repellent. Insect pests tend to attack plants that are weakened for some reason such as poor soil conditions, unbalanced nutrients, lack of water, or disease. As noted in chapter 6, good soil will maintain an active microlife in the first 6 inches of soil, which will include all kinds of predators that will attack insect-pest larvae when they are wintering over. Every predator you can maintain saves you time in pest control later.

INTERPLANTING AND COMPANION PLANTING

Chapter 6 covers this subject in some detail. By planting many different plants mixed among each other, we confuse the insect pest, which often uses its sense of smell to find its target plant. By giving it lots of different smells along with the smell of the target plant, we greatly reduce the damage caused by the pest.

PEST EMERGENCE TIMES

The first four steps in the IPM process deal in general with the condition of the entire garden and are directed toward preventing all insect problems with no focus on individual species of insect pest. Now we get to IPM in your particular garden. Most be-

ginning gardeners are overwhelmed by the problems of insect control. They know there are hundreds and thousands of insect varieties, so how can they possibly deal with them all? That is of course an erroneous image of the situation. Few vegetable gardens have more than five to ten insect pests, causing what could become serious damage. Of those, in a healthy garden, only three to five are particularly serious threats to the crop.

When you realize that the numbers of insect pests are not so overwhelming, then you can begin to imagine learning enough about those few bad guys so that you can control the situation. Every book on insect pests gives hundreds of different worms, bugs, and beetles that can supposedly raise havoc with your crops. The fact of the matter is that most of those insects don't even live in your area, since most books must try to cover all the insect problems across the entire country. So, your first task is to identify the pests in your particular backyard.

TABLE 8–2

INSECT PEST EMERGENCE TIMES

INSECT PEST	EMERGENCE PERIOD
Asparagus beetle	Late April through June
Bean aphid	May and June
Cabbage looper	May through July
Colorado potato beetle	April through June
Corn earworm	July and August
Japanese beetle	June and July
Mexican bean beetle	May and June
Pea aphid	April and May
Spotted cucumber beetle	May and June
Squash bug	May and June
Squash vine borer	June and July
Striped cucumber beetle	May and June
Striped flea beetle	April and May
Tomato hornworm	June through August

Note: First, determine if the pest is even in your neighborhood. Second, narrow down these ranges to at least a two-week period.

IDENTIFYING THE BAD GUYS

If you are an experienced gardener, you probably already know the five to ten insect pests that occasionally attack your little garden kingdom. If you are a beginner and can't figure out why your spinach is laced with holes, you can't find a solution to the problem until you identify the source—the insect pest making the holes. I suggest three steps to insect identification. First, buy a good book with lots of color photographs of insect pests (see the Bibliography). Secondly, if that doesn't work, talk to friends or neighbors who have vegetable gardens. The chances are fair to good that they have had the same problem and figured out a solution years ago. Finally, if all else fails, then call your county agricultural extension agent. He or she can often identify the insect just from your description over the phone. If that doesn't get the answer, the county agent may come to see you or ask you to bring a specimen to the office. Either way, the agent will know which bug is ventilating your spinach.

I can't emphasize enough the importance of accurately identifying your insect pests. Without good identification, the rest of IPM becomes more difficult to apply effectively. Don't try to identify every bug in your garden. Just worry about those that are doing damage. As you get to know how to deal with them, you will reduce or eliminate that particular insect problem, and you can move on to the next one. Remember, I am not talking about dozens of bad bugs—just three to five insects that represent your "most wanted dead or alive" list.

INSECT PEST EMERGENCE TIMES

Many gardeners don't realize that insects appear or emerge in their garden about the same time every year, year in and year out. The differences from year to year are in days not weeks. Their emergence is dependent on temperature, moisture, and the availability of food, and those conditions occur in your garden pretty predictably each year, plus or minus a few days. See table 8–2, which gives you some indication of when you might start looking for some of the most common insect pests in your area.

If you know when the bad guys will be arriving in your garden, then you are in a much better position to do something about repelling or controlling them. One of the benefits of using a home computer for managing the garden (see chapter 9) is the ease in keeping track of insect emergence times each year. I know when my Japanese beetles emerge every year. It is a few days on either side of June 2. So I have my Japanese beetle bug bag all mounted and primed with fresh attractant, so as those voracious bugs emerge from my lawn, a large percentage of them are immediately trapped and killed. I have few problems with Japanese beetles because I no longer have to wait until they become a serious problem before I begin my control activities.

INSECT MONITORING TRAPS

While plain old observation skills are a good way to spot the emergence of a particular insect pest, monitoring traps are starting to come on the market that will help us with this task and save us some time as well. If you know you have a particular insect, then in some cases it is possible to build or buy a little trap that will catch it when it first emerges, giving you that important emergence date.

RESISTANT VARIETIES

Once you know you have a problem with a certain insect, sometimes you can find a variety of the vulnerable vegetable that is resistant to that insect. A good example is the cucumber beetle. It can leave a virus that will wipe out your cucumbers in short order. There are now a number of cucumber varieties that are resistant to that virus. Table 8–3 gives a list of resistant varieties of vegetables. This is by no means an exhaustive list because there are new varieties coming out every year. One of the tips I give in chapter 9 regarding garden management is to keep a record of a new variety if it happens to be resistant to some problem you are struggling with this year. Next year you can get that new resistant variety.

Some insect problems can also be avoided by simply planting a particular variety when the insect is not active. Some crops planted in the early spring or late fall will avoid a particular insect problem. Whiteflies and aphids prefer warm weather and can be controlled somewhat if their host plant is grown in cooler times of the year. This is not always possible for all vegetables, such as tomatoes, but for zucchini I find that my late crop has fewer problems than my spring crop. The squash borer has run its course by September in my neighborhood.

BIOLOGICAL CONTROLS

Biological controls include a whole range of natural resources that are available to most gardeners. These include viruses, bacteria, predator or beneficial insects, birds,

TABLE 8–3

———— DISEASE-RESISTANT VARIETIES ————

CROP	VARIETY	DISEASE RESISTANCE
Beans, bush green	Blue Lake 14	Mosaic
	Provider	Mosaic, rust
	Romano 14	Rust
	Tendercrop	Mosaic
	Tenderette	Mosaic
Beans, bush lima	Thaxter	Downy mildew
Beans, bush wax	Kinghorn Wax	Mosaic
Beans, pole green	Kentucky Wonder 191	Rust
Cabbage	Golden Acre	Yellows
	Harris Danish	Yellows
	King Cole	Yellows
	Market Prize	Yellows
	Market Victor	Yellows
	Regina	Yellows
	Stonehead	Yellows
Corn	Golden Beauty	Bacterial wilt
	Golden Cross Bantam	Bacterial wilt
	Narrowgrain Evergreen	Bacterial wilt
	White Jewel	Bacterial wilt
Cucumbers	Belle Aire	Anthracnose, downy mildew, mosaic, powdery mildew, scab

(continued)

TABLE 8–3—*Continued*

CROP	VARIETY	DISEASE RESISTANCE
Cucumbers—*continued*	Bush Champion	Mosaic
	Gemini	Anthracnose, downy mildew, mosaic, powdery mildew, scab
	Marketmore 70	Mosaic, scab
	Pioneer	Anthracnose, downy mildew, mosaic, powdery mildew, scab
	Spacemaster	Mosaic, scab
	Tablegreen 65	Mosaic, scab
	Victory	Anthracnose, downy mildew, mosaic, powdery mildew, scab
Lettuce, romaine	Valmaine	Downy mildew
Muskmelons	Delicious 51	Fusarium wilt
	Harper Hybrid	Fusarium wilt
	Progress No. 9	Fusarium wilt
Peppers	Bell Boy	Mosaic
	Midway	Mosaic
	Pennbell	Mosaic
	Staddon's Select	Mosaic
	Yolo Wonder	Mosaic
Radishes	Scarlet Knight	Fusarium wilt
Spinach	Early Hybrid No. 7	Downy mildew, mosaic
	Hybrid 612	Downy mildew, mosaic
	Virginia Savoy	Mosaic
	Winter Bloomsdale	Blight
Tomatoes	Beefmaster	Fusarium wilt, root-knot, verticillium wilt
	Burpee VF	Fusarium wilt, verticillium wilt
	Gardener	Fusarium wilt, verticillium wilt
	Jet Star Hybrid	Fusarium wilt, verticillium wilt
	Roma VF	Fusarium wilt, verticillium wilt
	Small Fry Cherry	Fusarium wilt, root-knot, verticillium wilt
	Spring Giant	Fusarium wilt, verticillium wilt
	Superman Hybrid	Fusarium wilt, verticillium wilt
	Supersonic	Fusarium wilt, verticillium wilt
	Vineripe VFN	Fusarium wilt, root-knot, verticillium wilt
Watermelons	Charleston Gray	Anthracnose, fusarium wilt
	Petite Sweet	Anthracnose, fusarium wilt
	Summer Festival	Anthracnose, fusarium wilt
	You-Sweet-Thing	Anthracnose, fusarium wilt

and even toads. The principle of biological control is simple. The more beneficial predators of insect pests you have in your garden, the fewer insect pests can be found in your 60-Minute Garden. At the same time, it is critical that you have *some* insect pests so the predators have something to eat; otherwise they will go away. And even more important to the 60-Minute Gardener, these helpers work day and night saving you the time and bother of having to deal with insect pests.

MICRO PALS

Just as with humans, insect pests are vulnerable to many diseases. These are often caused by microbes or microfauna, which include viruses, bacteria, fungi, protozoa, and nematodes. These are the organisms that are smaller than the insect pest and often reproduce inside them. Many of these micro pals exist in healthy well-balanced soil, so

TABLE 8–4

COMMON INSECT PESTS AND THEIR PHYSICAL OR BIOLOGICAL CONTROLS

INSECT PEST	PHYSICAL OR BIOLOGICAL CONTROL
Aphid	Dormant oil
Cabbage looper	*Bacillus thuringiensis*
Colorado potato beetle	Handpick
Corn earworm	*Bacillus thuringiensis*
Cutworm	*Bacillus thuringiensis*
Harlequin bug	Keep weeds down
Hornworm	*Bacillus thuringiensis*
	Handpick
Imported cabbageworm	*Bacillus thuringiensis*
Japanese beetle	Handpick
	Milky spore disease
Leaf miner	Burn infected parts
Mexican bean beetle	Handpick
Mite	Dormant oil
Nematode	Increase humus
	Plant marigolds
	Rotate crops
Root maggot	Don't use manure
Scale	Dormant oil
Squash vine borer	Dig out of vine
	Burn infested vines
	Till in late fall
Thrips	Dormant oil
Whitefly	Dormant oil
White grub	Milky spore disease

TABLE 8–5

COMMON INSECT PESTS
AND THEIR INSECT PREDATORS

INSECT PEST	INSECT PREDATOR
Aphid	Aphidius wasp
	Green lacewing larva
	Lady beetle
Cabbage looper	Trichogramma wasp
Colorado potato beetle	Praying mantis
Corn borer	Lady beetle
	Trichogramma wasp
Corn earworm	Trichogramma wasp
Cucumber beetle	Praying mantis
	Soldier beetle
Cutworm	Ground beetle
Hornworm	Apanteles wasp
	Braconid wasp
Leafhopper	Green lacewing larva
Mexican bean beetle	*Pediobius foveolatus*
	Praying mantis
	Predator mite
Mite	Lady beetle
	Minute pirate bug
Scale	Chalcid wasp
	Lady beetle
Squash bug	Praying mantis
Thrips	Green lacewing larva
	Lady beetle
	Minute pirate bug
Whitefly	*Encarsia formosa* parasite
	Lady beetle
White grub	Ground beetle

that many larvae of insect pests never see the light of day because they were done in before they could emerge. One of the major benefits for having a healthy soil maintained by organic principles is that a good number of our potential insect pests are controlled without our ever knowing it.

At the same time, we have been developing the ability to introduce some of these microbes into our yards and gardens to attack particular pest problems. One pathogenic bacterium that is approved for use in this country by the United States Department of Agriculture is *Bacillus thuringiensis*, known as BT. It is available under such tradenames as Biotrol, Dipel, and Thuricide. It is a naturally occurring bacteria that causes disease in certain caterpillars, including the cabbageworm, the tomato hornworm, and many other garden pests. Gardeners dust BT onto infested plants, and when caterpillars eat it, BT enters the insect's stomach and penetrates the lining. It then multiplies in the bloodstream. The caterpillar stops feeding, becomes paralyzed, and gradually weakens and grows sick until it finally dries up and dies. BT is harmless to humans, other warm-blooded animals, and other insects.

Another micro buddy is *Bacillus popilliae,* called the milky spore disease. It is very effective against bad infestations of Japanese beetles, while being harmless to everything else. Considerable research is being done to find more microbes that are effective against certain insect pests but harmless to humans, other animals, and most other insects.

Illustration 8–1: Birds in your backyard will capture thousands of insect pests for their young.

BENEFICIAL INSECTS

You can easily acquire bugs from a mail-order house these days. Garden magazines carry advertisements for companies offering lady beetles, praying mantises, and numerous other insect predators guaranteed to rid your garden of insect pests. Unfortunately, this is an area for the buyer to beware. A great deal of money is spent and wasted in purchasing predator insects for controlling pests in the garden.

The prowess of the lady beetle and the praying mantis in devouring untold numbers of other insects is generally well-known. Lady beetles are particularly good in fighting aphids, and praying mantises will eat anything, even the beneficial insects. The biggest problem is keeping these hired guns in your own yard instead of spreading all over the neighborhood and into the next town.

I do not particularly recommend purchasing beneficial predator insects for dealing with pests problems outdoors in the vegetable garden (they do have some value in a greenhouse environment). If you wish to try this technique, you should read about the procedures very carefully and even then you have no guarantee of keeping the predators in your yard.

My approach is to offer an environment in my backyard that is varied and healthy, in the belief that predators will come in and hang around because of the positive environment and a steady source of food—that is, insect pests. I don't have lots of lady beetles, but I have some. I have not seen a praying mantis in my yard in several years, but I wouldn't be surprised to find one. I know I have lots of spiders, and I assume I have other insect predators that I never even see. I am fairly confident that I have a good population of predators because I don't have any serious populations of insect pests. Consequently, I don't spend any money buying boxes of lady beetles or praying mantises. I don't believe I need to.

BIRDS

One of the most overlooked controls for insect pests is the songbird. This delightful creature is an insect-controlling machine. A house wren can kill 800 to 1,000 insects in a day during the 12 weeks it is feeding its young. An oriole was seen eating more than 100 caterpillars in less than one hour! Many of us feed birds in the winter because we don't want them to go hungry; however, few gardeners have ever considered actually

TABLE 8–6

COMMON INSECT PESTS
AND THEIR BIRD PREDATORS

INSECT PEST	BIRD PREDATOR
Aphid	Chickadee
	Purple finch
	Warbler
Cabbage looper	Robin
	Sparrow
	Starling
Colorado potato beetle	Chickadee
	Purple finch
	Robin
Cucumber beetle	Purple finch
	Sparrow
	Warbler
Cutworm	Robin
	Sparrow
	Wren
Flea beetle	Chickadee
	Purple finch
	Warbler
Japanese beetle	Starling
Leafhopper	Purple finch
	Sparrow
	Wren
Leaf miner	Chickadee
	Purple finch
	Robin
Root maggot	Sparrow
	Starling
	Wren
Slug	Robin
	Starling
White grub	Cardinal
	Robin
	Starling

TABLE 8–7

WINTER FEEDING PREFERENCES OF BIRDS

BIRD	FOOD
Cardinal	Cracked corn, sunflower seeds
Catbird	Fresh fruits, raisins
Chickadee	Peanut butter mixes, sunflower seeds
Finch	Sunflower seeds, thistle seeds
Mockingbird	Fresh fruit, raisins
Nuthatch	Peanut butter mixes, suet, sunflower seeds
Purple finch	Sunflower seeds
Sparrow	Peanut hearts, white proso millet
Starling	Cracked corn, fresh fruit, peanut butter mixes, peanut hearts, raisins, suet, sunflower seeds, thistle seeds, white proso millet
Warbler	Fresh fruit, raisins

managing their backyard bird population in order to control insect pests in their garden. The design of the 60-Minute Garden not only attracts birds into its little ecological niche, but there is deliberate effort to increase the population density of birds in the garden compared to other areas in the neighborhood. This is a new idea!

The more birds you have that consider your garden as their territory, the fewer insect pests you will find throughout the growing season and the less time you will need to spend worrying about bugs. The average density of birds in this country is three birds per acre. Some people have increased that density to over 80 birds per acre by doing everything they can to provide an attractive environment for birds all year long. While the basic needs of birds are water, food, cover, and nesting sites, it is the diversity of these resources in your backyard that gives you a healthy and active bird population. Diversity of plant life around the garden, a variety of all kinds of insects (beneficial and pest), and many species of birds create a situation where insect problems in the vegetable garden are generally reduced. The winter birds will work

on thinning out the egg masses of insects, and the summer birds control the larvae and the adult insects in your backyard territory.

In my garden plan I include specific activities designed to increase the population of selected species of birds, commonly found in most backyards. Table 8–6 gives the most common birds that are particularly effective in controlling insect pests in your vegetable garden. I do everything I can to attract these particular species. I don't harm the other species, but I don't encourage them either.

BIRD MANAGEMENT PLAN

For those birds on my preferred list of beneficial predators that stay with us in the winter, I know which foods they prefer and that is what I offer in my feeders. Other birds enjoy the same foods, but I am sure of attracting numbers of my predator friends. Table 8–7 gives some of these foods.

In the spring, when most people stop feeding the birds entirely, I continue to feed my birds but at a reduced rate to avoid their complete dependence on me for their food. Also, in the spring I clean out the 11 bird-houses I have in the trees around my back-

Photo 8–1: This charming bird house sits just above the apple fence. The wren tenants raise several families each summer and eat thousands of insects in the process.

yard. These houses are designed especially for our selected predator species. Different species have different preferences for housing.

The birdhouse design at the end of the chapter (see illustration 8–5) gives you a chance to make slight adjustments to its size and to the position of the entrance in order to make the birdhouse attractive to a number of favored bird predators. The birdhouse should be mounted so that you can easily clean it each spring, since many birds will ignore a house that is full of last year's nest.

Each spring I also add a few more shrubs and plantings that I know are attractive to my bird buddies. And, as the late spring and breeding season arrive, I generally stop filling my bird feeders, but I have at least two birdbaths in and around my vegetable patch to give my birds a steady source of water. This is particularly critical in the hot summer months. I have one birdbath set at ground level with an emitter in my drip

irrigation system sitting over it to keep it filled. I set this out in the open so the cat can't get any special advantage from cover that might be too close.

Most people don't realize that most of the seed eaters, like the common sparrow, become voracious insect hunters during breeding season because they must have insects to feed their young. So those finches and sparrows that huddle around your feeder in the winter will be gathering aphids, various larvae, and many insect pests for their ever-hungry babies. It is a very nice coincidence that the breeding period of all birds happens to be the same time you have the most insects available in the garden.

All insects are not vulnerable to our feathered friends. Whiteflies have no bird predator that I know of, but aphids, cabbageworms, and all of the garden moths sure do. Japanese beetles are not considered a delicacy by most birds, but the ubiquitous and often maligned starlings and grackles will eat Japanese beetles with relish.

I've been managing my bird population for four years now, and I don't think it is an accident that I have not had a bad insect problem of any kind since then. I know that the other IPM activities also contribute to my lack of insect attacks, but I know that the birds carry their share of the load because I spend many moments throughout the gardening season watching them flit in and out of my garden to their nests and back again. I've seen as many as 30 birds in my garden at one time, and there are seldom moments when there are not at least a few sparrows or robins patrolling their territory in amongst my vegetables.

Later in this chapter you'll see that birds can become pests, as well, but there are measures you can take to prevent these problems (see illustration 8–3).

CHICKENS

Most backyard gardeners don't have chickens, but there are some vegetable gar-

BIRDS IN YOUR VEGETABLE GARDEN

Numerous birds have a positive impact in terms of controlling insect pests in your vegetable garden and backyard orchard. There are four categories of birds, according to how they find the insects they eat. Some birds feed while in flight. Some are bark gleaners, and others are foliage gleaners. And, there are birds that eat what they find on the ground.

BIRDS THAT FEED IN FLIGHT

Birds that eat in flight dine on gypsy moths, cabbageworm moths, codling moths, cankerworm moths, leaf rollers, locusts, leafhoppers, aphids, horseflies, winged ants, butterflies, and beetles. Included in this group are the following birds:

Catbirds
Flycatchers
Mockingbirds
Phoebes
Purple martins
Swallows
Vireos

BIRDS THAT ARE BARK GLEANERS

Several birds are helpful in an orchard because they eat insects found on the bark, including bark borers, hibernating insects such as codling moths, trunk borers, plant lice, and bark lice. These birds include the following:

Chickadees
Nuthatches
Warblers
Woodpeckers
Wrens

BIRDS THAT ARE FOLIAGE GLEANERS

Foliage gleaners feast on leafhoppers, aphids, leaf rollers, leaf miners, cankerworms, cutworms, hairy caterpillars, tent caterpillars, gypsy moth larvae, Colorado potato beetles, and flea beetles. These birds include the following:

Baltimore orioles
Blackbirds
Catbirds
Chickadees
Crows
Nuthatches
Purple finches
Warblers

BIRDS THAT ARE GROUND EATERS

Ground eaters may eat beetles, rootworms, leafhoppers, aphids, cutworms, cabbageworms, root maggots, grasshoppers, chinch bugs, white grubs, root borers, ants, root lice, and June bugs. These birds include the following:

Blackbirds
Bluebirds
Cardinals
Catbirds
Chipping sparrows
Crows
Phoebes
Purple finches
Song sparrows
Starlings
Vireos
Warblers
Woodpeckers
Wrens

deners who do have these insect-eating machines on their property or next door. I mention chickens because they are incredibly thorough devastators of virtually all insect larvae and eggs in the first 1 or 2 inches of garden soil. The problem, of course, is teaching the chickens not to eat your vegetables and to stick to scratching the soil for pesky bugs and caterpillars. One solution is to use the tunnel device again, only this time for controlling a couple of chickens. You can use the same bird netting you use to keep birds out of the strawberries to keep chickens *inside* a particular bed. You can set this temporary chicken coop up in a bed or in part of a bed and allow two or three chickens to function as veritable garden tillers. You can use chickens in the spring to work over a bed before planting it, or you can use them in the fall to clean out a bed before getting it ready for the winter. Either way, the chicken-cage device allows you to keep the cacklers away from your vegetable plants and focused exclusively on the piece of soil you want worked over by their great appetites for bugs and worms.

TOADS

Toads can eat over 100 insects a day during the growing season, so if you are lucky enough to have a toad in your vegetable garden, you want to do what you can to make it comfortable for the entire season. In just one season, your toad could knock off more than 10,000 insects free of charge. Toads like cutworms, caterpillars, beetles, sow bugs, squash bugs, slugs, grasshoppers, grubs, moths, and other insect pests. With a food preference list like that, every vegetable garden should have a whole toad family, and you can. While toads are not found in all parts of the country, in those sections where they do reside, the gardener can build a little toad house and give toads a shallow "pond" for the water they must have to survive.

A toad house is easy to make. The

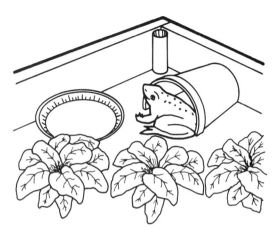

Illustration 8–2: A toad is perfectly happy living in a flowerpot that has been partially buried in the garden's soil.

timid toad simply needs to be protected from the summer sun in some cozy shady abode. So, a clay flowerpot half buried on its side makes an ideal toad house. The pond can be nothing more than a pie plate or other shallow dish set into the soil and kept filled with water. As with the birdbath, just place one of the emitters from your drip irrigation system over the pie plate, and you don't have to worry about remembering to keep it filled.

PHYSICAL CONTROLS

There are all kinds of physical controls that have been developed over the years to keep down and repel the population of insect pests in the vegetable garden. Some are more effective than others, but they are all worth considering if you are having a serious problem with a particular insect. I divide physical controls into three categories: handpicking, traps, and barriers.

HANDPICKING BUGS

If your IPM program is working well, you will still have a few insect pests among your vegetable prizes, but they should be few in numbers. Very often, what is left over after the birds, toads, and the beneficial insects have done their job can be picked off your plants by hand. Mexican bean beetles, Colorado potato beetles, and asparagus beetles are examples of pests that can be handpicked since they are fairly easy to spot.

The time to handpick your insect pests is early in their season before they can do much damage, so knowing their emergence times is a great help in alerting you to start looking for particular culprits.

TRAPPING THE INSECT PEST

You can use traps for two purposes. As I described earlier, you can trap to signal the arrival of an insect so that you can use other means of control, or you can try to trap the insect in sufficient numbers so that the trapping is in fact controlling the insect pest population. As I mentioned above, I use commercial Japanese beetle traps to actually control my beetle population. There are a number of traps to consider for actual control of certain pests.

Some gardeners have trouble with earwigs damaging young seedlings. These bugs are easily trapped by laying pieces of old garden hose around the bed where you are having a problem. Each day you can pick up those pieces of hose and dump their contents into a jar. You will reduce your earwig population pretty quickly with this technique.

Slugs can be trapped a number of ways. The traditional beer and pie plate trap is the most common device. A shallow dish or pie plate is set flush into the soil with a cup or so of beer in it. The slugs are attracted to the yeast in the beer and drown. Slugs work at night, so they seek cool shade during the day. You can trap them under boards, under overturned grapefruit rinds, or almost anything else that gives them protection. In the next section I'll describe a barrier for slugs.

Whiteflies can be a real problem in the garden, and they don't seem to be on the menu of any of the birds in my neighborhood. One trap, used effectively by greenhouse owners, is an object or a board painted bright yellow, about the same color as the common school bus yellow. The whitefly just loves that color and will land on that yellow surface when it is nearby. The trap is created simply by coating the yellow surface with a sticky substance such as min-

TABLE 8–8

EFFECTIVE TRAPS FOR COMMON INSECT PESTS

INSECT PEST	TRAP
Aphid	Sticky yellow board
Cabbage looper	Sprinkle with flour or salt
Corn earworm	Black light
Japanese beetle	Trap with sex lure
Nematode	Plant trap crops
Slug	Beer or yeast trap
	Trap under boards
Squash bug	Trap under boards
Whitefly	Sticky yellow board

eral oil, car oil, or a commercial product such as Tanglefoot. Every few days wipe off the layer of whiteflies stuck fast to the board and recoat your trap. This trap is most effective early in the season when the whiteflies are just getting started. Hang your yellow traps as close to the target plant as you can to be most effective.

SETTING UP BARRIERS FOR BUGS

If you know when to expect a certain insect pest each year (because you know about the mysterious emergence times I've been talking about), you can set up barriers to prevent them from actually getting to their target plants. The following describes a number of barriers that work very well against some pests.

SCREENS

The 60-Minute Garden is particularly adapted to making use of screening devices in many parts of the garden. There are several kinds of screens that have been described in other parts of this book. The design for the screen cloche is found at the end of chapter 6 (see illustration 6–7).

First let's talk again about birds. While having lots of birds living in and around the garden can be terrific for controlling pest insects, those very same friends can become pests themselves if you have a strawberry patch or just after you planted your corn. The simple solution is to screen off the strawberry patch or the corn patch, using the tunnel system described in chapter 3, so that the birds can't get near it. Instead of covering the ribs of the tunnel with clear plastic, use plastic bird netting. This makes your strawberry patch or corn patch free of

TABLE 8–9

BARRIER DETERRENTS FOR COMMON INSECT PESTS

INSECT PEST	BARRIER
Aphid	Reflective mulch
Cabbage looper	Diatomaceous earth
	Netting for moth
Cucumber beetle	Netting
	Wood ashes
Cutworm	Collar around base
	Diatomaceous earth
	Wood ashes
Flea beetle	Diatomaceous earth
Leafhopper	Netting
Leaf miner	Netting
Root maggot	Wood ashes in soil
Slug	Copper strip on bed
	Diatomaceous earth
	Hardware cloth
Squash bug	Wood ashes and lime

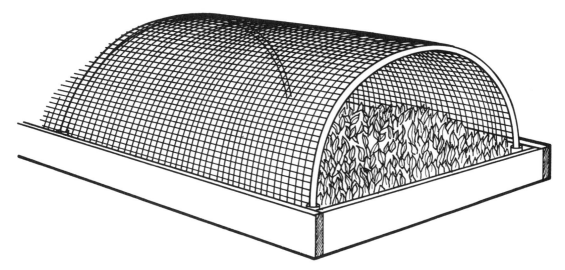

Illustration 8–3: Small-mesh plastic netting makes an excellent bird barrier when placed over the PVC ribs used for making tunnels.

birds, but in the case of strawberries, allows you to get in to pick the ripe fruit with ease. This same device can be used earlier in the season, when rabbits are still a threat to young seedlings. This net tunnel will keep everything out.

Another version of the same device is to use cheesecloth, instead of netting, over the tunnels, and you can screen out most insects as well as birds. Spunbonded polyester film is another material that is great for controlling insects, while allowing moisture to penetrate. It is normally used as an interfacing material in clothing manufacturing, but it is coming into more use in agriculture in recent years. Reemay is a similar material (see the Appendix for a source for this material). These new materials, cheesecloth, or tobacco cloth, while serving as excellent barriers to bugs, are also barriers to some sunlight. So, use them with care. In the heat of the summer, the cheesecloth screen makes an excellent cover for shading lettuce and other sun- and heat-sensitive plants. At the same time you may wish to isolate only a few particular plants in a bed for a critical period to fend off an emerging

pest insect. In that instance, the cloche screen device might be more appropriate (see illustration 6–7). This device allows you to protect a certain variety of vegetable while not screening off close neighbors that don't require protection.

Screens are most effective if used in conjunction with a growing awareness of insect's habits and emergence times. For example, root maggots come in many varieties, and some of those are larvae from flies that lay eggs at the base of seedlings. When the eggs hatch, the larvae or root maggots burrow into the stem and root system to begin feeding. Cabbages and other cole crops are particularly vulnerable to this pest in the early part of the season. The cheesecloth tunnel or the cheesecloth cloche may be the answer to some of the root maggot problems if it is erected before the fly arrives to lay its eggs.

Here is another example. Leaf miners can wipe out your spinach, Swiss chard, and beets. The leaf miner is the larva of a small black fly that arrives in early May to deposit its eggs on the undersides of the spinach or other target leaves. These eggs hatch into little maggots, which then chew up the insides of the leaves. There are no holes, just opaque spots in the leaves where these little pests have done their damage. The point here is that the fly can be prevented from getting to the spinach in the first place if the spinach plants are under a tunnel or cloche made with cheesecloth or tobacco cloth.

Before putting on the screen covering, check the young plants for clusters of from one to five small, white leaf miner eggs laid side by side on the undersides of the leaves. You don't want to close the barn door after the eggs have been laid. Another good trick is to leave a few spinach or chard plants outside the screen or cloche covering to check for the emergence of miners. Then when they arrive you can make a note of their emergence time for next year's mounting of the screen cloche. By the way, leaf miners have three to four generations per season, and the insects overwinter in the soil as pupae, so you need the protection for spinach in the fall as well.

SLUG BARRIER

The ubiquitous slug is a problem to many gardeners across the entire country. While the traps described earlier are helpful, the real goal would be to set up some kind of barrier that eliminates the problem entirely. There are two barriers being used today that have been successful. Neva Beach in Mendocino, California, developed a slug fence, using ¼-inch hardware cloth. She cut the hardware cloth into strips 8 inches wide, making sure to cut down the middle of the squares, leaving sharp points on the edges of the strips. Then she mounted those strips on the outside face of her boxed beds so that the sharp points of the edge stick up about an inch above the edge of the bed to serve as a vertical barrier to the slugs. She reports that slugs can't easily crawl up the mesh, and if they do manage to get to the top, they can't crawl over the tiny wire spikes. I think the same effect would be achieved with 4-inch strips tacked around your beds. That would require about 21 feet of standard 2-foot-wide hardware cloth for the 60-Minute Garden.

Another development in the battle against slugs is the use of a strip of copper flashing material. Gardeners have tacked a 2-inch strip of copper flashing material around the outside of their boxed beds about 1 inch from the top of the bed. This material has been a successful slug barrier because it carries a very mild electric charge at all times that humans can't detect, but it apparently tickles the slugs' bellies sufficiently to repel them.

ELECTRIC FENCE

There are very few backyard gardeners in this country who think of an electric fence as an option to use in fighting pests in their vegetable gardens. Perhaps you are in the group of gardeners who should consider using such a device. If your garden is harassed and destroyed by skunks, rabbits, raccoons, or groundhogs, your very best line of defense is to use the electric fence as a barrier. You can try all the other remedies such as mothballs, radios, and even chicken wire fences, but when you decide you want a sure thing that takes no time to manage, install an electric fence.

First, let me clear up some myths about electric fences. They are not designed to hurt anyone or anything. They are designed to surprise anything that touches the fence. Birds don't get shocked by sitting on an electric fence. You have to be in contact with the ground when you touch an electric fence to receive the shock. The shock of an electric fence is not really painful as much as it is a very strong buzzing feeling that you definitely want to have stop by letting go. The shock of an electric fence is in no way comparable to the dangerous shock you can receive from your home's electrical system. The zap of an electric fence is designed to be unpleasant rather than hurtful. It is more of a psychological barrier for animals than

Photo 8–2: This electric fence installation uses 24-inch PVC pipe supports for the two strands of wire surrounding the bed. In the foreground is the controller device that controls the voltage coming into the fence.

a physical one. Few animals that touch an electric fence two or three times will ever touch it, much less go near it, again. Some farmers can turn the power off in their fences after a few weeks because all the cows have learned about its zap and wouldn't go near that fence if you pushed them.

At the same time, an electric fence is definitely not a common tool for the backyard vegetable garden. I mention it because I know there are many potential gardeners and former gardeners who gave up their gardens because they couldn't beat the rabbits, or because the groundhogs took all the fun out of gardening. My friend Gene Logsdon, a wonderfully humorous garden writer, says fences are fine but electric fences are better.

So if you have a serious problem with attacks by four-footed pests in your garden,

the electric fence is definitely an option (see illustration 8–6). Most gardens need only two strands of wire—one at 6 inches and the second at 12 inches. Coons can climb wooden posts holding electric fencing, so PVC poles are better if you have very smart raccoons.

The only real problem with an electric fence in a vegetable garden is that it can be shorted out if it is touched by a wet leaf. All you have to do is remove the material that is touching the fence, and it will function again. In most cases though, the animal pests are only a problem when your plants are young and small. So that is when you should have your fence. If you give it juice for two or three weeks and then take away the power, the fence alone will continue to repel your furry nuisances, and you don't have to worry about anything shorting out.

The size of your fence depends a lot

on the layout of your garden. I use my fence selectively around only a few beds at a time as needed. I have power available near my garden, so I don't have to worry about using a battery. I use the fence in the spring to ward off the skunks who love to dig in my beds for grubs and in the summer when my corn is getting ripe. The raccoons always know when my corn is ripe exactly one day before I know, so to thwart their wiley clock, I rig my fence a week before I expect my first harvest of sweet corn. Some gardeners may find it more convenient to simply surround the whole garden with a fence and use it selectively when pests are expected to be a problem.

If you already have a chicken wire fence around your garden, the addition of a single-strand electric fence should be considered if you still have pest problems. Set up the single strand of wire 6 inches from the chicken wire and 4 to 8 inches off the ground using the PVC posts (see illustration 8–6). This combination fence has been 100 percent effective in excluding raccoons, groundhogs, rabbits, and surprisingly, even the deer.

Some gardeners only charge their fence at night to avoid surprising children during the day and because their problems from animal pests generally occur at night. In any case, the electric fence might mean the difference between having a good crop or not having a good crop if your furry pests are persistent.

REFLECTIVE MULCHES

One of the more exciting new developments in pest control is the use of reflective mulch. This is usually some type of tough paper covered on one side with an aluminum foil. It's available in rolls. This reflective mulch has been used very successfully in repelling a number of pesky insects harmful to our backyard crops, including aphids, leafhoppers, thrips, Mexican bean beetles, and even the fearsome squash beetle. For example, research has shown that the use of reflective mulch under a vegetable plant is 96 percent successful in repelling aphids. It works by tricking the insect into thinking the plant is really the sky. The mulch reflects the sun's ultraviolet rays, which the insects "see" instead of the blue grey light (color) of the plant. They think they are "seeing" the sky, and so they keep on flying and land in your neighbor's garden.

Some gardeners, bothered badly by the squash borer, have been finding that reflective mulch is helpful. The squash borer comes from eggs laid by a moth about the time your zucchini or cucumber plant goes into flower. By laying the reflective aluminum mulch around the base of the plant, forming a square, and by wrapping it around the first few inches of the stem, the moth gets confused and will generally not land there. If you can't find aluminum-coated paper mulch, aluminum foil will serve the same purpose. Use some of my "hairpins" (see illustration 5–5) to hold down the mulch so it doesn't blow away.

NATURAL SPRAYS AND BOTANICAL POISONS

I will not spend much time on these two final steps in the IPM process. You will only need these when everything else fails, and after a few years of IPM you will seldom have to resort to these approaches. At the same time, when the problem gets serious enough, natural sprays and botanical poisons should be brought into the fray.

Natural organic sprays, in contrast to what is called chemical sprays, include the hundreds of home remedies that have been developed by organic gardeners over the years. Some are designed to repel the insect, and others are designed to kill it. These sprays include such deterrents as soapy water, garlic, red pepper, and "bug juice," which is made by blending the insects themselves in water. Commercial organic sprays, especially the

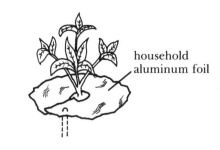

household
aluminum foil

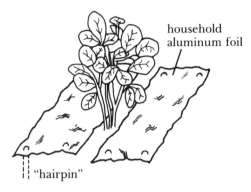

household
aluminum foil

"hairpin"

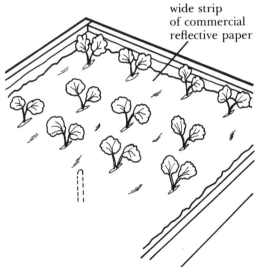

wide strip
of commercial
reflective paper

Illustration 8–4: Use reflective mulch in a number of ways to repel insect pests.

soap variety, are also available. Again, we want to know exactly which insect we are dealing with and select a natural spray that has been proven effective for that particular insect.

The botanical poisons are the very last resort in the battle of the bugs. While they are considered natural insecticides and are made with materials from nature, they still kill and often without respect for the good guys and bad guys. These insecticides are derived from plants for the most part and are poisonous to insects but generally harmless to humans and animals after a few days; however, they can be hazardous to people if they are not handled properly and according to directions on their packages.

These botanical poisons include pyrethrum, rotenone, and nicotine preparations. Pyrethrum is a contact insecticide effective against many pests, including leafhoppers, aphids, caterpillars, bugs, and various beetles. Rotenone is applied as a powder or a spray but does not have long staying power, so it needs to be reapplied fairly often. These sprays are definitely effective, but like chemical sprays they do not discriminate between harmful pests and beneficial insects.

I've covered a lot of territory in this chapter, but if you think about the total IPM process, it is not very time-consuming to manage, especially after the first year when your birdhouses are up, and you've constructed your screen panels and cheesecloth panels for the tunnels and the umbrella cloche. The greatest time requirement is those few minutes you spend each day or so taking care of the other management tasks in the garden. Your observation skills are probably your best weapon against the insect pests. Once you see one, you know how to respond, and you can avoid any serious problems right away. Learning about how the insects, good and bad, fit in to the amazingly complex ecosystem of my vegetable patch has been one of the more enjoyable and satisfying activities of my gardening experience.

TABLE 8–10

NATURAL SPRAYS AND BOTANICAL POISONS FOR COMMON INSECT PESTS

INSECT PEST	NATURAL SPRAY	BOTANICAL POISON
Aphid	Safer's soap	Pyrethrum
	Soap spray	
Cabbage looper		Pyrethrum
		Rotenone
Colorado potato beetle		Rotenone
		Ryania
Corn borer		Rotenone
		Ryania
		Sabadilla
Corn earworm	Dormant oil spray	Rotenone
	Mineral oil on tip of corn	
Cucumber beetle		Rotenone
		Ryania
Flea beetle	Garlic	Pyrethrum
	Hot pepper	Rotenone
Harlequin bug		Pyrethrum
		Rotenone
Hornworm		Rotenone
Japanese beetle		Rotenone
Leafhopper	Soap spray	Pyrethrum
		Rotenone
Mexican bean beetle		Rotenone
		Ryania
Mite	Dormant oil spray	
	Safer's soap	
	Soap spray	
Nematode	Liquid seaweed	
Scale	Dormant oil spray	
	Safer's soap	
Southern green stinkbug		Rotenone
		Sabadilla
Squash bug		Rotenone
		Sabadilla
Squash vine borer		Rotenone on base
Thrips	Safer's soap	Pyrethrum
		Rotenone
Whitefly	Safer's soap	Pyrethrum
	Soap spray	

An asparagus beetle.

Whiteflies underneath the leaves of a tomato plant.

UNIVERSAL BIRDHOUSE DESIGN

This birdhouse design will attract over a dozen birds that are beneficial to the vegetable garden. Use table 8–11 to make the necessary adjustments of measurements to build houses for the species you know are in your neighborhood.

It is important to make the roof of the house or one of the sides detachable so that you can clean out the birdhouse each winter without having to take it down from its mounting. Clean the birdhouse anytime after the first fall frost and before the early spring.

SHOPPING LIST

Lumber
1 pc. 1 × 8 pine board
Hardware
nails
2 hooks and eyes or a screw
   Total cost: $10 plus

TABLE 8–11

DIMENSIONS FOR BIRDHOUSES

HEIGHT FROM GROUND (FEET)	KIND OF BIRD	A SIZE OF FLOOR (INCHES)	B DEPTH OF BIRD BOX (INCHES)	C HEIGHT OF ENTRANCE (INCHES)	D DIAMETER OF ENTRANCE HOLE (INCHES)
5–10	Bluebird	5 × 5	8	6	1½
6–15	Chickadee	4 × 4	8–10	6–8	1⅛
8–12	House finch	4 × 4	6	4	2
6–10	House wren	4 × 4	6–8	4–6	1–1¼
12–20	Nuthatch	4 × 4	8–10	6–8	1¼
10–25	Starling	6 × 6	16–18	14–16	2
6–15	Titmouse	4 × 4	8–10	6–8	1¼

Source: United States Department of the Interior, Homes for Birds.

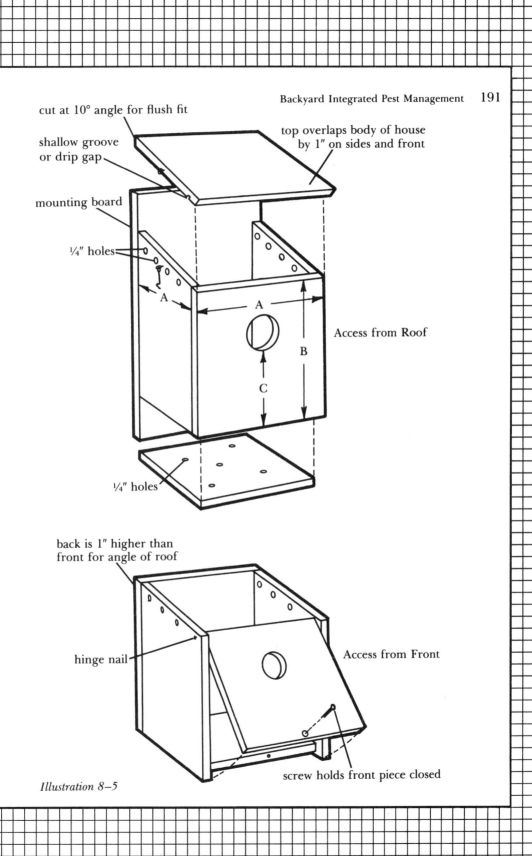

cut at 10° angle for flush fit

top overlaps body of house
by 1″ on sides and front

shallow groove
or drip gap

mounting board

¼″ holes

A

A

Access from Roof

B

C

¼″ holes

Access from Roof

back is 1″ higher than
front for angle of roof

hinge nail

Access from Front

screw holds front piece closed

Illustration 8–5

Photo 8–3: You can make the standard birdhouse out of all kinds of different materials. The best materials are the ones that are free.

Drill
Hammer
Hole saw
Saw

———————— *CUTTING LIST* ————————

Refer to table 8-11

CONSTRUCTION STEPS

1. Cut your pieces according to the sizes found in table 8–11 for the bird you are trying to attract to your backyard.

2. Assemble the parts according to illustration 8–5.

3. You don't need to paint your birdhouses. Some songbirds are repelled by bright colors on their houses. If you paint the house, don't paint the inside at all, and use earth colors like browns and greens.

ELECTRIC FENCE

This design eliminates the need for the insulator devices normally associated with installing an electric fence. This fence couldn't be simpler. Use the same rigid PVC material you've used in so many other projects in the 60-Minute Garden. The foundations in the boxed raised beds can serve as the base for the fence, or you can set it up outside the beds around the perimeter of your garden or part of your garden.

For the most effective operation, you must avoid allowing weeds or plants to touch the wire of the fence, since they will short out the circuit and make the fence inoperative.

_____ *SHOPPING LIST* _____

Lumber
4 to 8 poles 8′ × 1″ rigid PVC pipe
Hardware
1 electric fence controller device ($35 to $75)
1 roll annealed fence wire (as long as needed for your installation)
       Total cost: $60

_____ *TOOLS* _____

Hacksaw
Measuring tape
Pliers
Power or hand saw
Wire cutters

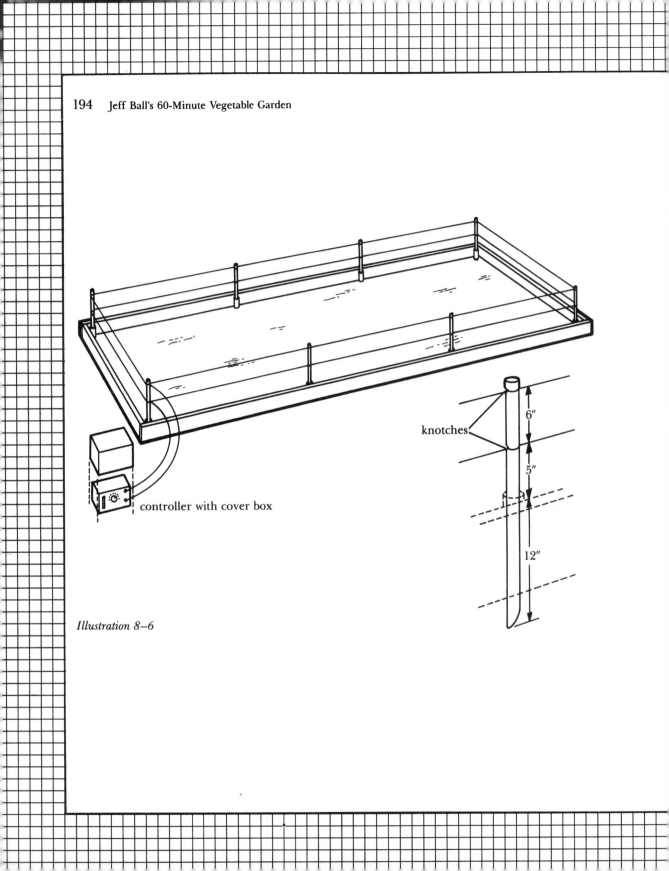

controller with cover box

knotches

6"

5"

12"

Illustration 8–6

CONSTRUCTION STEPS

1. Cut the PVC poles into 24-inch long pieces, using a hacksaw. Cut one end of each pole at a 45-degree angle so that the poles can be stuck into the ground or set into the garden's foundations.

2. In each PVC post cut a ⅛-inch notch at 1 inch and 7 inches from the top. This can be done with a power saw or a hand saw. These notches hold the wire in place as it is wrapped around each post.

3. Install the posts in the foundations or in the ground, as you choose. They should be 3 to 4 feet apart.

4. The controller should be located near one of the posts, in some kind of a box to protect it somewhat from the weather. Leaving enough wire to attach to the controller, begin wrapping the wire around the posts. Complete the stringing of the wire around the area at the lower level on the post, and then make the circuit of the area again, stringing the wire around the posts at the upper level. This should give you two strands of wire around your garden with one 6 inches above the edge of the bed or the ground, and the other 6 inches above the first.

5. Connect both ends of the wire to the controller as directed by the instructions with the instrument. Turn on the system and test it on both strands to make sure it is working. I test my fence by just barely touching it with my finger. I can quickly tell if it is working.

CHAPTER 9

GARDEN MANAGEMENT: PUTTING IT ALL TOGETHER

If you are truly interested in finding the ways to be able to manage a 200-square-foot garden in about 60 minutes a week, there are a number of garden management techniques that will help you. As in many things in a busy life, it takes a bit of time to save some time. A few hours devoted to some planning and scheduling in January can save considerable time in garden management throughout the growing season. Before we get to that planning and management process, let's talk briefly about the best way to go about building the 200-square-foot 60-Minute Garden in the first place.

CONSTRUCTING THE 60-MINUTE GARDEN

If you build all of the devices that are described in this book, you will have a very

complete and efficient vegetable garden system; however, there are only nine or ten devices that I consider essential to the design of the 60-Minute Garden. All the other devices contribute to timesaving and ease of the gardening activities, but they can be built later on as you get a chance to add them to your system. Those devices in table 9–1 are what you need to include in your first 60-Minute Garden.

The garden sink, birdhouses, compost sifter, and all the other handy devices listed in table 9–2 make a contribution to the total effectiveness of your garden, but are not absolutely critical to your being able to have optimum production in 200-square-feet, while taking only 60 minutes a week to manage.

The boxed beds with the PVC foundations and the compost bin are the basis for the entire garden system. They really should be constructed first. Building the beds and the bin in the fall has a number of advantages. You can double dig the soil in your beds and cover it with a thick layer of straw or other organic mulch, which will leave the soil in good condition for spring planting, with little need for any additional preparation. The first component of the 60-Minute Garden to be used will be the plastic tunnels, which can be erected as early as February in most parts of the country. February is not a good time to dig a bed, thus fall is the best time so you are ready to start your growing four to six weeks earlier than most of your neighbors. Fall is a good time to begin making compost since you have a ready supply of carbon material in the form of endless bags of leaves from your neighborhood.

Once the beds are dug and the boxes and the compost bin are constructed and installed, all the remaining projects can be completed during the winter months at your leisure. The drip irrigation system involves little construction effort and can be installed later in the season when watering becomes important; however, it is helpful to have your drip system available when you set up your early spring tunnels, even if you don't hook it up to water until later. Setting up the beds requires laying out the drip lines and then covering them with a black or clear plastic mulch that will stay on the bed during the entire season. To wait until later to install your drip system means reinstalling every bed, a definite bother and waste of time.

Once you have installed the basic garden system components, you can begin working on the other gardening devices over the next year or even two. Again, many of them are excellent winter projects for your workshop.

TABLE 9–1

INITIAL CAPITAL INVESTMENT IN TIME AND COSTS FOR THE BASIC 200-SQUARE-FOOT GARDEN

BASIC GARDEN	HOURS	COST ($)	PER SQUARE FOOT COST ($)
Build boxes and foundations	4	150	0.75
Double-dig beds	4		
Tunnels*	3.5	85	0.43
Hold-down pins*	1		
Vertical trellis*	5	100	0.50
Seedling lighting device*	8	20	0.10
Seed storage box*	1	20	0.10
Compost bin	8	80	0.40
Planting compass*	1		
Seeding board*	2		
Drip irrigation system	2	80	0.40
Seeds, fertilizer, etc.		65	0.33
Totals	39.5	600	3.01

*Ideal to build during winter to be ready for use in early spring.

TABLE 9–2

CAPITAL INVESTMENT IN TIME AND COSTS FOR ADDITIONAL FEATURES FOR A 200-SQUARE-FOOT GARDEN

ADDITIONAL FEATURES	HOURS	COST ($)
Standing board	1	4
Sitting board	1	4
Bed for special needs	15	75
Birdhouses*	6	10+
Bird screening*	1	
Shading device*	1	
Compost sifter*	2	20
Seedling box*	3	10
Outdoor seedling box*	2	10
Orchard fence	8	150
Garden sink	4	75
Electric fence	2	60
Cutting form	1	
Totals	47	418

Ideal to build during winter to be ready for use in early spring.

PLANNING AND SCHEDULING THE 60-MINUTE GARDEN

The key to keeping the time you need for managing your garden down to 60 minutes a week is planning things ahead. Planning does at least two things for you. It allows you to make better use of the limited growing space you have, and it saves you time by reducing the amount of repetitive tasks you would have to do without such planning. Many gardeners, especially those with large and complex gardens, have found that some degree of planning and record keeping is essential to a successful harvest. For some of us, those records and plans have been as much a nuisance as a help, primarily because we have to do them over again every year.

I have developed an approach to garden management that takes advantage of the power of a home computer to help me save time and to improve the effectiveness of my plans. All of the steps I describe for this planning system can be done with paper and pencil, but they cannot be done with as much ease as they can be with a computer.

HOME COMPUTERS AND THE 60-MINUTE GARDEN

Several hundred thousand vegetable gardeners in this country now have home computers and by the end of 1985, well over a million computers will be in the same homes that have a vegetable patch in the backyard. All home computers are not the same or have the same capabilities; however, all home computers can be a help in managing the vegetable garden to one degree or another.

The primary reason for using a home computer for managing your garden is that you do your master plan from scratch only *once.* After that you simply revise and refine it, allowing for a very customized and personal garden plan. If you put your planting schedule into the computer, you can make notes during the growing seasons about whether to plant something a bit earlier or later next year. Then next winter, when you are preparing your new garden plan, you simply refine those items you wish to change and leave all the other plans intact, ready to guide you for yet another year. This ability to simply revise instead of having to completely redo, is much more difficult with paper and pencil. With a paper record, it is generally easier to do the plan over again from scratch, than to revise it.

There are at least four different ways to use a home computer to manage your garden records and plans. The easiest way is to buy a computer program called *Garden Manager,* which is written by me and is forthcoming from Rodale Press. This inexpensive

program is designed to do all the things I discuss in the next section, in addition to containing a data file on 200 varieties of 50 vegetables.

The next best program to use is a simple data base manager or a time scheduler program. These programs allow you to introduce your many gardening activities in a random fashion as they occur to you, and then the program can sort out the activities in chronological order and print a schedule for you. Because these programs were not designed specifically for managing a vegetable garden, they have some limitations in terms of their capability.

While they offer some additional limitations, any word processing program and any spreadsheet program can be set up to handle your garden-planning and record-keeping tasks. Again, these programs are not designed to address the particular problems of garden planning, so their use will not give

Photo 9–1: While gardening can be very relaxing and satisfying, it is the harvest that makes all the effort worthwhile.

Photo 9–2: The 60-minute garden is a system. Each component—here composts bins and boxed raised beds fitted with trellises and tunnel ribs—can be used alone, but used together, they save time while producing bountiful harvests in a minimum of space.

you quite the full value found in a commercial garden software package, but they are still helpful.

SCHEDULING ON A WEEKLY BASIS

The primary purpose of doing any planning at all, besides being able to put together a seed order, is to be able to produce a schedule of events in the garden for the *entire year!* These events should be organized on a weekly basis and give you flexibility within the schedule to fit in the activities with your other time demands of job, family, and recreation. While some gardeners are interested in planning their gardens right down to the precise day for planting the peas, my life is so busy that if I get my peas into the garden plus or minus three or four days from the ideal day, I am happy and so is my garden.

As I said above, the key to making this planning process effective is to have the year's plan stored in your home computer so that you don't have to start all over from the beginning each year. You simply revise and refine your plan, and in a few years you can do your entire annual plan for the vegetable garden in less than half an hour. The first year's plan, however, will take a few hours to do properly. A garden management plan has a number of different types of information in it. The following explores each type carefully.

THE GARDEN MANAGEMENT PLAN

The easiest way to start your annual garden plan is to make some lists of the information you will want to include in your plan. These lists will then be put into the computer in random order for sorting out later.

VEGETABLE PLANTING SCHEDULE

This is the most important part of your plan. It determines first which vegetables and varieties you intend to plant, and it establishes the estimated dates for when these vegetables will be planted in the garden. Two pieces of information are needed to plan the seedling schedule: how much of each vegetable you will plant and when you will plant those vegetables. If the broccoli seedlings are going into the garden in late March, then you want to start the broccoli seeds indoors under lights in early February.

This process really takes two steps. You want to make a list of the vegetables you would like to grow and at the same time you need to begin making a rough sketch of where in your garden you will plant those vegetables. This dual approach tries to avoid plant-

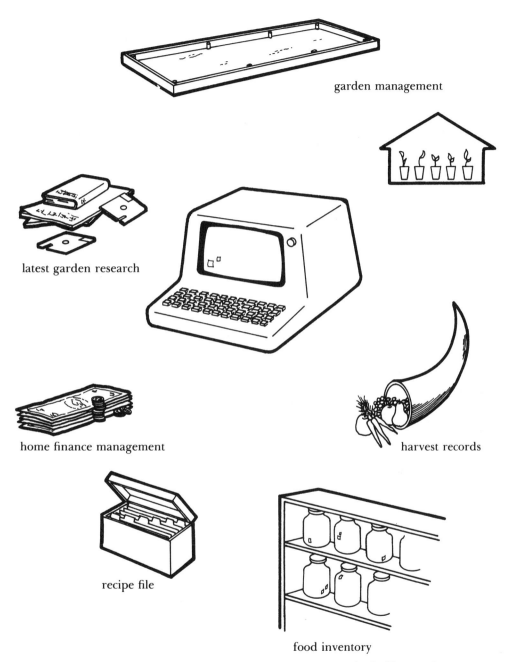

garden management

latest garden research

home finance management

harvest records

recipe file

food inventory

Illustration 9–1: The personal computer provides assistance in a number of valuable ways. In years to come, it will become even more helpful in producing and managing a family's food supply.

ing twice as many plants as you have room for in your vegetable patch.

The 60-Minute Garden has five growing seasons: early spring, spring, summer, fall, and early winter. In order to get maximum production from a 200-square-foot garden, you will plant vegetables during the first four of those five seasons. So, it doesn't do us much good to just make a note that you'll plant some broccoli this year. You need to know how many different succession plantings you will have and how many seedlings you need for each planting. This then gives two or three dates for starting seedlings, dates for transplanting seedlings into the garden, and projected dates for when to expect to begin harvesting the broccoli. Finally, you should try to estimate when the harvest will be finished so you can plan what to put in its place.

There is a complete and detailed garden management plan for a 200-square-foot garden later in this chapter (see illustrations 9–2, 9–3, 9–4, and 9–5). This plan shows the layout of the beds during the five growing seasons, and it gives a sample weekly schedule of events for the entire garden— 50 weeks in all! Reviewing that schedule should help you understand the kind of information you need to begin making your own annual plan. Having a list of the vegetables and their planting times is not the only information in the plan. There are a number of additional items that are almost as important to know about.

NATURAL EVENTS

One of the most important pieces of information in your garden plan is the last spring frost date and the first fall frost date in your garden. These two dates influence much of the planting schedule discussed above. Some gardeners also believe in the value of keeping track of the position of the moon as they determine when to plant or harvest their produce. You can easily add this information to your schedule if you are working with a home computer.

Your garden schedule is a perfect place to keep track of emergence times of insect pests so that you can anticipate possible problems (see chapter 8). When you see the Mexican bean beetle for the first time, note the date and put that date into your schedule for next year. When you spot your first beetle the next year, put that date in as well, to give you a range of two dates for the third year's plan. From then on you can begin to narrow down that range, as you collect information each year from your observations. Pretty soon, in three or four years, you have a pretty accurate ability to predict the emergence of your friend the Mexican bean beetle.

GARDEN MANAGEMENT ACTIVITIES

There are a number of other routine and periodic activities that you should include in your plan. Ordering supplies is an annual event, so note when it is time to order new straw mulch, plastic mulch, fertilizer, and even canning lids or freezer bags. These reminders simply take some of the burden of having to remember such details in the middle of a busy garden season.

Main garden events should be scheduled. When do you plan to get your annual soil test? When do you expect to set up the first tunnels in the early spring season? When will you put up the second-phase tunnels for the heat-loving crops? When do you expect to have to install your trellises? When do you expect to build another compost pile or turn the one you have? When do you prune your apple trees, and when do you bring in the flower bulbs? All these periodic activities occur every year. By including them in your schedule, you can spread them out a bit to make sure no individual week is overscheduled with activities. In this way, everything gets done, but your work load is spread more or less evenly throughout the season.

TABLE 9–3

60-MINUTE GARDEN PLAN FOR A
200-SQUARE-FOOT GARDEN

EARLY SPRING GROWING SEASON

WEEK NUMBER	EVENT DESCRIPTION	AREA (FT²)	NUMBER OF SEEDLINGS
Jan.			
1	Happy New Year!		
2	Recover from the holidays		
3	Celery (Tendercrisp)—start seedlings	6	10
	Chinese cabbage (Pak Choy)—start seedlings	3	9
	Onions (Yellow Globe)—start seedlings	9	150
4	Broccoli (Bonanza)—start seedlings	6	12
	Cabbage (Earliana)—start seedlings	6	12
5	Cauliflower (Early White)—start seedlings	6	12
Feb.			
6	Kohlrabi (Grand Duke)—start seedlings	6	10
	Set up tunnels for 100 square feet—early spring crops		
7	Lettuce (Green Ice)—start seedlings	3	12
	Spinach (Avon)—start seedlings	12	30
	Swiss chard (Rhubarb Chard)—start seedlings	6	15
8	Celery (Golden Self-Blanching)—start seedlings	6	10
	Onion sets—plant in the garden if ready	6	96
	Set up tunnels for other 100 square feet—spring crops		
9	Broccoli (Bonanza)—start seedlings	9	18
	Chinese cabbage (Pak Choy)—transplant	3	3
	Eggplant (Burpee Hybrid)—start seedlings	6	10
	Snap peas (Sugar Snap)—plant in garden	24	
Mar.			
10	Broccoli (Bonanza)—transplant	6	6
	Cabbage (Earliana)—transplant	6	6
	Cauliflower (Early White)—transplant	6	6
	Celery (Tendercrisp)—transplant	6	8
	Lettuce (Green Ice)—transplant	3	12
	Spinach (Avon)—transplant	12	24
11	Beets (Red Ace)—plant in garden	6	
	Summer squash (Burpee Golden)—start seedlings	3	5
	Sweet peppers (Tasty Hybrid)—start seedlings	6	8
	Tomatoes (Big Girl)—start seedlings	12	15
	Zucchini (Rich Green)—start seedlings	6	8

(continued)

TABLE 9–3—*Continued*

EARLY SPRING GROWING SEASON—*continued*

WEEK NUMBER	EVENT DESCRIPTION	AREA (FT²)	NUMBER OF SEEDLINGS
12	Cabbage (Copenhagen)—start seedlings	3	6
	Carrots (Danvers Half Long)—plant in garden	6	
	Kohlrabi (Grand Duke)—transplant	6	8
	Swiss chard (Rhubarb Chard)—transplant	6	6
13	Cucumbers (Burpee Hybrid)—start seedlings	6	12
	Lettuce (Green Ice)—start seedlings	3	30

EARLY SPRING PLANTING

CROP	AREA (FT²)	NUMBER OF PLANTS	YIELD (LB)
Beets	6	96	9
Broccoli*	6	6	5
Cabbage*	6	6	18
Carrots	6	96	12
Cauliflower*	6	6	9
Celery*	6	8	21
Chinese cabbage*	3	3	4
Kohlrabi*	6	8	6
Lettuce*	3	12	6
Onion sets	6	96	9
Peas, snap	24	192	48
Spinach*	12	24	9
Swiss chard*	6	6	17
Totals	96	559	173

*Seedlings
Note: There are a total of 79 seedlings transplanted into the garden.

SPRING GROWING SEASON

WEEK NUMBER	EVENT DESCRIPTION	AREA (FT²)	NUMBER OF SEEDLINGS
Apr.			
14	Beets (Red Ace)—plant in garden	6	
	Broccoli (Bonanza)—transplant	9	9
	Onions (Yellow Globe)—transplant	9	144
15	Predict last frost		
	Broccoli (Green Goliath)—start seedlings	6	10
	Celery (Burpee Fordhook)—start seedlings	3	8

(continued on page 206)

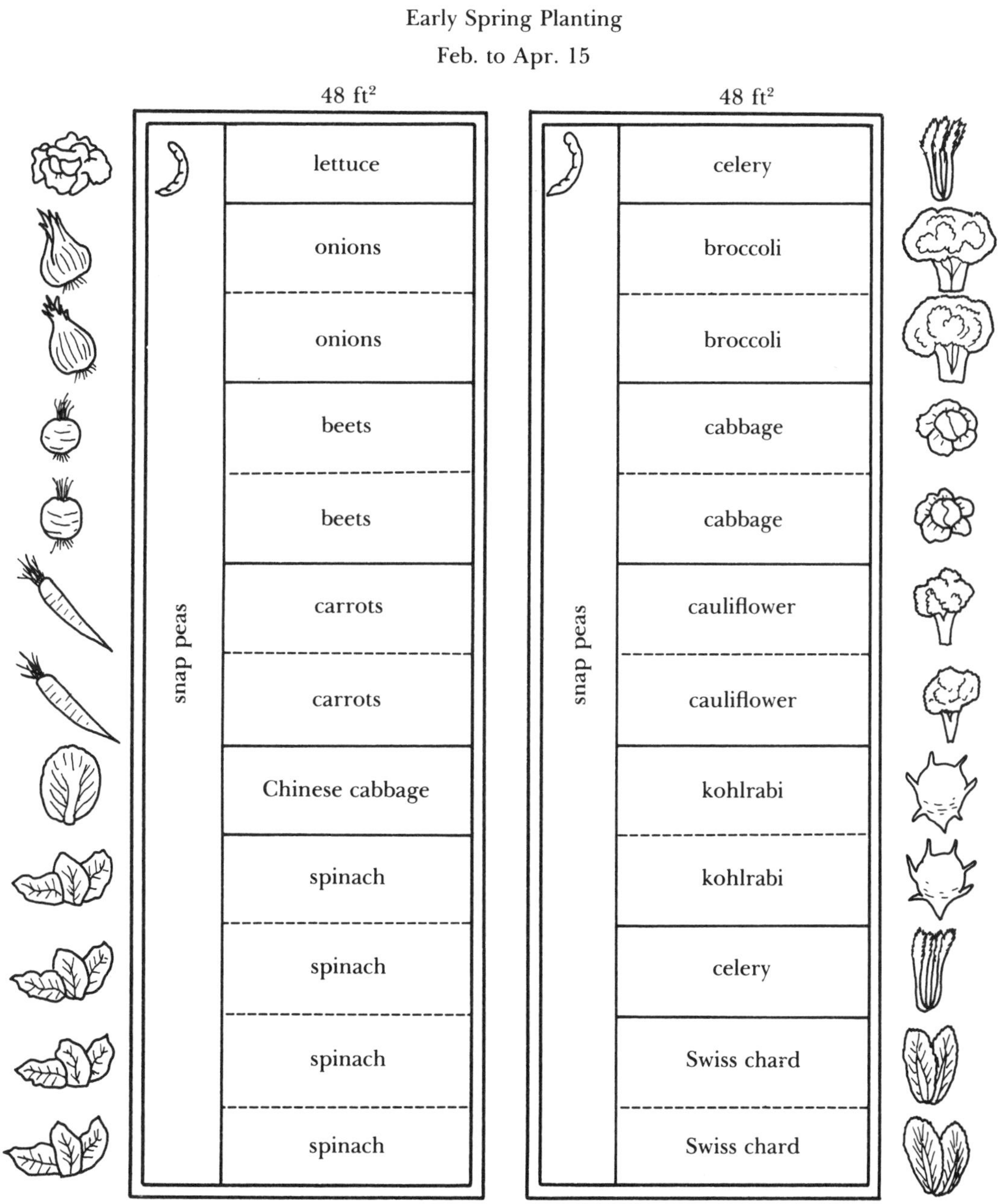

Early Spring Planting
Feb. to Apr. 15

48 ft²	48 ft²
lettuce	celery
onions	broccoli
onions	broccoli
beets	cabbage
beets	cabbage
carrots	cauliflower
carrots	cauliflower
Chinese cabbage	kohlrabi
spinach	kohlrabi
spinach	celery
spinach	Swiss chard
spinach	Swiss chard

snap peas   snap peas

Illustration 9–2

TABLE 9–3—*Continued*

SPRING GROWING SEASON—*continued*

WEEK NUMBER	EVENT DESCRIPTION	AREA (FT²)	NUMBER OF SEEDLINGS
16	Celery (Golden Self-Blanching)—transplant	3	5
	Eggplant (Burpee Hybrid)—transplant	6	5
	Summer squash (Burpee Golden)—transplant	3	3
	Zucchini (Rich Green)—transplant	6	5
17	Cucumbers (Burpee Hybrid)—transplant	6	6
	Lettuce (Green Ice)—transplant	3	12
	Sweet peppers (Tasty Hybrid)—transplant	6	6
	Tomatoes (Big Girl)—transplant	12	12
18	Cabbage (Copenhagen)—transplant	3	3
	Connect the drip irrigation lines to the house		
	Turn the compost pile		
May			
19	Cucumbers (Champion)—start seedlings	6	12
	Melons (Ambrosia)—start seedlings	6	12
	Pole beans (Kentucky Wonder)—plant in garden	12	
20	Winter squash (Butterboy)—start seedlings	6	12
	Winter squash (Early Acorn)—start seedlings	6	12
21	Broccoli (Green Goliath)—transplant	6	6
	Set up trellises on all beds		
	Broccoli (Green Goliath)—start seedlings	6	10
22	Carrots (Little Finger)—plant in garden	6	
	Celery (Golden Self-Blanching)—start seedlings	6	20
	Leeks (Titan)—start seedlings	6	100
	Swiss chard (Fordhook Giant)—start seedlings	6	18

SPRING PLANTING

CROP	AREA (FT²)	NUMBER OF PLANTS	YIELD (LB)
Beets	6	96	9
Broccoli*	6	15	12
Bush cucumbers*	6	6	12
Cabbage*	3	3	9
Carrots	6	96	12
Celery*	3	5	10
Eggplant*	6	5	12
Lettuce*	3	12	6
Onions*	9	144	27

(continued on page 208)

Spring Planting
Apr. to June

Illustration 9–3

TABLE 9–3—*Continued*

SPRING PLANTING—*continued*

CROP	AREA (FT²)	NUMBER OF PLANTS	YIELD (LB)
Peppers*	6	6	10
Pole beans	12	96	24
Squash, summer	9	8	30
Tomatoes*	12	12	48
Totals	87	504	221

*Seedlings
Note: There are a total of 216 seedlings transplanted into the garden.

SUMMER GROWING SEASON

WEEK NUMBER	EVENT DESCRIPTION	AREA (FT²)	NUMBER OF SEEDLINGS
June			
23	Beets (Detroit Dark Red)—plant in garden	6	
	Parsnips (Hollow Crown)—plant in garden	6	
	Turn the compost pile		
24	Brussels sprouts (Jade Cross E)—start seedlings	9	6
	Cabbage (Surehead)—start seedlings	9	12
	Watch soil temperature for laying straw mulch		
25	Celery (Burpee Fordhook)—transplant	3	4
	Cucumbers (Champion)—transplant	6	12
	Muskmelons (Ambrosia)—transplant	6	12
26	Celery (Golden Self-Blanching)—start seedlings	12	20
	Lettuce (Royal Oak Leaf)—start seedlings	3	30
	Lettuce (Burpee Bibb)—start seedlings	6	60
	Winter squash (Butterboy)—transplant	6	6
	Winter squash (Early Acorn)—transplant	6	6
July			
27	Kohlrabi (Grand Duke)—start seedlings	6	25
	Swiss chard (Fordhook Giant)—transplant	6	6
	Broccoli (Green Goliath)—transplant	6	6
28	Cauliflower (Burpeeana)—start seedlings	6	10
	Turn the compost pile		
29	Chinese cabbage (Burpee Hybrid)—start seedlings	3	6
	Chinese cabbage (Two Seasons)—start seedlings	3	6
	Collards (Georgia)—start seedlings	3	3
	Collards (Vates)—start seedlings	6	6
30	Celery (Golden Self-Blanching)—transplant	6	6
31	Kale (Blue Curled Vates)—start seedlings	6	30

(continued on page 210)

Summer Planting
(replaces early spring crops)
June to Aug.

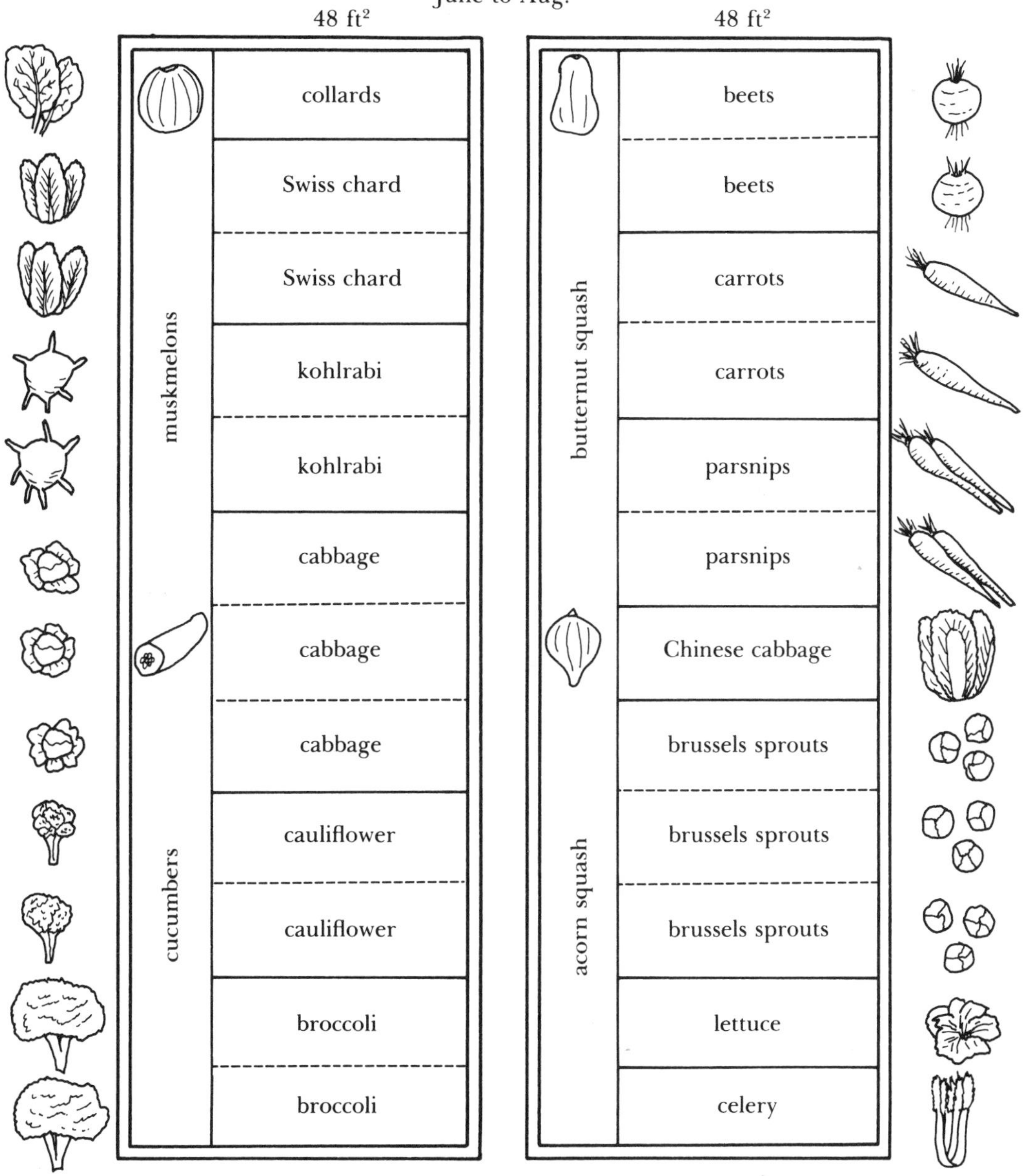

48 ft²   48 ft²

muskmelons / cucumbers		butternut squash / acorn squash	
collards		beets	
Swiss chard		beets	
Swiss chard		carrots	
kohlrabi		carrots	
kohlrabi		parsnips	
cabbage		parsnips	
cabbage		Chinese cabbage	
cabbage		brussels sprouts	
cauliflower		brussels sprouts	
cauliflower		brussels sprouts	
broccoli		lettuce	
broccoli		celery	

Illustration 9–4

TABLE 9–3—*Continued*

SUMMER PLANTING

CROP	AREA (FT²)	NUMBER OF PLANTS	YIELD (LB)
Beets	6	96	9
Broccoli*	6	6	5
Carrots	6	96	12
Celery*	9	10	30
Cucumbers*	6	12	18
Muskmelons*	6	12	12
Parsnips	6	96	10
Squash, acorn*	6	6	12
Squash, butternut*	6	6	12
Swiss chard*	6	6	17
Totals	63	346	137

*Seedlings
Note: There are a total of 58 seedlings transplanted into the garden.

FALL GROWING SEASON

WEEK NUMBER	EVENT DESCRIPTION	AREA (FT²)	NUMBER OF SEEDLINGS
Aug.			
32	Brussels sprouts (Jade Cross E)—transplant	9	6
	Cabbage (Surehead)—transplant	9	9
	Lettuce (Royal Oak Leaf)—transplant	3	12
	Lettuce (Burpee Bibb)—transplant	6	24
	Spinach (Bloomsdale Long-Standing)—start seedlings	12	48
33	Kohlrabi (Grand Duke)—transplant	6	10
	Leeks (Titan)—transplant	6	96
	Turn the compost pile		
34	Cauliflower (Burpeeana)—transplant	6	6
	Celery (Golden Self-Blanching)—transplant	6	10
	Collards (Georgia)—transplant	3	3
	Collards (Vates)—transplant	6	6
35	Chinese cabbage (Burpee Hybrid)—transplant	6	6
	Chinese cabbage (Two Seasons)—transplant	3	4
Sept.			
36	Spinach (Bloomsdale Long-Standing)—transplant	12	48

(continued on page 212)

Fall Planting
(replaces part of spring planting)
Aug. to Sept.

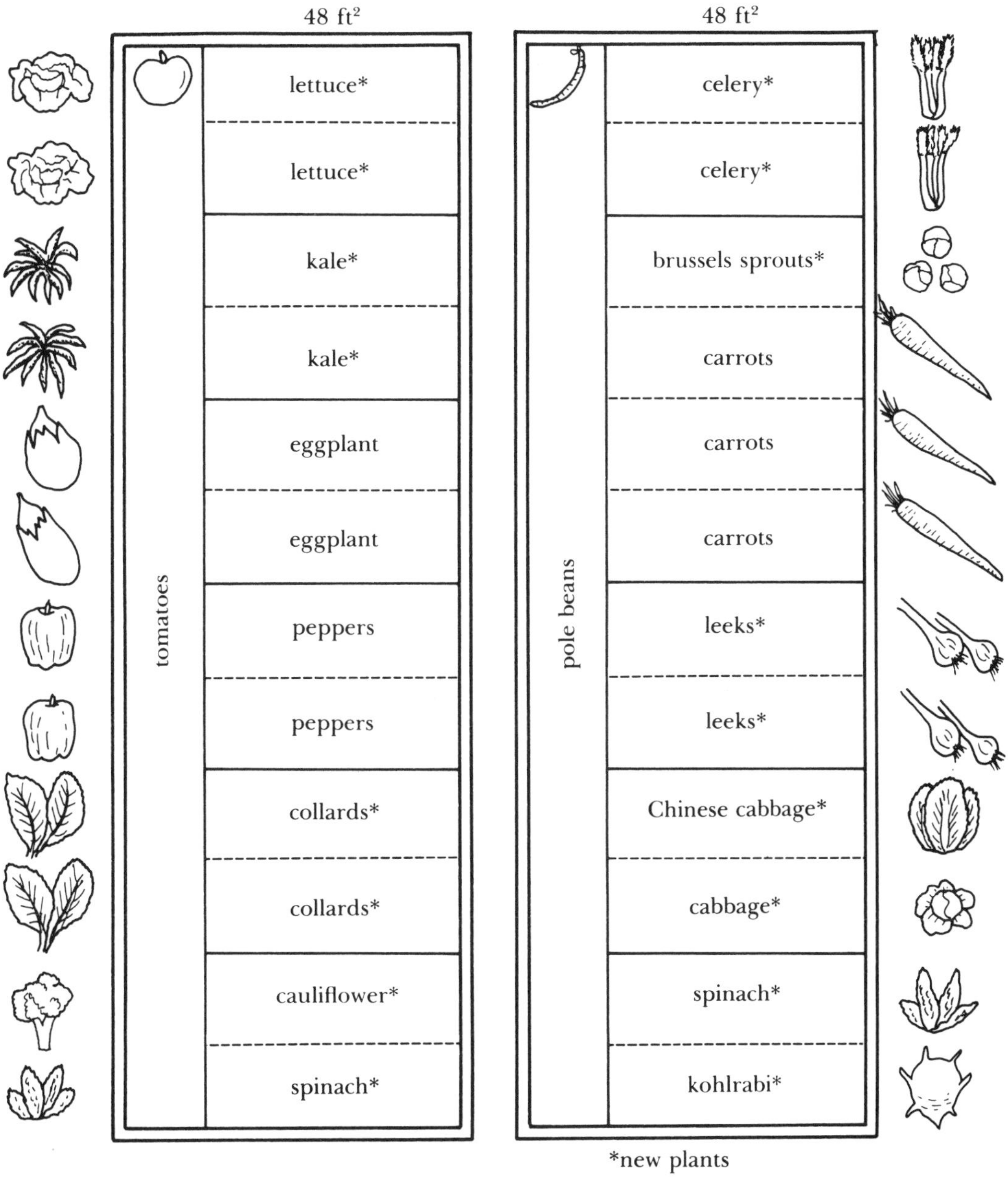

48 ft²
lettuce*
lettuce*
kale*
kale*
eggplant
eggplant
peppers
peppers
collards*
collards*
cauliflower*
spinach*

tomatoes

48 ft²
celery*
celery*
brussels sprouts*
carrots
carrots
carrots
leeks*
leeks*
Chinese cabbage*
cabbage*
spinach*
kohlrabi*

pole beans

*new plants

Illustration 9–5

TABLE 9–3—*Continued*

FALL GROWING SEASON—*continued*

WEEK NUMBER	EVENT DESCRIPTION	AREA (FT²)	NUMBER OF SEEDLINGS
37	Kale (Blue Curled Vates)—transplant	6	24
38	Order straw for winter mulch		
39	Build new compost pile for next year		
Oct.			
40	Set up the tunnels for the late fall season		
	Take down trellises		
41	Predict first frost		
42			
43			
44			

FALL PLANTING

CROP	AREA (FT²)	NUMBER OF PLANTS	YIELD (LB)
Brussels sprouts*	9	6	12
Cabbage*	9	9	27
Cauliflower*	6	6	9
Celery*	6	10	21
Chinese cabbage*	9	10	12
Collards*	9	9	9
Kale*	6	24	6
Kohlrabi*	6	10	6
Leeks*	6	96	12
Lettuce*	9	36	18
Spinach*	12	48	9
Totals	87	264	141

*Seedlings
Note: There are a total of 264 seedlings transplanted into the garden.

TABLE 9–3—*Continued*

EARLY WINTER GROWING SEASON

WEEK NUMBER	EVENT DESCRIPTION
Nov.	
45	
46	
47	
48	Most of the seed catalogs are in, so order next year's seeds
Dec.	
49	Finish harvesting the leeks, parsnips, collards, Chinese cabbage, and anything else that's lingering
50	Final cleanup for the winter; all beds under straw mulch

PRODUCTION SUMMARY FOR THE 200-SQUARE-FOOT GARDEN

SEASON	FLAT YIELD (LB)	VERTICAL YIELD (LB)	TOTAL YIELD (LB)	NUMBER OF SEEDLINGS
Early spring	125	48	173	79
Spring	149	72	221	216
Summer	83	54	137	58
Fall	141	0	141	264
Totals	498	174	672	617

Note: Vertical growing systems produce 26 percent of the yield.

HARVEST RECORDS

Here is where you can go wild with detail if you are so inclined. I have never been able to keep close track of my harvest in terms of pounds produced for each crop. I just knew whether I had *enough*. I had "enough" tomatoes, but I didn't have "enough" eggplant. But that level of detail is fine for me. I simply make a note in my schedule to increase my eggplant crop the next year, so next January when I revise my annual schedule, I remember to add a few more eggplant seedlings to my plan.

The home computer is a marvelous tool for those folks who enjoy keeping detailed track of their harvest. Even the simplest spreadsheet program allows you to set up a very effective record system that takes little time to maintain.

I also use my schedule to keep track of information I read in garden magazines and books. If I read about a new variety of cucumber that is resistant to cucumber beetle virus, then I make a note of it in my schedule so next year I will remember to

Photo 9–3: The 60-Minute Garden is definitely a productive system for growing fresh vegetables, but it is also a very attractive addition to the aesthetic value of your backyard.

order that particular variety so I can try it. I keep all my historical records right in my garden schedule. They are not extensive, but they are no good to me sitting lost in my filing cabinet. If they are not helpful, I just don't include them next year. I may read that I should water my celery a bit more frequently than I have been, so I'll make a little note in my schedule to add a watering reminder during the celery growing period. If I feel after a few years of being reminded to give the celery a bit more water that I don't need to be reminded, it is a simple task to edit out that item from my schedule. In a way, my garden schedule helps me to learn about my garden a little more every year.

Table 9–3 offers a sample garden management plan for a model 200-square-foot garden, using the 60-Minute Garden system. The varieties are not necessarily recommended for everyone; however, they do represent fairly popular varieties in the country. The plan is not presented for you to follow closely in your own garden. It is just an example to give you ideas about how you might construct your own plan.

MANAGING ON 60 MINUTES A WEEK

When you read table 9–3, you will ask yourself, Can this garden plan actually be accomplished with 60 minutes of work a week? It seems like a lot of activity to fit into just one hour a week. Well, there are some one-time activities that I don't include in my 60-minute figure. At the same time, I know that most of them can be accomplished along with your weekly management activities, and you won't exceed 60 minutes a week very often. Remember, the 60 minutes are based on the assumption that you are looking for

TABLE 9–4

TIME REQUIREMENTS FOR THE
60-MINUTE GARDEN

ONE-TIME ACTIVITIES	TOTAL TIME (MIN)	
Plan garden	120	
Order seeds	30	
Prepare black plastic	30	
Remove winter straw	15	
Lay black plastic	10	
Set tunnel ribs	5	
Cover tunnels	30	
Mount trellises	30	
Add straw mulch	30	
Remove straw mulch	15	
Reset tunnel ribs	5	
Cover tunnels	30	
Make compost pile	120	
One-time total	470	(7.83 hr)

WEEKLY ACTIVITIES	TOTAL TIME (MIN)
Start seeds	5*
Water seedlings	5
Transplant seedlings	12†
Water garden	3
Feed garden	5*
Maintain garden	10
Harvest	20
Weekly total	60

*15 minutes every 3 weeks
†36 minutes every 3 weeks

optimum production from your garden rather than maximum production. If you get into interplanting, spot feeding, spot watering, and some of the other tricks for increasing production to the limits, you are adding some time to your weekly totals. You should be aware, however, that four or five hours a week in a 200-square-foot garden is easily sufficient time to get maximum production from your vegetable patch. If you have the time, go to it!

The 60-Minute Garden is a system that can be built slowly over time. If you like to eat fresh vegetables, and you enjoy growing some of them yourself, you should get the best return for your time and money by investing in a gardening system that gives you great food and one that will give you much pleasure for many, many years! A 60-Minute Garden is sure to do that for you.

APPENDIX: SOURCES FOR SUPPLIES

CHAPTER 3

POLYETHYLENE FILM

A. M. Leonard, Inc.
P.O. Box 816
Piqua, OH 45356
(800) 543-8955
(UV-type film)

Ken-Bar, Inc.
24 Gould St.
Reading, MA 01867
(617) 944-0003
(Eskay-Lite UV-type film)

Martin Processing, Inc.
P.O. Box 5068
Martinsville, VA 24112
(703) 632-9853
(LLumar UV type-film)

CHAPTER 4

TWINES FOR TRELLISES

A. M. Leonard, Inc.
P.O. Box 816
Piqua, OH 45356
(800) 543-8955
(various twines)

CHAPTER 5

COMPOST SIFTERS

Smith & Hawken
25 Corte Madera
Mill Valley, CA 94941
(415) 383-4415
(compost and soil sifter)

COMPOST SUPPLIES

Necessary Trading Co.
Suppliers and Consultants for Sustainable
   Agriculture
620 Main St.
New Castle, VA 24127
(703) 864-5103

DIGGING TOOLS

Gardener's Supply Co.
133 Elm St.
Winooski, VT 05404
(802) 655-9006
(Wolf-Terrex digger)

Green River Tools
P.O. Box 1919
Brattleboro, VT 05301
(802) 254-2388
(Double Digger)

Smith & Hawken
25 Corte Madera
Mill Valley, CA 94941
(415) 383-4415
(U-Bar Digger)

—— SOIL THERMOMETERS ——

Brookstone Co.
300 Vose Farm Rd.
Peterborough, NH 03458
(603) 924-9511

CHAPTER 6

—— SHADING MATERIALS ——

Gardener's Supply Co.
133 Elm St.
Winooski, VT 05404
(802) 655-9006
(Reemay shading film)

— SOIL BLOCKS AND MAKERS —

Ball Jiffy
1400 Harvester Rd.
P.O. Box 338
West Chicago, IL 60185
(800) 323-1047
(Jiffy-7 Plant Starter Pellets)

Green River Tools
P.O. Box 1919
Brattleboro, VT 05301
(802) 254-2388
(soil block maker)

Mellinger's, Inc.
2310 W. South Range Rd.
North Lima, OH 44452
(800) 321-7444
(soil block maker)

CHAPTER 7

———— DRIP SYSTEMS ————

Aquatic Irrigation Systems Inc.
619 E East Gutierrez St.
Santa Barbara, CA 93103
(805) 965-5125
(kit available)

Chapin Watermatics Inc.
P.O. Box 490
740 Water St.
Watertown, NY 13601
(315) 782-1170
(drip hose system)

Drip Irrigation Garden
1264 W. 2d St.
Los Angeles, CA 90026
(213) 250-9318
(kit available)

Gardener's Supply Co.
133 Elm St.
Winooski, VT 05404
(802) 655-9006
(porous soaker kit available)

General Irrigation Co.
P.O. Box 776
Carthage, MO 64836
(417) 358-8171
(emitter system)

International Irrigation Systems
155 Third Ave.
Niagara Falls, NY 14304
(416) 688-4090
(kit available)

Irridelco Corp.
3081 E. Hamilton St.
Fresno, CA 93721
(209) 485-7170
(kit available)

Meredith Enterprises
231 S. Lincoln Way
Galt, CA 95632
(209) 745-3247
(kit available)

Misti-Maid, Inc.
P.O. Box 4607
Mountain View, CA 94040
(415) 961-7448
(kit available)

Raindrip, Inc.
14675 Titus St.
Panorama City, CA 91402
(818) 988-0303
(kit available)

Richdel, Inc.
P.O. Drawer A
Carson City, NV 89702
(702) 882-6786
(kit available)

Submatic Irrigation, Inc.
P.O. Box 246
Lubbock, TX 79408
(806) 747-9000
(kit available)

Trickle Soak Systems
P.O. Box 38
8733 Magnolia Suite 109
Santee, CA 92071-0038
(619) 449-6408
(kit available)

The Urban Farmer
2121 Taraval St.
San Francisco, CA 94116
(415) 661-2204
(some kits; mostly components; manual)

DRIP SYSTEM TIMERS

Brookstone Co.
300 Vose Farm Rd.
Peterborough, NH 03458
(603) 924-9511
(computer timer)

Galcon, Inc.
6400 Variel Ave.
Woodland Hills, CA 91367
(818) 703-1240
(battery-operated Drip Thinker)

Gardena, Inc.
6031 Culligan Way
Minnetonka, MN 55345
(612) 933-2445
(battery-operated computer timer)

Rain Matic Corp.
P.O. Box 3321
Omaha, NE 68103
(402) 345-8400
(battery-operated computer timer)

Water Watch Corp.
131 S.W. 156th St.
Seattle, WA 98166
(206) 244-0956
(programmed by microprocessor, battery
   operated)

FERTILIZER SIPHON DEVICES

Hyponex Corp.
P.O. Box 4300
Copley, OH 44321
(216) 666-1145
(brass siphon mixer)

LIQUID ORGANIC FERTILIZERS

Necessary Trading Co.
Suppliers and Consultants for Sustainable
   Agriculture
620 Main St.
New Castle, VA 24127
(703) 864-5103

CHAPTER 8

BENEFICIAL INSECTS

Necessary Trading Co.
Suppliers and Consultants for Sustainable
   Agriculture
620 Main St.
New Castle, VA 24127
(703) 864-5103

BIOLOGICAL PESTICIDES

Necessary Trading Co.
Suppliers and Consultants for Sustainable
  Agriculture
620 Main St.
New Castle, VA 24127
(703) 864-5103

Reuter Laboratories, Inc.
14540 John Marshall Highway
Gainesville, VA 22065
(800) 368-2244

ELECTRIC FENCE SUPPLIES

Parker McCrory Mfg. Co.
2000 Forest St.
Kansas City, MO 64108
(816) 221-2000
(solar-powered controller)

INSECT TRAPS

Brookstone Co.
300 Vose Farm Rd.
Peterborough, NH 03458
(603) 924-9511
(yellow stakes for whiteflies and other
  insects)

Consep Membrane Inc.
64550 Research Rd.
Bend, OR 97701
(503) 382-4100
(pheromone traps)

Hercon Div. Health-Chem Corp.
200 B Corporate Court
South Plainfield, NJ 07080
(201) 755-7730
(pheromone traps and food bait traps)

Insects Limited Inc.
10505 N. College Ave.
Indianapolis, IN 46280
(317) 846-5444
(pheromone traps)

Kenco Chemical and Manufacturing Corp.
P.O. Box 6246
Jacksonville, FL 32236
(904) 359-3005
(pheromone traps)

Mellinger's, Inc.
2310 W. South Range Rd.
North Lima, OH 44452
(800) 321-7444
(pheromone traps and sticky stakes)

Necessary Trading Co.
Suppliers and Consultants for Sustainable
  Agriculture
620 Main St.
New Castle, VA 24127
(703) 864-5103
(numerous traps including pheromone
  traps, sticky strips, apple maggot traps,
  animal traps, fly traps)

Reuter Laboratories, Inc.
14540 John Marshall Highway
Gainesville, VA 22065
(800) 368-2244
(pheromone traps, floral-scented lure and
  pheromone traps, yellow sticky bars)

Trece, Inc.
P.O. Box 5267
Salinas, CA 93915
(408) 758-0205
(pheromone traps)

BIBLIOGRAPHY

Ball, Jeff. *The Self-Sufficient Suburban Garden*. Emmaus, Pa.: Rodale Press, 1983.

Bartholomew, Mel. *Square Foot Gardening*. Emmaus, Pa.: Rodale Press, 1981.

Bubel, Nancy. *The Seed-Starter's Handbook*. Emmaus, Pa.: Rodale Press, 1978.

Carr, Anna. *Rodale's Color Handbook of Garden Insects*. Emmaus, Pa.: Rodale Press, 1979.

———. *Good Neighbors: Companion Planting for Gardeners*. Emmaus, Pa.: Rodale Press, 1985.

Chan, Peter, with Gill, Spencer. *Better Vegetable Gardens the Chinese Way*. Portland, Oreg.: Graphic Arts Center Publishing Co., 1977.

Dennis, John V. *Beyond the Bird Feeder*. New York: Alfred A. Knopf, 1981.

Editors of *Organic Gardening* magazine. *Getting the Most from Your Garden*. Emmaus, Pa.: Rodale Press, 1980.

Fryer, Lee. *The Bio-Gardener's Bible*. Radnor, Pa.: Chilton, 1982.

Hill, Lewis. *Pruning Simplified*. Emmaus, Pa.: Rodale Press, 1979.

Logsdon, Gene. *Wildlife in Your Garden*. Emmaus, Pa.: Rodale Press, 1983.

Minnich, Jerry. *The Earthworm Book*. Emmaus, Pa.: Rodale Press, 1977.

Minnich, Jerry, and Hunt, Marjorie. *The Rodale Guide to Composting*. Emmaus, Pa.: Rodale Press, 1979.

The New Alchemy Institute Staff. Hirshberg, Gary, and Calvan, Tracy, eds. *Gardening for All Seasons*. Andover, Mass.: Brick House Publishing, 1983.

United States Department of the Interior. *Homes for Birds*. Conservation Bulletin 14. Washington, D.C.: United States Government Printing Office, no date.

Yepsen, Roger B., Jr. *The Encyclopedia of Natural Insect and Disease Control*. Emmaus, Pa.: Rodale Press, 1984.

INDEX

Page references in italic indicate tables. Boldface references indicate illustrations and photographs.